INDIAN FEMINISMS

INDIAN FEMINISMS
Individual and Collective Journeys

Edited by
Poonam Kathuria
Abha Bhaiya

zubaan

ZUBAAN
128 B Shahpur Jat, 1st Floor
New Delhi 110049
Email: contact@zubaanbooks.com
Website: www.zubaanbooks.com

First published by Zubaan Publishers Pvt. Ltd 2018

ISBN: 978 93 85932 01 4

Zubaan is an independent feminist publishing house based in New Delhi with a strong academic and general list. It was set up as an imprint of India's first feminist publishing house, Kali for Women, and carries forward Kali's tradition of publishing world quality books to high editorial and production standards. *Zubaan* means tongue, voice, language, speech in Hindustani. Zubaan publishes in the area of the humanities, social sciences, as well as in fiction, general non-fiction, and books for children and young adults under its Young Zubaan imprint.

Printed and bound at Raj Press, R-3 Inderpuri, New Delhi 110 012

*This book is dedicated to the voices of dissent,
the sane and seemingly insane voices that have made the women's
movement in India today what it is, a voice for justice,
a voice for peace, a voice for inclusion and for humanity.*

Contents

Acknowledgments

This book is the result of a collective feminist endeavour, coordinated by the Society for Women's Action and Training Initiatives (SWATI).

We would like to thank the Global Fund for Women for the trust they placed in us. Your untied grant made us more committed to using this fund as productively as possible. Thank you.

We would also like to thank the authors for being part of this project and putting their faith in it. We hope the end product will help to make up for the delay.

Introduction: Through a Feminist Lens

Women's Voices, Modes of Campaigning and Non-Violent Ways of Resistance

Poonam Kathuria

In 2011 SWATI[1] initiated a discussion with a small group of feminists around Mahila Nyaya Samitis[2] (NS) and the increasing interest by the state[3] in promoting them as alternate redress mechanisms. The purpose of the meeting was to reflect on the implications and fallout of this state-driven expansion of an institution that evolved out of a process of women's empowerment and was rooted in rural women's movements. The question we wanted to address was: how could we influence the government's attempt at replicating the NS and ensure that it retained the gender just and feminist perspective of the NS? The group decided on an action plan that included the development of protocols for the functioning of the NS; and the creation of an operations manual/material that codifies the gender just feminist approach of NS. Somewhere along the way the idea metamorphosed into a collection of essays that focused on events post the 1980s[4] in the Indian feminist movement, its ways of resistance and its engagement with rights and justice. This edited collection is the result. This book is thus about women's movements, women's leadership, their struggles, campaigns, the gains they have made, the challenges they have faced, and those they continue to confront. This book is about Indian feminisms. It is not a cohesive collection in the thematic sense. But it is not an eclectic collection either. Its interconnectedness lies in feminist analysis and advocacy through legal and socio-political means.

What has been unique to India, and for that matter to South Asia, is that much, if not most, feminist writing has been done by feminist activists who have drawn theoretical understandings from their own experiences and practice. Therefore, it is no coincidence that each of the authors who came into this project of capturing feminist ways of advocating for issues through legal and socio-political means, is walking the practice and has put forth a specific feminist approach/ way of advocating for change. The range is wide and the landscape of issues that this book covers is significant for their contemporary nature, their relevance at both the regional (South Asia) and global levels and the critical feminist perspectives that they bring.

Feminists, by and large, have the ability to be self-critical, to introspect and analyse past actions, to recognize the differences, contradictions and to locate common cause beyond women's equality and rights. This has allowed them to constantly forward their perspective and analysis in a holistic way instead of remaining stuck in a groove, holding on to ideas that are no longer current. This has also made them targets of intense criticism at times. Feminism's success has been in being able to critically look not only at patriarchy and gender but also at other structures of domination such as caste, class, sex, ethnicity, race, religion etc., that intersect to produce multiple forms of subjugation, not only for women but also for men and sexual minorities. It is the feminists who have stood up against capitalism, against war and violence, against destruction of the environment, against fundamentalism; and it is they who have forged alliances with varied movements on these issues, thus strengthening them and infusing them with a feminist analysis. This makes the women's movement one of the most successful movements in the world. And that is why it is important that its struggles and challenges are documented for the future generations as a part of feminist history and for the young feminists, who are often looking for inspiration and an analysis that can help anchor their experiences.

This book has eleven essays arranged into four broad 'sections'. The first section comprises personal reflections on the dilemmas experienced in working with survivors and the questions they pose to feminists and to feminist work in evolving a new perspective. The essays point to the continuing interaction between the patriarchal order and the feminist endeavour.

The second section describes women's 'art' of protest and their demands for justice. The courts of women held in varied contexts – one questioning the global developmental paradigm and the other challenging the male prerogative over religion and its interpretation – open this section. They show how feminists have conceived of alternate ways to protest against violations and organized themselves to claim rights and ownership on their own terms. The third section examines feminist engagement with the law in the Indian context and the success and challenges thereof. It looks at feminist organizing and successful building of common cause across constituencies. The fourth section exemplifies feminism's success in being able to bring its understanding, analysis and methodological approaches into state institutions. Together, the essays illustrate some of the key events and issues that feminists have engaged with that have shaped feminist consciousness of the women's movement, influenced institutions of the state and challenged and changed social sensibilities in the last three and a half decades.

In this introduction I have tried to locate the essays in a broader social or geo-political context. In keeping with the slogan that the personal is political, the essays are organized in an intersectional (subjective to me) chronology of individual to society to institutions – both social and state.

TO BE BUT HOW TO BE? FEMINIST DILEMMAS AND CHALLENGES

The book opens with a poignant reflection by a grassroots activist, Suneeta Thakur. Her profound piece 'My Journey is Our Collective Destination' encapsulates the spirit of the book. Suneeta expresses her own dilemmas and travails of working as an activist-cum-counsellor in a feminist organization and the conflicts she experienced. In so doing, she embarks on a journey of recovering the woman in her. In its telling, her personal story is interwoven with experiences of working with women survivors. The article symbolizes the sisterhood of women, where Suneeta is constantly seeing her own self, with all its dilemmas, reflected in the women who come to her for support. And this is what makes it a collective journey, no matter who started earlier or who joined later; who has reached a destination and who is still searching for a route. It is still a collective endeavour of recognizing organized suppression, powerlessness, compulsions as well as discovering desire, empowerment and joy.

Marriage and Matrimonial Law

Matrimonial (family) litigation in India has been and continues to be a contentious and traumatic matter for most women. While it has been possible for women to get a divorce and to free themselves of the restraints of an unhappy or abusive marriage, many women also find themselves on the brink of destitution as the concept of joint ownership of property is sorely lacking in Indian personal laws and most laws privilege a separate property regime i.e. ownership of property and family assets by the husband as his exclusive property.

The straitjacketed process of law is unable to factor in the complexities and differing contexts of the women. The 'one size fits all' compulsion of the law demands that women fit their complex realities into this uni-dimensional but extremely complicated and hostile process. Many give up. But some women do continue to fight and they learn to work the system on its terms. While such women are empowered in being able to deal with the system, to use a Frerian analysis, they do so by becoming 'like the oppressor'. For the women's movement this represents a deep dilemma: the woman is a survivor, but survival does not necessarily mean victory.

The essay 'The Interface between Life and Law' by Flavia Agnes is a personal reflection on this engagement of life and law, reiterating that while one may end up with nothing much on the legal justice front, the empowerment that one gains through this engagement has its own value. Flavia's essay provides the backdrop to conversations and dilemmas expressed by several women's organizations who, in the process of helping women survivors, are faced with predicaments of women learning 'the tricks of the trade' and deal with this adversarial system on its own (not necessarily ethical) terms. She illustrates and analyses this in depth through a particular case and comes to the conclusion that all said and done, the answer still lies in continuing to use the law as that is the only way law gets interpreted and challenged for its purpose and impact. This is resonant of the position of the Indian women's movement that has continued its engagement with the law as a major strategy to advocate for a feminist reconstitution of the law. And this success was evident in The Criminal Law (Amendment) Act, 2013.[5] However, this is not to say that we have arrived; the journey has been going on for a while and we are moving ahead.

Towards a Feminist Jurisprudence[6]

Feminism not only refers to an awareness of women's oppression and exploitation in society, at work and within the family, and conscious action by women and men to change this situation;[7] it also implies a struggle for the attainment of women's equality, dignity and freedom of choice in order for women to control their own lives and bodies within and outside the home. Legislation and law reform, both at international and national levels, have been an essential arena for setting standards of equality, dignity and freedom.[8] The feminist critique of law revolves around law not just as a site of patriarchy, but advances the principle of neutrality, universality and equality as laid out in the Constitution, contesting these claims and proving that law is essentially male[9] in its perspective.[10] Feminist jurisprudence[11] thus can be loosely understood as feminist writing on the law, analysing it for its implications for women and women's lives. Feminist jurisprudence revolves around a number of questions and features a diversity of focal points and approaches. However, its main characteristic is the goal of bringing the law and its practitioners to recognize that law as currently constructed does not acknowledge or respond to the needs of women, and must be changed.

Progressive women's movements are united around a common cause of challenging gender inequalities and injustices in society with a view to ending patriarchal domination. Not all women's movements or activists allied with movements for women's rights and ending patriarchy identify with the term 'feminism'. However, it is useful to consider that 'the consciousness of sexism and sexist oppression is the essence of feminist politics, and it is this politics that energises women's movements, whether or not the word 'feminist' is used.' [12]

Thus, the idea of feminist jurisprudence was no longer confined to the formal legal system but was now being applied to social jurisprudence systems (community codes/charters/norms) that were completely unfair to women and that influenced the formal jurisprudence systems. The Indian context was no different, in spite of its promise to the contrary. In practice the state mirrored society. As an integral strategy, it was imperative to strengthen women's collective and individual agency. Unless women took leadership in the social sphere, the promise of the 'equality before law' would never be realised. For this it was important to strengthen the individual and collective agency of women. Abha Bhaiya's essay, titled 'Legitimately Ours – The Parallel Systems of Feminist Jurisprudence' traces the difficult and complex journey of women demanding there rightful place in society. Working independently within their own organizations as well as in collaboration with a national state programme,[13] many feminist groups forged ahead with finding alternative and parallel systems to shape feminist jurisprudence at the community level, thus translating the promise of 'equality before law'. In this personal account Abha Bhaiya acknowledges the important role that state actors played in shaping the agenda of women's empowerment, making the Indian women's movement a truly national movement, and one that encompassed both the urban and the rural. She shares how these parallel systems conducted by rural and urban poor women have become the norm rather than an exception, because they demonstrate how the promised justice can be brought closer home.

This was amply visible in India in the unprecedented level of mobilization to protest against the gang rape of Bhanwari Devi, a worker of a women's development programme of the government of Rajasthan. Women's groups across the country gathered to protest against the state and the judiciary who trivialised the cause of Bhanwari and abdicated state accountability.

The case brought into focus the issue of sexual harrassment of women at the workplace and led to the historic set of guidelines on sexual harassment, issued by the Supreme Court in *Vishaka* v. *State of Rajasthan*.[14] The court gathered feminist vision from the UN Convention on Elimination of All Forms of Discrimination Against Women (CEDAW), Directive Principles of State Policy, affirmative action policy under Article 15(3) and the idea of human dignity as inputs for its reasoning. It is because of this vision that the extraordinary type of judicial law making[14] in this case became non-controversial and acceptable.

The essay, 'Challenging the Collusion of Caste, Class and Patriarchy Embodied by the State' by Kanchan Mathur is perhaps one of the first systematic attempts at documenting the Bhanwari Devi case and the series of events that shaped the struggle of the women's movement around women's right to work and safety at the workplace.

The formal hierarchical legal systems have mostly remained unresponsive and unaccountable to the specificity of women experiences of violence. In response to the failure of the legal system, the practice of alternative/parallel feminist jurisprudence emerged more than three decades back. Within women's organizations as well as in collaboration with a national state programme, many feminist groups forged ahead with finding alternative and parallel systems to shape feminist jurisprudence at the community level, thus translating the promise of 'equality before law'. As an integral strategy, it was imperative to strengthen women's collective and individual agency.

Given the promise of a fairly egalitarian Constitution, the women's movement in India has always turned to laws for achieving equality of social, political, economic rights and opportunities.[15] In her essay 'The Women's Movement and Legislative Reform on Violence Against Women' Madhu Mehra traces this movement for law reform in the face of the law's inability to capture, leave alone remedy, patriarchal subjugation. Her essay provides an overview of the feminist engagement with law and the constitutional promise of the right to life, liberty, dignity and equality in relation to law reform campaigns on sexual and domestic violence. She traces the legislative advances and aspects that these have highlighted. This is followed by a discussion on institutional reform at the formal level of the police and the judiciary, and the informal level of creating alternative mechanisms of justice. In doing so, she analyses the evolution of the Mahila Nyaya Panchayats and Nari Adalats which are women-led, informal feminist strategies and which challenge the concepts of retribution and punishment as the only ways in which survivors can seek justice.

In conclusion, she looks at different views and positions on engaging with the law, and indeed, the value of law reform in creating visions of feminist futures. The feminist critique of the law also points to the importance of an evolving law reform agenda that has grown and will continue to grow with the intersectionality of new movements and concerns such as those relating to caste, communalism and sexuality rights.

Assertion and Resistance

Alternate redress mechanisms, as institutions like the women's courts are very unimaginatively called in global parlance (robbing them of their politics), are a space for organized women's resistance against injustices they have experienced during war and peacetime, in both private and public spheres. They are spaces where women get their voices heard, demand accountability and name and shame their violators.

The imagery of the court has been effectively used by women at local, national and international levels as a platform to focus attention on violations of women's fundamental rights to safety, equality and dignity by the family, community, the state and by one country against the women/men of another country. This book has two powerful articles that focus on women's courts of justice. While both draw on very different contexts, the politics underlying them is rooted in justice, non-violence and a feminist vision of a different world.

'Courts of Women: Re-imagining Justice', is a lyrical piece by Corinne Kumar, one of the founders of the International Courts of Women. It describes the idea and impact of a feminist imagery of non-violent forms of resistance against the violence inherent in the international order for which no remedies are provided by local, national or international judicial systems. The imagery of the court, in this case, is bereft of the symbolic power of the law, and is more a creative expression to symbolize collective voices of human rights violations, abuse and repression of women by state actors and the failure of recourse to the international judicial system that is composed of the powerful/economically dominant states who themselves are the biggest violators of human rights.[16] Founded in 1989 by a group of activists and artists, the Courts of Women have become a comprehensive form of protest against violence inherent in the international order. In these courts, the collective disempowerments and violations become an empowering/powerful tool of exposing national and international justice systems that serve to render invisible the massive and continuous violation of rights, particularly those pertaining to women.

The purpose of the Courts of Women is to give voice to those made invisible by the international justice system. The 'violence against women', denounced by the Courts is based on issues such as war-related violence and nuclear testing, 'development'-induced violence, the violence of poverty, domestic violence, trafficking, HIV and AIDS, migration, destruction of the environment and food sovereignty.

Feminism is often perceived to be a western construct and anti-religion because of feminism's intense critique of the role of religion in naturalizing/legitimizing women's subjugation and secondary status. However, Muslim women outside the West have been active in modern forms of feminism since the 19th century. Different feminist movements reflect the cultural contexts in which they arise, and Muslim feminists have adapted their own ways of working within an Islamic framework, allowing women to counter gender oppression and expectations as a part of their faith.[17]

Umm Yasmin of the Centre for Muslim Minorities and Islam Policy Studies at Monash University, Australia defines a Muslim feminist as 'one who adopts a worldview in which Islam can be contextualized and reinterpreted in order to promote concepts of equity and equality between men and women; and for whom freedom of choice plays an important part in the expression of faith.'[18]

According to those who follow the Islamic feminist movement, female Muslims see two things standing in the way of their emancipation. On the one hand, they find a conservative Islam that prevents women from having access to religious knowledge and hampers the achievement of equality as prescribed by the Quran. On the other, there is what they call 'colonial feminism', which was born in the North and was laced with Orientalism. This type of feminism dictates to the women of the South the manners and framework of their emancipation, arguing that it is impossible to be both subject to God and freed from the power of men. India, like some other countries such as Malaysia and Turkey, has proved to be a particularly fertile ground for Islamic feminism for many reasons. Although there is a dominance of Hinduism, India remains a pluralistic democracy, which has created a conducive environment for women to challenge Quranic teachings and Islamic jurisprudence.

'Justice In The Name Of God: Organizing Muslim Women In Tamil Nadu', by V. Geetha, illustrates how the Tamil Nadu Muslim women's *jamaat* (or assembly) successfully bridges the dichotomy of faith and equality, as more women speak up against their oppression by reinterpreting and appealing to Islamic law. The women's jamaat of Tamil Nadu is powerfully symbolic of Islamic feminism,[19] justice for women and resistance against patriarchal interpretations of Islam. The women's jamaat and mosque movement (not unique to India) is seen by many Muslim women, including Houda,[20] as liberating as women are active and they're asking questions and claiming intellectual ownership of Islamic teaching.

The Communal Violence (Prevention) Bill

In the Indian subcontinent, politically motivated communal violence peaked in 1946 and thereafter, the carnage during and after the Partition (of Pakistan and India) shattered the lives of hundreds of thousands of people. Since then sectarian violence has raised its ugly head with systematic regularity. Some of the worst moments of such violence include the Nellie massacre 1983, the anti-Sikh violence 1984, Mumbai 1992, Gujarat 2002, Kandhamal 2007–8, Assam 2012 and Muzaffarnagar 2013.

The United Progressive Alliance[21] (UPA) government came to power in 2004, in the wake of the 2002 Gujarat carnage. Understandably so, UPA had, as one of its electoral promises,[22] a model, comprehensive law on communal violence that would generate faith in state institutions among minority communities. While many termed this hypocritical (considering the Congress' own involvement in the anti-Sikh violence of 1984) several civil society groups, including human rights activists, lawyers, and women's groups, saw this as an opportunity and became active in the formulation of an alternative draft Bill, with the intent to influence the government's Bill.

The Communal Violence (Prevention and Reparation) Bill, is perhaps the first of its kind drafted in order to bring justice to victims/survivors of targeted, sectarian violence and enforce state accountability. The close engagement of women's rights activists and feminist lawyers' with this process of drafting, and campaigning for the law was intended to bring in a perspective of impunity and denial of justice to women, and recognition of the disproportionate impact on women of such violence, but was by no means limited to that.

Saumya Uma's essay, titled 'A Beacon of Hope: Reflections on Engagements of Women's Rights Activists With the Communal Violence Bill', traces the trajectory of the Bill, through her own involvement in the discussions around its making over a period of ten years from 2004 to 2014. She presents the varied (often oppositional) positions, contestations, debates and critiques among civil society groups in formulating and reformulating the several drafts. She highlights the rigorous and long drawn out process with the untiring efforts of activists who, at every level, broadened the ambit of the Bill, not only to incorporate women's concerns but also to include the concepts of reparations and command and superior responsibility, drawn from international criminal jurisprudence. This, in itself, is a major achievement in terms of expanding the boundaries of rights-based justice and state accountability. The UPA government, in spite of its commitment to bringing in the Bill, could not do so due to several reasons, all of which have been analysed in the essay.

The involvement of women's groups in the formulation of the Communal Violence Bill created the impetus and support for women to assert the importance of their direct participation in the traditionally male spaces of decision-making associated with conflict resolution and peace building.

I wonder whether it is possible to work on progressive projects, for progressive outcomes, while also being deeply critical of the same institutions, laws and policies that we expect to produce the outcomes. This has been demonstrated to us time and again. Caribbean-American feminist Audre Lorde famously answered this question in the negative many years ago when she offered the insight that the master's tools will never dismantle the master's house. Given the mixing of religion with politics for power, this adage is particularly true in the context of the CV Bill. But then the other moot question is, do we have a choice of not engaging with the state?

LGBT+ Rights: Two Steps Forward, One Step Back

It is estimated that the global LGBT+ population is somewhere between 250 million and 500 million people (5–10 per cent of the world's population aged over 16). Most of these people – hundreds of millions of them – are forced to hide their sexuality, fearing ostracism, harassment, discrimination, imprisonment, torture and even murder.

Total criminalization of homosexuality continues in nearly 80 countries – including most of Africa, Asia, the Caribbean and the Middle East – with penalties ranging from a one-year jail sentence to life imprisonment. Half of these countries are former British colonies and current members of the Commonwealth.[23] The anti-LGBT+ laws in these Commonwealth nations were originally legislated by the British government in the 19th century during the period of colonial rule. They were never repealed when these nations won their independence from Britain.[24] They instilled in these countries an intolerance of homosexuality that continues to this day.

Despite this discrimination, persons of 'alternative sexualities', as they used to be known in the past, are gaining increasing visibility everywhere in the world as they begin claiming their rights and appropriating public spaces. LGBT+ people have made huge strides in many parts of the world.

A mere four decades ago, 'queers' were almost universally seen as 'mad, bad and sad'. Same-sex relations were deemed a sin, a crime and a sickness. It was only in 1991 that the World Health Organization declassified homosexuality as an illness, and Amnesty International agreed to campaign for LGBT+ human rights and to adopt jailed LGBTs as prisoners of conscience.[25] To address the rights of the LGBT+ people is seen by many as one of the last great undone tasks of the civil rights movement. And there does seem to be a growing international support for change.[26]

Jaya Sharma's poignant semi-personal account of the repeal of Section 377[27] of the Indian Penal Code, titled 'Voices Against 377', is an acknowledgment of the importance of the law in so far as it is a useful instrument to rule in favour of recognition and to fight discrimination. While law is the location, the substance of this article is in its description of the anxieties, fear, rejection, distress and exploitation, and amidst all that, the courage and the tenacity to continue the fight; to do so, not in a violent way but with persistent plodding to talk, engage in dialogue, logically argue with the most illogical and build alliances beyond just the LGBT+ rights to embrace a broader political agenda and solidarity with all oppressed groups.

The 2009 judgment brought gay and lesbian people out of the closet and the issue into public debate. This coming out, quintessentially 'personal is political', provided the gay and lesbian liberation movement a sense of self respect and an army of enlistees. The right wing's fears that visibility to the issue would encourage others to either experiment with homosexuality or at least be tolerant of it, turned out to be true. While the Right may shudder at that fact, the widening visibility and confidence of the LGBT+ movement paved the way for others to come out and has transformed public consciousness ever since.

Institutionalizing The Feminist Analysis/Institutionalizing Feminism

The success of feminism has been in being able to embed its values, ideas and principles across sectors in transforming responses to women's issues. This is at the heart of two chapters in this book, and they focus on shaping institutional responses to violence against women. While the criminal justice system has been and continues to be the major focus, in the last two decades, state institutions that are responsible for providing health services,[28] good governance and civic infrastructure have come into the ambit of the ongoing attempts by feminists to draw attention to and disrupt the philosophical and political separation between public and private life.[29]

Anjali Dave, Yashoda Pradhan and Taranga Sriraman's essay, 'Special Cells For Women and Children: Redefining Scope and Strategies For Intervening On Violence Against Women', focuses on this very successful process of institutionalisation of the Special Cells for Women and Children and infusing them with feminist practice and response. They coin the term 'feminist social work praxis', which amalgamates feminist values in social work practice.

The emergence of 'feminist counselling' as distinct from 'counselling' is one of the most important examples of the feminist praxis that also informed all other feminist interventions at various levels, be it the criminal justice system, the health or the governance systems. Feminist counselling emerged out of a critique of the bio-medical approach, and the awareness that counselling theory and practice had developed in a highly patriarchal manner. Together, they treated distress and mental health problems as disease and as the individual's responsibility. The feminists not only asserted the link between personal and social identities but also the need for an integrated analysis of varied forms of oppression (race, gender, religious beliefs, biases, age, disability etc.).

The second essay in this section by Sangeeta Rege and Padma Deosthali, titled 'Domestic Violence: Women-centred Approaches and the Need for Feminist Counselling', traces the differential evolutionary paths of feminist counselling in the West and in India. Based on their own experience of institutionalizing a feminist counselling framework in public health institutions, the authors have succinctly put together the principles of feminist counselling. In this framework, counselling is understood as a multi-dimensional intervention involving therapy, analysis and advocacy, while encouragement and acknowledgement of women's agency is at the core of informing development of protocols to address the issue of all forms of violence faced by women.

The Dilaasa initiative and Special Cells set up by Tata Institute of Social Sciences could very successfully place the issue at multiple levels in the health and criminal justice systems and therein lies the feminist success.

Feminist activism may be defined as embodying elements of dissent, resistance and rebellion.[30] Hands interprets dissent as a protest against something, resistance as refusal to go along with something and rebellion as a productive response to change something. Each of the essays in this book points at this creativity of feminist activism that upholds rebellion and resistance, while simultaneously understanding the contradictions of the patriarchal world order as is seen in working with survivors, or the compassionate strength displayed by the international courts of women and the non-adversarial nature of the Nari Adalats. The other aspect is the inclusive nature of the movement and its ability to forge solidarity with other causes, as can be seen in the Communal Violence Bill and the LGBT+ campaigns. This is reminiscent of the feminist debates of the eighties when they decided that the role of the feminist would be to infuse all other movements with feminist thought.[31] This has remained the character of the movement and has made it what it is: one of the most dynamic and complex movements in the world.

Notes

1. Society For Women's Action And Training Initiatives works in Gujarat for the rights of women and the marginalised.
2. The Mahila Nyaya Panchayats-(women justice platforms) are gender just, women led informal jurisprudence mechanisms at the community level.
3. Delhi government initiated 81 Nari Adalats.
4. The eighties are generally seen as marking a new moment, often identified as the third wave of the women's movement in India.
5. In the wake of massive protests post the gruesome rape of a young woman, the government set up the justice Verma Committee to look into provisions of the rape law. Many longstanding demands of the women's groups were included in the Committee's recommendations to the government. The amended law now includes crimes such as stalking, voyeurism, acid throwing, and disrobing, recognizes the structural and graded nature of sexual crimes against women, defines consent by saying submission can not be understood as consent, redefines and expands the notion of rape to all forms of non-consensual penetrative sexual acts that violate a woman's bodily integrity and tries to tackle the issue of impunity through directing the state to set up support services for sexual assault. Also, the Evidence Act has been amended and it now disallows the bringing in of 'a woman's past history or character' to be invoked in the trial.
6. I take this title from a paper by Ann Scales (Scales, A. 1981. 'Towards a Feminist Jurisprudence,' Indiana Law Journal, 56, Issue 3. See also West, R. 1988. 'Jurisprudence and Gender,' University of Chicago Law Review, 55.1)
7. Kamla Bhasin and Nighat Saiyyad Khan, 1986. *Some Questions on Feminism and Its Relevance in South Asia* New Delhi: Kali for Women.
8. See Naysa Ahuja, 2010. 'The need to understand the women's question and its implications on women in the Indian patriarchal society'. Women's Studies and Development centre, University of Delhi.
9. Feminists (all) argue that legal concepts of 'impartiality' and 'objectivity' are just viewpoints of dominant groups, and therefore hide male bias: 'if the sexes are unequal, and perspective participates in situation, there is no ungendered reality or ungendered perspective.' See Katherine A. MacKinnon, 1989. 'Method and Politics', in *Toward a Feminist Theory of the State*, Cambridge: Harvard University Press, p. 114.
10. See Ann Scales, 1986. *The Emergence of Feminist Jurisprudence: An Essay*, 95 Yale L.J. 1373, College Pune, 11–20 January.
11. The first recorded use of the phrase 'feminist jurisprudence' was in 1978 at a conference celebrating the twenty-fifth anniversary of women graduates of the Harvard Law School by Professor Ann Scales, then a Harvard student herself. More recently, Professor Robin West has claimed that 'feminist jurisprudence is a conceptual anomaly'. Existing jurisprudence is masculine,

according to West, because it is about the connection between patriarchal laws and human beings, who are presumed by those laws to be male. Feminist jurisprudence cannot exist until patriarchy is abolished. ('The virtual abolition of patriarchy is the necessary political condition for the creation of non-masculine feminist jurisprudence.' (Ibid. p. 60.) See Patricia A. Cain, 1989. 'Feminist Jurisprudence: Grounding The Theories', 4 Berkeley Women's L.J.191,Available at http://scholarship.law.berkeley.edu/bglj/vol4/1ss2/1)

12. See Peggy Antrobus. 2004. *The Global Women's Movement: Issues and Strategies for the New Century*. London: Zed Books, p. 16.

13. Womens development program was first initiated in the state of Rajsthan. Its success led to the program being replicated from the center. The program was called Mahila Samkahya – Education for Women's Equality.

14. The court proposed guidelines to alleviate the problem of sexual harassment till the government of India enacted a law. The law – The Sexual Harassment of Women at Workplace (Prevention, Prohibition and Redressal) Act – was enacted in 2013.

15. See: Radha kumar, 1993. *The History of Doing: An Illustrated Account of Feminisms and Women's Movements in India 1800–1990*. New Delhi: Zubaan.

16. The exclusion of the United States from the International Criminal Court Jurisdiction, along with the Court's unwillingness and inability to consider trying the U.S. and Great Britain for aggression and the actions of their troops in Iraq and Afghanistan undermine the notion that international law could be anything more than an instrument in the hands of powerful states.

17. For details, see The Light in Her Eyes at Obxpeaceandjustice.org/category/documentaries/light-in-her-eyes/

18. ibid.

19. Because some secular Muslim feminists are less interested in reforming Islam and more concerned with promoting gender equality within a secular society, the term 'Islamic feminism' arose to distinguish those women who work specifically within Islam. Islamic feminism also aims for the full equality of all Muslims, male and female, in both public and private life.

20. Houda al-Habash is an Islamic preacher, who challenges conservative male clerics and believes that Islam demands that women be educated in all areas and insists that education itself is a form of worship. Houda's school (of Quranic teaching for girls) is part of a resurgence of Islam across the globe known as an 'Islamic revival' See 'The Light in her Eyes' in Context: The Women's Mosque Movement, op. cit.

21. The UPA is a coalition of centre-left political parties in india formed after the 2004 general election, led by Indian National Congress, whose chairperson Sonia Gandhi is also the chairperson of the UPA.

22. Later part of the UPAs common minimum programme.

23. An association that is supposedly committed to uphold democracy and human rights. Same sex sexual activity remains illegal in 41 0ut of 53 common wealth countries.

24. 'Britain's own record was not always so positive. And UK had the largest number of homophobic laws of any country on earth – some of them dating back centuries. Thanks to an astute 20-year twin-track campaign of direct action protest and parliamentary lobbying, today the UK is one of the world's most progressive countries on LGBT+ rights.' from http://www.lgbt-today.com/news-a-articles/featured-articles/259–lgbt-rights-the-global-struggle-for-queer-freedom.

25. Prisoner of conscience (POC) is a term coined by Peter Benenson in a 28 May 1961 article ('The Forgotten Prisoners') for the London Observer newspaper. Most often associated with the human rights organisation Amnesty International, the term can refer to anyone imprisoned because of their race, sexual orientation, religion, or political views. It also refers to those who have been imprisoned and/or persecuted for the non-violent expression of their conscientiously held beliefs.

26. While fundamentalist religion is still a major threat to the LGBT+ equality, the community has been able to look outward and express solidarity with groups working on other forms of oppression and thereby build alliances.

27. The Indian Supreme Court reinstated an 1861, colonial era law criminalising consensual sex between same sex adults. The decision was made on 10 December 2013, World Human Rights Day. The apex court ruled that it had been struck down improperly by the lower court (which had ruled the 1861 act unconstitutional in a 2009, decision).

28. In 1996, The World Health Assembly passed a resolution and declared violence as a leading public health problem. Source- http://www.who.int/violence_injury_prevention/resources/publications/en/WHA4925_eng.pdf

29. Margaret Thornton, 1998. 'Development of Feminist Jurisprudence', paper presented at the Winter Workshop on Law, Development and Gender Justice, ILS Law College, Pune, 11–20 January.

30. Feminist activism may be defined as embodying elements of dissent, resistance and rebellion (Byerly, Carolyn M., and Marcus Hill. 'Reformulation Theory: Gauging Feminist Impact on News of Violence Against Women.' *Journal of Research on Women and Gender 5* (2014). https://journals.tdl.org/jrwg/index.php/jrwg/article/viewFile/71/36.)'

31. Kumar, Radha, 1993. *The History of Doing: An illustrated Account of Movements for Women's Rights and Feminism in India, 1800–1900.*.New Delhi: Kali for Women.

ONE

My Journey is Our Collective Destination

Suneeta Thakur

This narrative is not simply a story. It is a journey that I have lived. It is not my journey alone but that of all women, my soul sisters, who I came to know as part of my work with Jagori's violence intervention programme. What we believe inwardly is often in constant conflict with our outward lives. In living this battle raging within us, we experience the essence and truth of life. This essential truth may be that of knowledge, or of our rights, or of change, but to obtain it, we have to endeavour to come together, teach each other and be taught by one another, for nothing can be achieved without struggle, and no struggle can be won without a united front. Only then can we claim that we share the same thoughts and believe in the same transformation. This story is the record of my inner travels, of my association with Jagori, the relentless efforts towards creating awareness about violence against women, and the struggle for change.

Facing the Mirror

So many years have passed in this struggle. The cause is still with us in all its specificity and its uniqueness. In trying to recall the beginnings of this struggle, I am flooded with memories of myself as a free spirit when I was a child, but also of my cheeks smarting with father's stinging slaps and harsh scoldings, my indignant sobs and my youthful, impetuous plans to run away from an oppressive home.

At the time, I often imagined that the fault was mine, but now, after many years I have realized that the rebellion I felt at the unfairness of it all was what feminsim is about. When I began to understand this, the fire raging within me received some respite, my mind was relieved that it was not I who was in the wrong, but it was they, the ones who always tried to stop me. I was merely speaking out for my rights. If to articulate one's rights as a woman is feminism, then I have been a feminist right from my childhood, and there must be so many more like me, who are passionately committed to a world where everyone's rights are respected.

I see so many childhood memories being reflected in the lives of thousands of women engaged in battle, sisters like me. 'Didi, why should I tolerate all this? I have obeyed every whim of Papa's, but this time I will not be silent. I want to study. My brother does not study, but he is given every opportunity to do so, while I am ordered to sit at home; why should I do that? I don't want to remain shackled and bound to the home! Help me, help me, please!'

Countless are the brave and the battles we have supported them in, echoing their words, breaking boundaries, going beyond the limits of our knowledge, joining hands in sisterhood, and finding some way or the other to carry forward the struggle for asserting ourselves, our existence, our individuality. At home, families are quite fed up.

'She just doesn't stay at home! The very mention of office makes her get up and go!'

'She is ill, but she will not rest or let others be.'

'Are these 'women' or some kind of a scourge let loose by heaven who are hell-bent on a rebellion against men?'

We have smiled in response to every such accusation. We've said our battle is not against men; it is against the societal structure they have created, which elevates them to being gods, and renders us their slaves and worshippers. We don't want to change men. Let them do that themselves. We want to change this world that looks at two equal beings with such discriminatory and prejudiced eyes, forcing them to live life in such unequal ways.

If our claim for justice is labelled 'feminism' and we are accused of being obstinate, domineering, arrogant, fanatical and homebreakers, then so be it. There are many battles against discrimination and there are as many ways to fight discrimination as there are battles; and as many strategies to address the issues facing us. But all have one goal: women have endured injustice, have lived lives of deprivation, have been forced to tolerate discrimination, but they will not let the same happen to other women.

Perhaps this fire rages inside every woman, but she is not able to name it. If this were not so, why would all women be suffering the same agony, have the same demands, be equally adamant and be fighting the same bitter battles?

Why Does the Scale Never Tilt in My Favour?

After a long and arduous day of serving every family member and pandering to their whims, drained of all strength, as I lie down in bed, he arrives, all sweaty and stinking of alcohol. He usually never remembers anything but he never forgets to 'sleep' with me. If I don't sleep with him my bones are broken, if I do, my body is wrecked! I let him do what he likes with me—at least this way there will be food to eat for the children, otherwise he will stop giving me money even for that. Or he'll go to some other [woman], and the little money that he doles out will also stop and then what will I do Didi? That is why I stay silent. Please call him and pull him up properly. Ask him not to beat me, to understand my pain and my plight.

Her words transcend the age barrier and move me deeply. Perhaps that is why the woman in me is at once ready to help her: 'Don't fret, dear sister, we'll call him, we'll talk to him; if he understands, good, otherwise there are other ways to make him realise his mistake.'

Her anxiety at hearing the words, 'other ways' is understandable. We often hesitate to talk of the legal rights of women. The woman seated in front of us, even though aware of legal rights, panics at the thought of engaging with the procedures that legal recourse entails. 'Didi, the police, the courts! No, no. I have not seen these. I don't even know them. The police in any case will lecture me, they never say anything to the husband. Even if they take him away to the police station, they will release him after a few hours. He return will and break some more of my bones. Police, courts, law...these are for the rich; who listens to us?'

Endless Struggles and Small Victories

Listening to this soul sister's words, reflecting on the difficulty of keeping faith in a broken and failed legal system, I fall into deep thought. The clamour of the woman in me surprises me. I find myself thinking, I wish there was a washing machine which could cleanse the mindsets of these men. Unfortunately neither you nor I can do this. That's why we have to fight. Nothing will change overnight. The structure is rusted metal. Hitting at it will only break it but will not remove the corroding rust—we'll have to keep filing away at it. 'Change will be slow but it will come and we'll fight this battle together.'

Riding the boat of family and social pressures, these women search for themselves. Sometimes they manage to stay afloat, at other times they nearly drown. There are times when decisions are really difficult, they cannot step out of their families – for where will they go? This is why, for them, the courts, the police stations, legal action, all these remain last resort options. And yet, for us, as activists, while we understand this, sometimes there's impatience: 'Stop! Why do you continue to tolerate all this? There is no need to suffer like this. Go, work, earn; it's not so difficult to rear your children. Tell us if you need help.'

But a look at their silent gaze stops us in our tracks. We know, as they do, that this is not an individual battle, but one which addresses society and the ways in which it is organized. And in this battle, the woman has to fight strategically and we have to be her support. When she understands this, there is relief, satisfaction and confidence, and this empowers us.

I am reminded of my own trajectory and my first tentative steps, my encounter with Jagori. I recall that Abha di (Abha Bhaiya) was seated at the front desk, writing something when I went in. We began talking. A long and deep discussion about family, home, upbringing, education, marriage followed. I remember her probing questions and perceptive gaze as she explored strategies to fit employment into my future, as my inquisitive little daughter's tiny fingers played havoc with the papers on her table. I remember her laughingly asking, 'how will you manage this little storm?' The assurance that she would be with me made me feel much lighter, as I shed the weight of worries and climbed down the steps of the office.

I remember telling myself, 'I lost out on so many opportunities in trying to please you, but no longer! Enough! I will leave this house but not Jagori, never!'

The storm raging within me abated, and even today, Abha di's smile revitalizes my faith: 'Didi, I will not suffer any more, enough is enough! You are right; but please, stay by my side!'

I am Waging War for Peace

Today I am not just a woman but a living campaign. Home, neighbourhood, family, friends—it is as if every breath of mine has become a campaign. Taking feminist action has become a habit, be it while walking the street, in the bus, in some neighbourhood, or in my own relationships. When I hear my feminist friends echo the same words, I feel as if the formula of 'two and two make twenty four' is gaining currency in this patriarchal society. Slowly, but surely change is happening.

It has become a habit with me now, if I see any injustice, any violation of any woman, I refuse to stay silent. People chide me, they say 'Why do you speak? It is none of your business.' I tell them, 'it may not be my problem, but she is a sister, a woman like me! Keeping quiet will only embolden the oppressors. Even if we don't take action, it is important to point out that something is wrong. Isn't that right, Didi?'

In those words is reflected a silent affirmation of feminist principles. The one thing that we all know is that by breaking the silence, not just the perpetrators of injustice, but also those around them, the bystanders, the neighbours, get to know that violence against women is a crime, whether inside the home or anywhere else. This first step towards preventing injustice, creating awareness and sensitizing people is really important. Often, a sister's anguished cry for help as she suffocates in the four walls of her home, seems like my own helpless voice, echoing down the passage of time. My experiences become a protective shield for her to convince her to believe in her own words. We listen, understand, feel and become one with each other.

Sometimes, feminist arguments and definitions of feminist principles seem to be meaningless. After all, it is not so easy to break off from one's family, or one's relationships and carve out your own identity. Every woman's thoughts, personality, limits, strengths, society, class, religion, creed is different, so how can the strategies be the same? Being women, their pain may no doubt be the same, but each one's situation is different, and so each one's strategies to counter patriarchal values and institutions are sure to be located in their familial and in social situations, which must be recognized. Is the knowledge and the awareness about our violation not the first step to claim our rights? To begin the journey of feminist politics and principle?

Women on the Chessboard of Power

Sometimes I think that if I had to choose between the safety of power and opposing the tyranny of power, perhaps I too would, like most women who come to us, opt for the safety offered by that power, even if that protection was gained at the cost of injustice and violation.

It would seem to be a more effective choice to fight from the security of home and strategize to counter its injustice from inside that situation, rather than to deal with the insecurity and uncertainties of the outside world. And there's nothing wrong with this, if some women do think so. Especially when they really have no option of security or refuge if they leave their homes and families. Therefore, we must respect a woman's choice, because the problem is hers and the resolution must also be hers, it is she who will ultimately have to face the consequences of her actions.

We can only offer safe, rational solutions, explain the positives and negatives of every action, but the ultimate step will have to be taken by her alone. As counsellors, we have deliberated, contemplated, argued and debated endless times over such issues. As women, as case workers, we have to continually struggle with our own selves. And in this, sometimes the 'woman' wins and sometimes the caseworker learns new things from the same women who come to us for help. This mutual learning and teaching goes on against the background of the conflict between principles of feminism and pragmatic choices.

Often, this is not easy. She demands, 'Please call my mother-in-law and sister-in-law and make them understand that they instigate my husband. He does not beat me, does not drink, and he brings home a decent income. This somehow irritates them and under some pretext or other, they provoke him and he begins to fight. It is they who incite him to demand dowry.' Or, 'I want to teach my husband a lesson by putting him in the police lock-up—he should also experience the pain and humiliation of being beaten.'

In such situations, how can we tell a woman what is right or wrong? The principles of counselling and the reality of her situation put us at a sort of crossroads, and sometimes, against our wishes, we have to keep quiet and accept her decision, 'We are with you, whatever happens. But it is possible that your decision may not get the response you are seeking, and if that happens, you'll have to think of other options.'

I believe that mutual rapport and trust are essential principles of feminist counselling, and these can come from our shared experiences of being women. My experiences have helped me immensely in my work as a counsellor. One can proceed further by bringing one's own feelings, problems and thoughts in tandem with others' experiences and ways of thinking but not by imposing one's ideas. Only then can change be initiated from the inside out and from the self to all.

Change Persists Against Obstacles

As their understanding of the social and structural nature of violence grows, a lot of women who come to us with their problems become our co-travellers. At the organizational level these women form support groups. In this way, as survivors, they become catalysts in social change.

'Didi, the shopkeeper is a crook, the way he looks at women makes me want to gouge his eyes out. I get angry and speak up, fight, but when others don't speak up with me, I can't decide how much I'll be able to take. They should also protest.' I know of so many women who were initially not willing to listen to a single word against their husbands or families, but they now participate in our meetings and are ready to take the lead in helping other women. They are familiar with the difficulties faced by women in the community, the need for improved implementation of public services, the means of redress, social welfare and health schemes, and are eager to take the initiative and work for change. Their names, religion, social strata, caste, are immaterial for them. They have recognized the feminist in themselves.

Raima was married at sixteen; at twenty, she was the mother of three children. Raima had never thought that she would be able to see a new dawn in her life. 'Didi, if nothing else, I'm gaining a lot of knowledge in these meetings with you. I feel inspired to do something. The children have started going to school; and I can go back to my studies now.' In three years Raima cleared Class XII, and enrolled for a Bachelors in Social Work, where she is now in her second year. Initially her husband supported her, but now, seeing her determination, her involvement and leadership in other activities beyond the home and her changed thinking, he has started resenting her. Raima says, 'Didi, now I will not step back; you have given wings to my innermost desires—now I will soar high, and shall take him along the same path.'

Sometimes I think society has created restrictions on women simply to curtail their boundless vivacity and buoyant energy. Families and relatives (whether in the parental or the marital home), have no problem with women as long as they do not disturb the status quo. They accept everything till their influence in the family and in society is not threatened. As soon as these women begin to question the family, community or the way institutions are organized, they are subjected to control and even violence.

Another woman, Suman, secured excellent marks in her Class XII exams. Had she been alive, she would have been overjoyed! Her friends say 'throw the report in her parent's face now.' All she wanted was to achieve something, but she was not allowed to study or to play. And as soon as they learnt that she was friendly with someone, they forbade her from going out. She was sent off to her maternal grandmother's place. No one knows whether she died of natural causes or was deliberately killed. What can they do now— she's gone.

I have often found myself standing with united youth groups, agitated and shocked at the untimely death of their friends. Though helpless and wounded, they are determined to remedy the wrong. 'You must learn from this tragic event. Do not keep things to yourself; you can talk to us. If she had spoken even once, we may have been able to find a way out for her. Please don't think of dying. There are a thousand ways to live! Whether or not others are willing to help, we are with you, no matter what. Always remember that. The only true homage to your friend will be to ensure that you never let this happen to anyone else. If someone is victimised or terrorised, or is being wronged, tell each other, bring it to our notice, we will find a way out.'

One Plus One Makes Eleven

This is feminist math. And truly one plus one does add up to eleven for women, because of the strength of their solidarity. It's good to hear someone say, 'Didi, no one except you understands what I want. When I come here I feel as if I have come to a place that is my own. I will never leave your side.'

Rama was married at a very young age. Her husband was an alcoholic and a habitual gambler. Despite her best efforts,

Rama could not please her husband—he resented the fact that she was literate, and continually forced himself upon her. Fed up with his excessive physical demands, she left the house. But he followed her to her parents' place. Her parents too blamed her. She was left with two options—go back to her husband or leave her parents' home and go elsewhere. Rama chose to leave her parents' home. Things did not work out even with Jagori's intervention and efforts at mediation. Rama was placed at a shelter. However, she fell sick very often. The shelter authorities refused to keep her. She was diagnosed with tuberculosis, and was bereft of a shelter.

Since no shelter home was willing to take her, and sending her to her parents or husband posed a threat to her life, it was decided to make arrangements for her stay at Jagori's field office[1] for a few months till her treatment was complete. The finances and medical care were managed collectively by the women of the group, each taking turns to stay and look after her at night. In a few days, Rama was every woman's friend. Their daughters were her friends and the mothers her aunts. With so much love and care, Rama soon started recovering. Today her treatment is almost complete.

Rama no longer stays at the Jagori field office. She has rented a small place close by and works part-time in one of the field programmes. The group members continue to take care of her and encourage her to pursue her dreams. Rama is now studying to clear her Class X exams. She aims to become a lawyer. The past is behind her, and she has no time to dwell on it.

There are innumerable such stories that stand as testimony to our work. We don't know how people view us—and we really don't care. But people, both women and men, have now started supporting us. People have begun to understand that whether the idea is to keep track of what is going on in people's homes, or to improve social services, or offer assistance on issues related to women's rights, the creation of a safe and equitable society is not just the responsibility of women but that of men too.

This task cannot be undertaken by any one organization or a handful of women. All stakeholders (leaders, legislators, councillors) need to support this enterprise. The problem arises when politics and power threaten to take over. We may have been able to find ways to approach the police through using contacts but our real dream is a day when any woman will be able to walk into a police station without hesitation or fear, and receive support for any problem that she faces. Is it too much to hope that the doors of justice will open for women and will remain like that?

The Unfinished Struggle

Sometimes it seems that the relationship between women and power is that of a master and a slave. Be it the family or society, everyone is ready to grant favours at an individual level, but people are not willing to look at the problem at a general level. I am reminded of what Marx said in an entirely different context: 'the bourgeois can bestow beneficence on the proletariat, but cannot give them equality.' For if the boureois do give equality, all power play will stop and when has anyone voluntarily given up power? The truth is that as much as this struggle is with society, it is also with the institutionalisation of thought which, in the name of a few compromises, has habituated us to a comfortable life, has rendered us slaves of our own conditioning. So though we may want to, we are unable to make decisions about ourselves.

Sometimes our children's needs and happiness weigh more than our own and sometimes conventional lessons drown our inner voice. The advice to preserve the status quo, retain security and comfort, ends up being valued more than our dreams and desires.

But who is to blame for this? The woman who is suffocating inside, who only wants to be recognized as a human being, or the bewildered woman who is battlling the external world and trying to make something of her life.

Can a woman achieve contentment by neglecting the truth of lived experience? It's really difficult to listen to a woman say things like, 'Didi, if it wasn't for the children, I would have left long ago and lived anywhere. I keep quiet and I suffer when I see the faces of my children and my parents. I am willing to live off scraps, but I can't bear to see my children subjected to injustice.'

Why don't we want to do anything for our own selves? Why don't we give our selves the same respect and value that we accord to all our relationships? The woman in me often screams, 'if you don't respect yourself, no one will respect you. Don't hide your own weakness in the name of your children and parents! If you are determined, your children can become your support.' The gap between simply listening and really understanding can only be gauged from the decisions women take—the decisions which are theirs alone.

There Are No Simple Answers

I do believe we women have spirits akin to those of ants in our determination to do what we have decided to. We carry loads that are heavier than our capacity and our body weight, and we have challenged head-on the might of the elephant, the power of patriarchy.

We stand like unvanquished champions. We have no time to stop and let defeat overtake us, and we will continue to fight, till no woman is left alone, helpless or in pain.

So we continue to fight, with ourselves and with society and its ideology that renders us weak and meek; we continue to fight the thinking that binds us to tentacles of power and uses not just men but also women as pawns. It is often said that 'women are women's worst enemies', but if both men and women are equally ready to continue the circle of violence, why is it that only women are blamed? The politics of accusing and insulting women as weak, rendering them helpless, is something we don't understand, but when we do, the whitewash over patriarchy is wiped out and it stands exposed before us. Challenging it, then, becomes our compulsion. If man and woman are governed by the same rules of life and death, then how can the rewards and penalties, opportunities and rights be different for them?

The blame for this lies entirely on the organization of society in a manner that perpetuates exploitation and wrongdoing. Before we indulge in the rhetoric of nationalism, let us talk of being 'selfish'; before we talk of protecting our country, let us first talk of protecting our families; before we denounce terrorism, let us condemn the domestic violence that pervades our homes.

My inner voice often protests that we invoke the anti-terrorist law against those who threaten the security of our country and society; then why don't we also mete out harsh punishment to those who threaten the very foundations and security of our homes and of society? The bedrock of a country is its homes, its families. If families are unsafe, then what is the point of talking of the safety of society? After years of struggle, we finally find that we are not alone. Today, those who have tried to bring change within their families are with us, They tell us, 'Didi, if the family's perceptions and attitudes change, then the coming generations will live the change. Even if my whole life is put at stake in this endeavour, it is not a losing proposition if it means that the girls of upcoming generations will experience the happiness of security!'

Transcending the family and relationships, and charting the course of their lives in their own way, these women have their own logic. Their methods might be different, but all have fought the battle for their identity and their rights in their own ways.

There is happiness and satisfaction that violence against women is at last being recognized at the level of the family and social structures and is being seen as a barrier to development. Reforms are being initiated. But there is a long way to go because it is not enough to recognize a problem and make laws, there needs to be good implementation too. Those who hold power are the ones who can be effective in changing the balance of power. Therefore, it is important that men discard their masculinised selfish ideology and move towards a new era.

It is heartening that a lot of men are with us in spirit. They too face violence at the hands of patriarchy. It is important to understand that this is not a battle between men and women, instead this struggle is against an unequal and deeply discriminatory ideology, which, is as harmful for men as it is for women.

Our fight is not against society but against the abuse and exploitation of women that pervades it. Those willing to recognize the termite that has eaten away the foundations of this society and to think afresh, lay down new foundations and correct the centuries-old system of oppression and denial, and those who are desirous of forging new relationships based on equality, partnership and co-operation, according dignity to each individual and creating a harmonious, violence-free society, come and join hands with us. What is stopping you?

Translated from the original Hindi by Iqbal Judge, Poonam Kathuria and Abha Bhaiya.

TWO

The Interface between Life and Law

Flavia Agnes

The Context: A Personal Journey

My engagement with domestic violence has been a personal journey. Starting as a 'battered woman', or in other words, as a victim of domestic violence, moving on to acquire the label of a 'survivor', a litigant, a support person to other victims/survivors, a lawyer for women's rights, a legal scholar, constantly challenging some accepted premises within the women's movement, heading the NGO which provides legal advocacy to women, getting involved in framing policies and statutes, on to monitoring and evaluating government schemes and programmes to help survivors of violence – I have had an exhausting and complex journey filled with challenges and obstacles, but also an ultimately rewarding one. This essay attempts to briefly capture this journey from the personal to the public, from individual struggles to the broader canvas of working with state structures.

The story dates back to 1967 when, as a naïve 20-year-old, starry-eyed bride, I entered into an arranged marriage, oblivious of the dangers it entailed. But my dreams were shattered soon enough, when the hard reality of coping with a violent marriage hit me very early into it. No one had warned me, but even worse, no one believed me. I raised three children while being trapped within it, always feeling guilty and responsible for the violence which lasted for thirteen long years because I did not know how to break out of that cycle.

Not that I didn't try. I did. I tried all avenues that were open to me – family, relatives, neighbours, the parish priest, the church hierarchy, counselling centres. They all had just one piece of advice for me – adjust, be submissive, do not assert yourself, gradually it will fade away. But it didn't. All my efforts to find a solution were in vain and the violence persisted – acute battering, deep gashes, fractures, bruises all over the body, violence and the threat of it, sexual abuse, financial depravity, all woven together into a death-like grip wringing the life out of me. Bruised body, wounded spirit, shattered soul, there seemed to be no way out. I felt as though only death would loosen that grip, but the imploring faces of the three innocent children kept haunting me. I continued, always nurturing the hope that one day, it would vanish, but it did not.

Though its frequency reduced, its intensity and its unpredictability continued. I lived in constant fear that it could erupt any moment and all hell would break loose. Any odd reason could act as a trigger. I had no control over it. I did not get used to it, but over the years I learnt some coping mechanisms, some survival instincts.

As the children were growing up, the violent environment was affecting their psyche. I realized then that I had to break free, if not for my sake, at least for theirs, from that vicious cycle of violence that continued from generation to generation. We were all entrapped within it, each contributing in our own way to the power dynamics within which domestic violence flourishes.

It was not a smooth, linear process. There were many leavings and returnings, back and forth. For years on end, it seemed that I was just going round in circles. Much later, I realized that they were spirals. Each time helped me get wiser until finally I was able to make that final transition. The entire process took 13 long years of trial and error.

Drawing support from the fledgling anti-rape movement of the early 80s, I walked out. This was the next major step in my life. It kindled the hope of a new possibility and glimpses of an alternate lifestyle. My contribution to the movement was to place my own personal struggle into the public domain to make a case for foregrounding domestic violence to bring about a shift from the earlier narrow and limiting focus on 'dowry deaths'.

An important marker of this phase was the writing and informal publishing of my autobiographical essay, *My Story .... Our Story ... of Rebuilding Broken Lives* in 1984.

Not just personally for me, but also for the women's movement in general. Subsequently, this essay has been translated into almost all major Indian languages and continues to be a source of inspiration to women embarking upon the winding journey towards a violence-free future, in and through various social and legal institutions.

The essay is not a legal text but a personal statement about how a woman negotiates violence, the kind of support she seeks, the responses she receives, the challenges she encounters and the setbacks she must endure, to reach her goal. The liberation here is not a linear progression but a process in which one goes back and forth, and 'success' comes in small and almost invisible measures, and at some point, the process itself transforms into a journey of survival without a clear beginning or an end. Of course, some give up, only to become statistics in crime records. But a few brave ones struggle to move on. I was fortunate to be among them.

Completing my formal education and acquiring a law degree was part of the process of moving on. This too was not easy. There were no role models to emulate. The path was untrodden, the route, long and winding. It took an entire decade from 1980 to 1990 to rebuild myself, become confident and self reliant, shed off the label of 'battered woman' and transform myself into a women's rights lawyer.

There were several hurdles to cross before I reached my goal. It was extremely challenging to get back into the formal education system to get the required degrees. I had to start from the bottom, at the age of 34. It was humiliating and also taxing, especially when one had to also look after the educational and emotional needs of the two teenage girls with meagre resources. Then there were the harrowing legal battles, with their own ups and downs. There were so many things to cope with, all at the same time. Often I faltered, went off track, thought I could never make it to the end. Yet I persisted, slowly, just one step at a time. (This is the advice I give to my clients – just one step at a time and you will go a long way ahead. The autobiography becomes a useful tool in this process.)

Finally I was almost there, a graduate! Then an LLB. I heaved a sigh of relief, I had made it! Starting as a junior lawyer at the age of 40 again had its own challenges, jostling for space with 20-year old fresh graduates, who were around my daughters' age. But I convinced myself that I was not entering as a novice. I was bringing the wealth of my personal experience and the confidence that comes with having faced life on its own terms.

I started as a junior with a well established human rights law firm, but couldn't last long. At that time there was no space for exclusive women's rights litigation. Again there were no precedents. I was destined to be a pioneer. (During the early nineties, the word 'women's rights lawyering' had not yet gained currency. But a decade later, it became an important buzz word for many NGOs. In fact all human rights NGOs included this in their basket of rights.) I realized that it could not be accomplished at an individual level, it needed organizational backing.

Majlis and the Framework of the Legal Centre

So in 1990, Majlis, a legal-cultural centre, was initiated by me and a close friend, with support from a few friends from the women's movement, who had professional expertise in various fields, more particularly in the field of art and culture, laws and rights. An unusual combination – law and culture. The name also was unusual. An Urdu word denoting association.

My partner in this project was my close friend, Madhusree Dutta, a theatre director, with an interest in curating political art and producing socially relevant films. The partnership worked well for 25 long years, was dynamic and productive, with both units working on innovative and path breaking projects within the broad sphere of law and culture.

In 1991, while registering the organization, we chose the name 'Majlis' as it was non-conformist, and meant a move away from the then prevailing culture of choosing words rooted in Sanskrit/Hindi, to better reflect the pluralistic and composite cultural traditions.

However, a year later, when after the demolition of the Babri Masjid, riots broke out in Mumbai and we got involved in relief work, turned out to be a major political statement. We added a new dimension to law and culture, that of secularism. We produced the film, *I Live in Behrampada*, directed by Madhusree which won the prestigious Filmfare award in 1994. Within a communally vitiated atmosphere, the innocuous sounding name became suspect. We had to pay a price in terms of securing the required official permissions, but we stood firm in our political ideology and continued.

For the next decade, we were able to meet the many challenges of our times through a vibrant and dynamic partnership between law and culture, hold seminars on the themes of secularism, and take the demand for a Uniform Civil Code head-on. We were able to provide the theoretical argument against it and suggest that within a pluralistic culture, such a move would, in fact, be anti-minority. We pressed for litigating for rights within the existing framework of personal laws and subscribed to the notion, 'reform from within'. Gradually, this position was accepted by several women's rights and human rights groups, particularly after the Gujarat riots of 2002.

However, after 2003, the two units – the cultural centre and the legal centre – functioned as autonomous units, each with its own area of specialization, constantly striving to break new ground.

Within the legal field, we persisted with our initial ideology of building an all-women team of lawyers, activists and support persons. Over the years, some young law graduates who were part of the team during the initial years, continued with their engagement with women's rights and human rights, as independent lawyers, rights activists or legal scholars, even after they left the organization. Hence I feel that Majlis has had a significant contribution in shaping the modern day discourse on women's rights through its activities, its underpinning philosophy and theoretical moorings.

Despite the fact that we had won several landmark cases, especially in the realm of the right to residence in the matrimonial home as well as securing the rights of women from minority communities, funding for litigation was a major constraint, as the legal profession is considered to be lucrative by donor agencies. They could not understand that litigating on behalf of women from marginalized sections could never be a self supporting activity. In order to secure funding for litigation, we included a range of other activities – trainings, research, publications, seminars. This turned out to be a blessing in disguise as it helped us evolve as a comprehensive legal centre with a multi-pronged approach towards securing women's rights.

There were several organizational setbacks too. In 2007, when three senior lawyers left the organization, and our funding had almost come to an end, I decided to wind up. I was 60, I had made significant strides, both in my personal life as well as within the organization. However, I was also heartbroken that the organization initiated by me could not sustain itself beyond me.

At this moment, a new light dawned in the horizon and a new beginning was made. My close supporter and associate, Audrey D'Mello, joined with an entirely new area of expertise, much needed to build an organization which could be sustained. With this the process of reinventing the legal centre started. This brought in a wave of new enthusiasm as a few young, enthusiastic lawyers joined and we were able to start new projects such as litigation under the newly enacted Domestic Violence Act, government collaboration to monitor the implementation of the Domestic Violence Act and RAHAT, the survivor support programme for rape victims. Securing the rights of minority women has been a consistent engagement over the years.

Today, we are a team of around twenty five persons – lawyers, social workers and a support team. Within this new structure, my role is vastly diminished and reduced to mentoring team leaders, and providing direction so that the organizational ideology seeps down.

The RAHAT Survivor Support Programme

Though our major intervention has been in the realm of matrimonial rights and domestic violence, in 2011 we tentatively ventured into a new area, of providing socio-legal support to survivors of sexual violence. Today, it has become a major flagship programme.

We were accidentally thrown into it when we had to provide support to an illiterate, migrant mother, seeking justice for her four-year-old who had been raped by an elderly watchman in a school in the vicinity of our office. Though the mother had rushed to the police station immediately when she noticed that her child had been crying and was in pain, and noticed the redness around the thighs and pelvic area, the police, under pressure from the lady principal, had refused to register an FIR (First Information Report). It was only when a doctor in a public hospital, where the mother was advised to take the child for treatment, noticed the swelling and redness around the vaginal area, and referred the matter to the police that a complaint could finally be lodged, three days later. Reports in the press had already stated that the mother was insane, that she had demanded Rs.10 lakh from the school authorities to 'settle' the case, or that the 'false' complaint was filed at the instigation of a local builder who wanted to encroach into the school property.

The mother was determined to get 'justice' for her daughter, but had no clue what she was up against. We looked around to explore if there was an NGO providing this type of socio-legal support. When we could not find any, we stepped in and pitched ourselves against the influential school authorities, and secured a conviction against a high-profile criminal lawyer, where the prosecutor had thrown in the towel. At that time, 'rape' was not a major obsession for the media. The work of most NGOs revolved around issues of domestic violence. The constant refrain in the media was that women file false cases of rape due to which most cases end in acquittal. We entered into an extremely hostile environment.

Following up this case for over two years, we were able to grasp the intricacies of the criminal justice system, and identify the gaps within it which posed an obstacle to securing justice for victims, especially those from marginalized communities. We had not only succeeded in securing the conviction against all odds, but had familiarized ourselves with criminal courts and trial procedures. In 2012, we set up the RAHAT survivor support project, as a collaborative project with the Mumbai Police. By the time rape became a national concern after the gruesome Delhi gang rape, we were well established within the criminal justice system. Through systematically following up rape cases we were able to shatter some popular myths and were also able to evolve a model for a mobile outreach programme, which could be accessed by the survivor at her residence, where she is most comfortable, as soon as a rape case is reported and explore the assistance she needs to sail through the daunting criminal legal system.

After following up 490 cases (2012–15) and analyzing 140 judgments of trial courts (2011–12) we brought out a report which provides an in-depth socio-legal analysis of victims, abusers, the crime and the trial. The key findings are:

- Around 74 per cent of the victims are below the age of 18 years.
- Girls between the ages of 10 and18 are the most vulnerable.
- Of those who were pregnant at the time of reporting, 31 per cent were in the age group of 10–15 years and 36 per cent were in the age group 15–18 years.
- Most victims belong to marginalized sections and come from poverty stricken backgrounds. Many victims are 'out of school' children. The incident of rape serves to push them several notches down the social ladder as there are no mechanisms for victim support. Several of these cases end in acquittals as the NCRB rate of conviction is only 25 per cent.
- Cases of fathers and stepfathers raping daughters are as high as stranger rapes. Young girls trapped in such situations are the most vulnerable as there is no 'safe' space left for them.
- Through our intervention programme we have been able to reverse conviction rates. In cases where we have provided support, the conviction rate is around 80 per cent.

The RAHAT survivor support progamme which aims to transform victims into survivors has been one of our major success stories.

A Glimpse into Litigating for Women's Rights

Litigating for women's legal rights within the formal legal realm is extremely daunting. Despite the odds, we have persisted with a firm conviction that the litigation space is an important arena where not only are rights protected, but the law also gets reconstituted. We believe that through the litigation process, we must hold on to the gains secured through public campaigns and law reforms.

However, we are also confronted with the reality that women's lives are complex and it is not easy to fit these complex experiences within the linear mould of law. Women move constantly between the formal and the informal spaces and are constrained to negotiate for their rights, both in the formal and the informal realms. In order to approach the court, the complexities of the lived experiences have to be constantly flattened out to fit within the confines of 'law' as laid down in statute books or have to be dressed up and inflated to meet its requirements.

The women approach us through different routes – client referrals, word of mouth, newspaper reports of our work, television debates over women's rights in which we are invited to participate and more recently, through the internet. The number of women who actually file cases in court is small compared to the women who approach us for consulting. In the initial years, while around 300 women approached us, only around 50 ended up in court. The ratio has remained the same while the number has grown over fivefold in Mumbai alone.

The work has extended to other cities and district towns through the district lawyer training programme which was initiated in 2003 and continued till 2009. As an outcome of this programme, today we have a network of around 100 lawyers who also continue to be engaged in activities similar to the ones that the core group conducts in Mumbai. They not only litigate on women's rights in courts but also spread legal awareness among community-based organizations, publish articles in local newspapers and spread knowledge of rights in schools and colleges. This has greatly enhanced our outreach in Maharashtra.

The Comparative Context of a Legal Narrative

While conscious of the domain of rights and the processes of litigation, we are also acutely aware of its limitations, and the daunting problems which those who enter the system, must endure. The profile of a legal case discussed here reflects these complexities and provides a glimpse of negotiations that are carried out during the litigation process, both within and outside the justice mechanism.

While the context for my own personal journey towards freedom was set within the women's movement of the eighties, the case I discuss was set in another era, three decades later. By then the women's movement had achieved significant gains through various campaigns focusing on the issue of violence against women. Important among the achievements was the enactment of the *Protection of Women from Domestic Violence Act* in 2005 (which came into effect in 2006), enacted with much fanfare and jubilation. It was supposed to revolutionalise court processes and bring instant respite to women victims, thereby helping curb domestic violence in society.

When I set out, cruelty was not even a ground for divorce for Christian women (it became a ground for divorce for Christian women only in 2001 after a sustained campaign that lasted over two decades!). The case for judicial separation had to be given up half-way as the legal system had very little to offer and the losses through the legal battle in terms of costs, hardships and mental trauma were far greater when weighed against the gains. Even the order of meagre maintenance of Rs.150/- each for the two daughters and Rs.500/- for myself could not be enforced as the husband chose to give up a lucrative job rather than pay maintenance. The matrimonial residence was a flat provided by the company and the constant threat one faced was that the husband had the option of giving up the job and relinquishing the occupancy of the flat.

The gains were outside the legal and religious institutional structures and more within the context of the social movement for women's rights, which helped to bring an attitudinal change within. Despite this, dealing with institutional processes was a herculean task and a great learning experience.

Against the positive developments and across the time gap, I now set out to discuss the journey of a Muslim woman from a lower middle class background, in and out of the legal institutional processes. The question that frames this discussion is: what have been the actual gains for women victims of domestic violence from the time when I set out on this journey to the time when she sets out on hers. I have named her Farzana, to conceal her identity.

Farzana – Reconstituting the 'Self' through the Legal Process

Farzana, a frail woman in her mid-thirties, approached us one evening in 2008 with a strong sense of urgency. She was fully covered in a burqa and refused to take it off even while speaking to a young Muslim lawyer, within the environment of an all women legal chamber, functioning under a familiar-sounding Urdu name, Majlis.

She was perturbed that her husband was plotting to divorce her. He had approached the *mohalla*[1] committee for mediation and the committee had decided that the husband should divorce her by pronouncing oral *talaq*. The husband was extremely abusive towards her. He also suspected her fidelity and though the allegation was baseless, the neighbours were in agreement with the husband. Despite the violence, Farzana was opposed to the divorce as it would render her and her four children destitute. She had no other support in the city and had nowhere to go. She was referred to us by a Muslim women's support group whom she had approached for help.

After the initial consultation, we decided to file for an injunction restraining the husband from dispossessing her of the matrimonial home and for a protection order restraining him from causing cruelty to her, under the Domestic Violence Act (DVA).[2] We had to obtain an urgent order before the divorce was pronounced because Farzana believed that, according to the tenets of Islam, it would be *haraam*[3] for a divorced woman to live under the same roof as her former husband.

Little did she know that the right of residence of a divorced woman is protected under the DVA. We felt that even if her husband pronounced talaq after we had obtained the initial order of injunction, we could challenge the validity of such a divorce and she could not easily be evicted from her home due to a pre-existing order in her favour. This would help to change her mindset, as a court order has a certain formality and sanctity attached to it. It would also give her a better bargaining power at the time of negotiations. We decided to advance the plea that the constant threats of pronouncing talaq constituted 'legal cruelty'.

The next evening Farzana was back in our office, accompanied by her four children. This time she removed her burqa to show us the black eye, the blue patches on her face, and the bruises on her arms. The children were hungry, as they had not eaten since the previous night. Farzana herself was on the verge of fainting. Our first response was to offer her some food before proceeding with the task of taking down the facts and preparing the court papers. Her situation had become even more precarious since the previous evening. We decided to move fast and file an application in the magistrate's court the very next day. Our lawyer worked through the night and the papers were filed the next morning. The magistrate however, was not swayed by our pleas of urgency and declined to grant an urgent, *ad-interim, ex-parte* order.[4] He adjourned the matter for seven days so that the husband could be served with a notice. The young lawyer dealing with her case was dejected as she perceived this as a major setback to the case. There was nothing to be done other than keeping our fingers crossed and waiting for the seven days to pass off peacefully without any major violent eruptions.

On the next date, the court had not received the police report regarding service of summons. However, since the concerned magistrate was absent, we decided to press for urgent orders before the magistrate who was in charge of the court for the day. This turned out to be a blessing in disguise. The magistrate was far more sympathetic and passed an ad-interim injunction restraining the husband from dispossessing her from the matrimonial home. We had won the first round. Our young lawyer was elated. This was her first case under the newly enacted DVA. This was followed by another victory four days later. The husband had received the court summons and was present with a lawyer. He was asked to file his reply. On the following date, a fortnight later, we argued the case and secured an order for an interim monthly maintenance of Rs.3,000, an order of residence in the matrimonial home and an order of compensation of Rs.1,000 for her medical expenses. Since the husband was earning only Rs.7,000 per month, we considered this to be a very good order.

It seemed that Farzana had won yet again. The new statute with its provisions of quick remedy was working in her favour. But as the case progressed, we realized that this was only a minor victory and the major battle was still ahead. Since they were both living under the same roof, a month later the violence erupted again. The husband had flouted the order and had brutally beaten her. Armed with a medical report from a public hospital, we filed an application under Section 31 of DVA for violation of the protection order and pressed for his immediate arrest.[5]

Instead, the magistrate ordered an inquiry to ascertain the veracity of our allegations. The police report was favourable and it seemed that we had won yet again. But this did not lead to any concrete response from the magistrate and our application lay dormant in the court for several months. Meanwhile, Farzana continued to be beaten, but we noticed a change in her. She was gradually gaining confidence. Now she knew that she could call her lawyer for advice. However, we felt helpless that despite a favourable order we could not provide her any protection. Farzana, however, had learnt one lesson. She knew that every time she was beaten she had to rush to a public hospital and get a medical report. She had learnt the 'law of evidence'. She was gradually learning the ropes of litigation.

In our desperation, we evolved yet another strategy for her. Since the magistrate was unresponsive to our plea, we advised her that the next time she was beaten she should directly approach the court and present herself before the magistrate, remove her burqa and show her bruised face to him. Magistrates' courts are crowded with under-trials who are brought in for remand accompanied by their lawyers, all of whom are mostly men.

This is very different from the environment within the family courts, which is crowded with women litigants, some of whom come with their children and there is an overwhelming presence of women lawyers. Cases under the DVA are not dealt with in these courts, but instead, in the magistrates' courts. Farzana's action of removing her burqa in the witness box within this court setting evoked the right response. The magistrate was moved and issued directions to the police to arrest the husband for assault under the relevant sections of the Indian Penal Code (IPC). But he was still not prepared to pass an order of imprisonment for flouting the court order of protection as stipulated by the statute.

When the husband appeared, he revealed certain facts of which we were not aware. He submitted that Farzana should move out since she had another dwelling in a slum which had been leased out on rent. She also had the support of her father and brother who were in a position to provide her an alternate shelter. We were taken aback. Had we known these facts perhaps we might have evolved a different strategy for her rather than advising her to continue residing in the same house and exposing her to extreme physical violence. But since the course of the litigation was already sealed, we could not now retract. So we decided to proceed with our original strategy.[6]

We were stuck as the case was not making much headway. The magistrate refused to frame charges for the offence of flouting the orders as this offence carried a fine of Rs. 20,000 in addition to imprisonment of one year. When a legal provision mandates stringent punishment, the courts are extremely reluctant to act.

Farzana continued to be beaten while the case kept dragging on in court. The husband and his lawyer were countering our every move and were using delaying tactics to defeat her rights. One day the husband would be absent, on the next date the lawyer would not be present and on the third date there would be yet another excuse. And of course on the fourth date, predictably, the court would be vacant. Over time we realized the hard reality that it is easy to obtain orders under DVA but extremely difficult to enforce them.

In the meanwhile, the relationship between Farzana and her husband had become extremely contentious. Both had developed a familiarity with the court and the local police station. They approached these places as they would approach the local community centre or the marketplace. Every week, one of them would lodge a complaint against the other. The situation had become volatile as by now Farzana had become bold and would not take the beatings lying down. One day when the husband thrashed her, she retaliated and both received minor injuries.

The husband complained against her and got himself admitted in a public hospital. When Farzana approached the police station to file her complaint she was arrested. To teach them a lesson, the police filed cross cases against both for assault. While Farzana spent a night in jail, the children were left at the mercy of the neighbours. This is the first time that any of the women we were defending had been arrested for assaulting her husband. We were extremely perturbed. The next day we were able to get her released on bail. The husband remained in police custody for 15 days as there was no one to bail him out.

Thereafter, Farzana had to appear in court as an accused in these proceedings and needed a criminal lawyer to follow up her case, but she had no money.[7] So we felt that it was best that the matter was settled. We convinced the husband and his lawyer to come for a settlement meeting where it was agreed that the residential premises would be sold and the proceedings would be divided equally between them. The 'residential premises' in question was a small 10 x 12 feet room in a *chawl*[8], adjacent to an open drain, but given the exorbitant price of real estate in Mumbai, Farzana and her husband estimated that it would fetch around Rs. 600,000. Following this, certain consent terms were drawn up.

Thereafter, Farzana stopped contacting us and even stopped responding to our calls. She would not appear in court and we had to constantly make excuses on her behalf and take dates. The magistrate noticed this and was curious but did not comment. But we were relieved as we thought that things had settled down between them.

Suddenly, after eight months, she appeared again with bruises all over her body. She told us that the husband had stopped paying her maintenance. We called him for the settlement but this time he was adamant. We were back to square one, following up the court case. By now the husband did not have money to engage a lawyer and started appearing in person, which gained him the sympathy of the magistrate.

After a few days Farzana was beaten up again. She retaliated by hitting him with a bamboo stick. The husband suffered injuries. She rushed to the police station and filed a complaint that he had brutally beaten her and while chasing her, had fallen down and injured himself. She also went to a public hospital and got herself admitted. In her own way Farzana was learning to defend herself against her husband and was also learning to manipulate the system. The husband also admitted himself into the same hospital and they both spent the night in adjacent wards. We were amused at Farzana's boldness.

We moved the court again. This time the magistrate issued an arrest warrant, and the husband was given a short prison sentence. He came out and made allegations that we were unnecessarily harassing him and instigating his wife to assault him. But the magistrate appeared sympathetic towards Farzana and disregarded these allegations.

When we met Farzana next, she had changed. The burqa had gone. She was well groomed and wore light make up. Her salwar-kurta was of the latest fashion, with short sleeves and a wide open neck. The frail woman who had approached us on the first date had been transformed into a confident and assertive one. She informed us that she had got a small job and was managing the house with her earnings. She also told us that her boss was sympathetic and was willing to support her.

On her next visit, she mentioned that her boss was willing to marry her and that she was now agreeable to talaq. The young lawyer dealing with her case who came from a conservative Muslim background was taken aback at the ease with which Farzana was narrating her involvement with her boss. Overall, we were happy for her, but asked her to proceed cautiously. After a few weeks she was back again, and this time without a job. She said that her boss had evil intentions. Perhaps he didn't want to marry her but only sexually exploit her, perhaps not.

In the process of interacting with courts and lawyers, Farzana had learnt to live life. She had become an active member of the women's group which had referred her to us and was part of their support network. She had made new friends, attended courses in photography and spoken English. This exposure transformed her into a new person. She continued to be beaten on and off but she had learnt to deal with it. The violence no longer had the capacity to consume her or destroy her entire life. She had even overcome the shame and stigma attached to being a victim of domestic violence.

Interestingly, Farzana did not want to fall back on her father and brother for support and in doing so, she was challenging the popular stereotype of the 'dependent' Muslim woman, shunted between the father and brother on one side and the husband on the other. She wanted to negotiate her claims and entitlements outside the purview of patriarchal controls.

She constantly challenged our notions of 'law' and 'justice'. The 'facts' always came out in bits and pieces, and we had to struggle to fit them together into a composite frame and dress them up for legal scrutiny. But she was honest and forthright and did not deliberately suppress them. It is just that she could not fathom the 'relevance' and 'irrelevance' of 'facts' as we understood them in the context of legality. She expected us to be there for her as and when she chose to approach us. In any case, the court case was not bringing her much solace. At times we felt 'used' by her casual attitude towards us and towards her own case. But gradually we too learnt to accept her and respect her choices.

While the gains in court were limited and far below our expectations, Farzana had used the process to rebuild her own life. She had learnt to deal with formal institutions and meet their requirements. The law, the courts and the support group – all had a role to play in this process. Her struggle becomes emblematic of what Ewick and Silbey (1998) refer to as the interaction between structure and agency, where state authority and local action encounter, and where law, self and social practice are mutually constituted.

Comprehending the Litigation Arena

Matrimonial litigation is an emotionally charged arena. Balancing the claims of contesting parties is like walking a tightrope. There is seldom a 'right' and a 'wrong' that gets decided since the litigation extends far beyond statutes and rights and spills over into the domain of intimate human relationships. The negotiations and settlements and the fine tuning of rights and claims become as important as the legal arguments based on legal precedents and statutory provisions. This may be true for other realms of law as well, but within family law and matrimonial disputes this becomes an overarching concern. Most often, the legal strategies evolved in the lawyers' chambers and the settlement meetings held in bar rooms determine the fate of a case. Timing is a critical factor. The interim orders secured at the initial stage of litigation often seal the fate of the case.

There are several strands in this legal narrative that can be flagged for further analyses. The agency of women, their perceptions and articulations, the incidents that are foregrounded in the context of the claims and held up for legal scrutiny, the dynamics of client–lawyer relationships and women's interactions with the state machinery and legal institutions, to list a few.

The narrative challenges popular notions of victimhood and our ideas of legality and morality. 'Facts' and 'truth' acquire a different hue as we enter the complex terrain of litigation. The game has its own set of rules. The manipulation of 'facts', admission of guilt and flouting of orders can be done only within its confines. One cannot stray too far from this confined space or one may run into rough weather, or, in other words, invoke the wrath of the court.

Sexuality and morality form the base upon which the entire edifice of matrimonial litigation is mounted. Within the patriarchal framework, this game too has its own set of rules and its own grammar. Women cannot easily win this game, even when they choose to play it. But for men, it is an easy game to play. The hypocrisy of a blatantly patriarchal social order is striking. Different sets of rules apply to men and women. In this realm, the diverse sets of personal laws are rendered insignificant and invisible, and contemporary social norms, perceptions and values become governing principles. Contestations over legality of marriage and legitimacy of children become highly volatile. For most women, their children are their weakest links. It is here that the game is toppled. Beyond this, there is no game left to play. There is only emptiness.

The local socio-economic realities constantly hover over the matrimonial claims. In a city like Mumbai, with skyrocketing real estate prices, shelter becomes the primary concern which runs through the legal narratives and becomes a focal point of legal contestation. Directly or indirectly, legal strategies revolve around notions of ownership, possession and occupation – the general concerns under property laws. The urban realities also get contextualised – slum rehabilitation projects, government directives of joint occupation, division and sale of matrimonial homes which may comprise just a small room in a slum, joint ownership of premises to secure a higher bank loan, and so on. Land records of rural agricultural land and several other collateral concerns crowd the domain of matrimonial litigation.

When mundane and ordinary lives are transposed to the legal domain, they are subjected to a mighty power that can render the familiar strange, the intimate public, the violent passive, the mundane extraordinary and the awesome banal. The terrain is also full of contradictions. It can be deadly serious and, at the same time, a source of humour and entertainment. It can also transform into a game of treachery, bribery and deceit and suck into its web all the players. Then there is no neutral ground to stand on.

Life experiences do not neatly correspond to formal institutional locations. There is a constant shift from the formal to the informal, from the civil to the criminal, from contests to negotiations, from the legal to the extra legal. At times the water becomes murky and the doctrine opaque. It is through these lived experiences that the law gets constituted in a 'bottoms up' manner as opposed to the top down process of law-making by legislators and judges.

Legal narratives are mediated stories constructed in a legal chamber with a definite focus of litigation, constantly keeping in view the law's mandates and requirements. This results in a yawning gap within the legal narratives. These gaps point towards women's culpability and bring us back, yet again, to the claims of facts and truth, legality and morality. Uncomfortable questions loom large on the horizon and continue to haunt us: Did Farzana deliberately suppress the fact that she had alternative accommodation? Was she justified in assaulting her husband and then lodging a false complaint against him?

But the moot question remains – through their culpability, do women become undeserving of their rights and entitlements enshrined in the Constitution and legislations as citizens? Here the perception of law as a set of rules that can be manipulated to one's own advantage becomes the supreme concern. If the rules are already set, then the players must play within their confines as consumers of law. As Martha Fineman argues (1995), law is a crude and limited device and is circumscribed by the dominant ideologies of the society in which it is produced. The perception of law as an arbitrary and capricious product of power confronts you. The space for claiming rights is limited and a lawyer must perform within its narrow confines.

The test of legal acumen lies in tailoring the experiences of the subaltern woman within an acceptable legal discourse, so that her voice reaches the higher echelons of the legal edifice and the law gets constituted within the realm of her realities, and not as a distant and sublime domain far beyond her reach.[9] The claims of legal provisions come alive only when they are tested against the experiences of women. The legal narratives provide us with a link between social processes and legal domains and compel us to examine the interface.

Reaching out to those at the Margins: The PLUS Course

Though one of the primary concerns of the women's movement has been the campaign for legal reforms, it is obvious that legal institutions often preclude women at the margins from accessing them. These institutions are formidable and time consuming. This forces us, as a legal chamber committed to protecting the rights of women, to explore solutions which lie outside the formal court structure. Nevertheless, even while negotiating these rights, we believe a thorough grasp of laws, their boundaries and their linkages with rights is essential. Without all this, efforts of counselling or mediation become futile and may even result in the loss of crucial rights.

One way in which we tried to deal with this dilemma was through our district lawyer training programme; educating women lawyers in smaller towns so that the gains of campaigns for law reform could help shape the litigation in smaller courts located in rural areas. This programme has met with measurable success over the years. But even here the strategies continue to be within the framework of the law, which has its own limitations. We are faced with constant demand for 'teaching rights' outside the framework of law and courts, in what we term as negotiations 'under the shadow of the law'.

But awareness of rights needs to be built into the realities of women's lives. Only then will rights become accessible to women at the margins. Starting a Para-Legal Understanding course for social workers (PLUS for short) or grassroots activists was an innovative way of responding to this need.

The course tries to break down laws and the litigation process into easily comprehensible modules of four hours each, which can be taught to grassroots activists with primary level education. Though the lectures are delivered by lawyers, they are based on real life situations and include strategies for the protection of rights through community level interventions, without approaching the formal court in the first instance. As an empowerment strategy, particularly for women who seldom venture out of their 'bastis' exposure trips to local police stations and important government offices are built into the course, as per the needs of the participants. It is also interspersed with practical lessons on how to conduct a simple legal awareness training in the community on any relevant issue such as the provisions under the Domestic Violence Act or the recently enacted Protection of Children from Sexual Offence Act, 2012 (POCSO).

The strength of the course lies in its attempt to dispel the anti-women biases and misconceptions that dominate all community level negotiations over rights for women. It hinges on the belief that if accurate legal information is provided to women from the community, they can become powerful mediators of rights for women in informal situations and the need for approaching a court and the dependency on lawyers is reduced.

The course ends with a simple test to assess the level of transmission of legal knowledge from the lawyer to the participants. Armed with the legal knowledge, they become better negotiators of rights within the community. Our interaction with the group does not end here, but continues over a sustained period, to help them solve intricate disputes which may need the intervention of lawyers. Only a miniscule number of cases actually proceed further to the courts, but the assurance that reliable legal assistance is available is greatly reassuring to the concerned woman as well as to her support person.

Deconstructing Sexual Assault

The participants of this group have been a great support in our programme for survivors of sexual abuse because they are able to alert us immediately after such an incident has taken place in the community. Here I must narrate in detail one of my most enlightening experiences while interacting with a group of participants. While discussing the provisions of POCSO, which lists various types of penetrations, and not just the conventional peno-vaginal intercourse, but also object penetration, anal and oral sex etc., I decided to start with the conventional definition of rape with its emphasis on peno-vaginal penetration.

At that time we were dealing with the rape of the four year old (discussed earlier) who was abused by the school watchman. While describing the incident, the child had said, '*Buddha uncle ne keeda dala.*'[10] The police had not bothered to ask further details about the *keeda*. Though we were successful in securing a conviction, the crime under Section 376 could not be proved, as the term *keeda* was not explained and hence the judge was constrained to convict under Section 377 (unnatural sex which includes insertion of objects), though medical evidence proved vaginal injury. (The incident occurred in 2011, prior to the POCSO Act in 2012.)

The group members, middle aged married women, were not novices, they had taken a number of victims to police stations and had successfully registered their cases. While they were familiar with the term 'rape', when asked to explain the word, they could come up only with '*balatkar*' or '*izzat lootna*' (taking away your honour), '*zabardast*' (using force), and '*galat kaam*' (wrongful action/deed). When asked to explain what action is involved they could not go any further and there was great discomfort within the group. As I was relentless in my insistence that they would have to explain the act to me, reluctantly they came up to the stage of disrobing the victim but could go no further. They were not ready to name a single sexual organ either male or female. They thought I was being vulgar and immodest to press them further for an explanation.

So I decided to move away from rape and asked them to explain normal sexual activity that is involved in the conception of a child. Though most were married and well versed with childbirth, cultural barriers prevented them from speaking of sexual activity. The participants were an active group who had reported cases even to the media. Despite this, the blushing and discomfort continued but finally we were able to extract the following sentence from them, '*zabardastise purush ladki ke kapade uthar ta hai, aur uske oopar sota hai, aur apna ling ladki ka yoni ke andhar dalta hai*' (The man forcibly removes the the woman's clothes, lies down on top of her and inserts his penis into her vagina). It took around 90 minutes for us to reach this level of communication but it turned out to be a powerful session for all of us in understanding the barriers faced by women while reporting rape. It gets worse under POCSO where one has to describe not conventional rape but a range of other sexual perversities.

If this was the level of discomfort within a group of married women between the ages of thirty and fifty, who were social workers of their area, one can only imagine what transpires when a young girl in her early teens approaches the police to lodge an FIR. Add to this the fact that the task of preparing this all-important document (indeed, the most critical piece of evidence in a case) is left to a young, untrained and often reluctant head constable, and the mind truly boggles!

When we explained that the victim/survivor should not wash herself, the clothes, including the blood-stained undergarments worn during the offence, that these should be taken in the same state to the police station and that the crime scene should not be disturbed, the women were shocked. They were unaware of the legal relevance of these precautionary measures. In none of the cases reported by them to the police station, had they followed these precautionary measures.

We also provided some important tips to the participants such as in a case of sexual assault, the victim need not be taken to the police station. If it is a recent incident, it is better to go straight to the hospital for treatment. Hospitals – both public and private – are duty bound to conduct the medical investigation, collect forensic evidence and also provide treatment to the victim. Further that an FIR can be filed by a relative, neighbour or a social worker. The police cannot conduct a pre-FIR investigation. This is based on our experience that the victim suffers the worst humiliation at the police station and is made to wait for hours before the FIR is filed which is very traumatic when the law specifically provides that the FIR can be recorded by anyone else. The victim's statement must be recorded at a place and time which is convenient to her. These are small but significant tips which will help women, especially those on the margins, to negotiate the criminal legal system on better terms.

The PLUS course helps us to transmit the practical knowledge gained from following cases of rape to grassroots activists, so that the way they respond helps the legal standard required for securing convictions.

In Conclusion

We are conscious of the monumental task that faces us. Yet we are confident that experimenting and thinking outside the box is the only way forward to protect the rights of women.

Over the last two decades our challenge has been to render the formal court atmosphere more sensitive to women's rights and to also demystify legal provisions and deconstruct biases that operate at the community level. The challenge has been to maintain the balance between the formal and the informal, constantly moving from one to the other, in the pursuit of protecting women's rights.

However, increasingly, we are aware of the challenges involved in litigating in formal courts and many times, women are unable to endure the rigour of it. Hence we are constantly in search of mechanisms through which rights can be safeguarded by empowering women from the community.

Through wide ranging and varied experiments, we have been responding to contemporary challenges as and when the need arises. I cannot say that we have evolved a model that can be followed by others in this sector. The position we occupy is unique as being an exclusive women oriented litigation center, a legal NGO encompassing within it a rights based framework of broader concerns – campaigns, policy changes and evolving protocols and guidelines for stake holders. The canvas is very broad and the framework is challenging.

Can this be a sustainable model for a legal centre working on women's rights? It is difficult to predict at this juncture. The future of the organization will be moulded by those who are steering its activities, and are involved in bringing newer visions of organizational structures, frameworks and ideology in these troubled times.

Notes

1. A mohalla is a colloquial term used to refer to a lower class neighbourhood.
2. Protection of Women from Domestic Violence Act, 2005.
3. Haraam is an Arabic term meaning sinful.
4. An order passed without giving notice to the opposite side. The court can pass an interim order before the final order under Section 23(1). An ex parte order can be passed under Section 23(2) of the DVA. This is done only when the judge is convinced of the urgency.
5. The breach of a protection order is a cognizable and non-bailable offence under Section 31 and Section 32 of the DVA; the person breaching the order can be

arrested, produced before the Magistrate for further directions, including a penalty of upto 1 year imprisonment, Rs. 20,000 fine or both.

6. By way of explanation, Farzana stated that the dilapidated room was located in a far off area and was too small for her to live along with her four children. In any case, it belonged to her father and was kept in her name only for convenience. The father was receiving the rent and neither he nor Farzana's brother were supportive of her.

7. We could not defend her through our legal aid programme as the work is confined only to civil and matrimonial matters.

8. A large building divided into several tenements, offering cheap accommodation to labourers.

9. Here I am borrowing the analytical framework of Gayatri Spivak (2001), from her seminal essay titled 'Can the Subaltern Speak?'

10. The old uncle inserted a worm.

References

Agnes, Flavia. 2014. 'My Story … Our Story … Of Rebuilding Broken Lives'. (informal publication – 5th Edition) Mumbai: Majlis.

Ewick, P. and S. Silbey. 1998. *The Commonplace of Law: Stories From Everyday Life.* Chicago: University of Chicago Press.

Fineman, Martha Albertson. 1995. *The Neutered Mother, The Sexual Family And Other Twentieth Century Tragedies.* New York: Routledge.

Spivak, Gayatri Chakravorty. 2001.'Can the Subaltern Speak?' in Cain, Peter J., and Mark Harrison (ed.) *Imperialism: Critical Concepts in Historical Studies Vol. III.*London: Routledge.

THREE

Legitimately Ours: The Parallel Systems of Feminist Jurisprudence

Abha Bhaiya

Introduction: Recalling Her Story

Every now and again, we come full circle and begin all over again. Like a home maker, an activist's work is never done. In this essay I try to put together my recollections of moments and movements in the history of the feminist movement in India that I have been engaged in. What I provide below is just a small window into a much larger tapestry of feminist activism of the last four decades. There is much more that needs to be recorded, but unfortunately, words set the limit.

It was sometime in 1983 that as a volunteer for the women's collective, Saheli,[1] I found myself sitting in the court for a hearing. The case in question was that of a 20-year old construction worker from Rajasthan who had been gang raped at the construction site by the contractor and some workers. The courtroom was cold, the lawyers and judges 'very male', the survivor almost invisible. I knew this case was not going to give us what A and I wanted to hear. The rapists were acquitted. The court held that there were no marks on A's body that could provide evidence that she had fought back. The medical examination had been delayed. What held me together was A's courage and determination. I came out seething in anger.

Later, another case that became important for the Saheli collective and for many other autonomous groups was the case of the murder of Sudha Goel.[2] Sudha had been at the receiving end of continuous harassment for dowry by her in-laws and in the end was burnt alive by them. At the time, she was in an advanced stage of pregnancy. Almost all dowry murder cases brought to Saheli those days by parents of young women victims, had a common script. Our question to the parents always was, 'why did you not bring her back home, why were you so indifferent to the signals that she kept sending, why did you not report the case while she was still alive?' The answer was always the same, 'We did our best. We spent a lot of money trying to fulfil all their demands. How long can we keep the daughter in our house? After all her husband's home is her home. But now we want to take revenge, teach them a lesson.' The question that went round and round in our minds and that we wanted to put to the parents was, 'Is it not too late? Why did you not help her when she so desperately needed your help? Do you realize that you are also responsible for what happened to her?'

Sudha Goel's story was no different from that of countless other women. The letters she had written, the phone calls she had made were not heeded by her parents. She had pleaded with her father to take her back as she feared for her life. Her last letter was heartbreaking: she asked her parents to employ a maid for her and pay her since she was heavily pregnant and therefore was unable to bend and do all the housework. Sudha's fears were not unfounded. She was soon brutally murdered by her husband and her mother-in-law, both of whom had colluded in planning her death. As I sat in the court, I wondered whether the judge, who read Sudha's letters (these were placed as evidence in the court), understood what it meant to be so advanced in pregnancy and to be the sole household worker for the entire family. How humiliating it must have been for her to have to beg her parents to pay for a maid who could take some of the load off her. Sudha Goel's story made me wonder why women's voices were so inaudible to their families, more specifically their parents and also to society at large as well as to the entire justice system. Are not homes and courts a continuum of a patriarchal system that is indifferent to the exploitation and abuse of women?

As I sat in on the hearings, I was not just seeing the accused and the complainant on opposite sides of the fence but also hearing the deafness of the legal machinery. It was clear that judges, lawyers, people sitting in the courtroom, were all bonded by patriarchal, caste and class biases. How could they then ever experience the total disfranchisement of women from their marital, maternal, familial and social citizenship?

NO SAFETY ZONE

The violence that confronted women was complex. The most pervasive form of human rights abuse in the world, violence against women includes a range of acts. In most cases, the perpetrator is known – and sometimes close - to the victim. According to a number of studies, domestic violence is endemic and comprises the highest number of crimes against women. According to the National Crime Records Bureau (NCRB),[3] violence against women by partners has been steadily increasing. Therefore, the fact that the violators are not necessarily strangers but men well-known to women had to be put out on the family and public chessboard for all to see and acknowledge.

Women's inability to voice their violation, to walk out of violent homes and to seek alternatives is fraught with systemic impediments and ideological doctrines learnt by them in their patriarchal schooling in the first, and the most culpable institution, the family. This internalization is so deep that women often find it difficult to even recognize it as a violation of their rights as human beings. The divide between what was seen as the public, and what is defined as private played a major role in maintaining silence about such violations. Thus speaking out is the first step towards seeking redressal.

Understanding the theoretical underpinnings of violence against women helped activists to bridge the gap between private and public violence. Initially, a number of activists from different feminist groups began sharing their personal experiences. A self-disclosure process in intimate and secure spaces allowed them to share experiences of child sexual abuse, of discrimination, neglect and denial in homes. This starting point paved the way for solidarity and a conceptual understanding of the family as a patriarchal institution, one that sought and gained strength from religious and cultural practices. It took a while to realize that instead of guaranteeing safety, as received wisdom would have it, confinement inside the home ensured silence and slavery, increasing women's tolerance and acceptance of suffering and injustice. The other hard-hitting realization was that neither the parental nor the marital home belonged to women. In spite of being burnt, beaten, sexually abused by the husband and other family members, a majority of women survivors still believed that this was the only socially legitimate place for them.

Notwithstanding these realities, the state institutions did not recognize the family as the most culpable institution for serious crimes against women. Indeed, the much-acclaimed democracy had failed to provide safe citizenship to women.

Galvanizing the Movement

Two incidents mark the genesis of the feminist movement of the late seventies. The custodial rapes of Mathura,[4] a young tribal woman in 1980 and, two years earlier, that of Rameeza Bee,[5] a young Muslim woman (Kannabiran 1980) galvanized the movement towards national campaigns demanding legal reform. In both these landmark cases, the emphasis in the trials was not on evidence of rape but rather on the victims' sexual history and their characterization as promiscuous, leading to the acquittal of the police officers charged (Kannabiran and Menon 2007). The Rameeza Bee judgment led to widespread protests across India and many women's groups came together to demand a review. A Mumbai based group called the Forum Against Rape (whose name was later changed to Forum Against the Oppression of Women) organized a national conference where the question of legal reform was widely debated. Activists spoke of the failure of the judicial process. A wider set of discussions took place on the nature of patriarchy in which violence against women was located within the framework of the systemic oppression of women by men. In the aftermath of the acquittal of the two accused in the Mathura rape case, four lawyers wrote an open letter to the Chief Justice of India expressing concern about the judgment and its violation of the rights of women. This letter became a catalyst for a nationwide campaign for reform of the rape law, and resulted in the first set of reforms in 1983. [6] The campaign against rape eventually led to the first amendments (since colonial times) on the law on rape; the mobilization of activists across the country played a role in the emergence of a number of autonomous, non-party affiliated, women's groups.[7] At the same time, there was also a nationwide debate on the anti-dowry law, and several amendments were proposed. Section 498A[8] was the direct result of the active role of feminists as vigilant pressure groups.

The eighties and nineties were significant as years of learning by doing, evolving our collective spaces for action and reflection. Most women's collectives began with study circles that helped activists to build a conceptual foundation for their praxis. Several of the groups simultaneously started engaging with women from poorer and marginalized communities in the slums and villages. As more women came forward to report their cases, campaigning and supporting women in crisis also helped women's groups to gain public legitimacy.

The decade of the nineties saw an exponential increase in the number of women's groups across the country. Many of these groups echoed the slogan, 'the personal is political', and affirmed that everything that takes place inside the four walls of the home is linked to a broader political reality. This led to a more nuanced and complex understanding of the institutions of the state such as the police, the judiciary and the bureaucracy. At the same time, feminist groups strengthened their demands for more stringent state accountability. They also directed their efforts towards law reform, and the incorporation of women's perspectives in the policy and planning processes, putting pressure on the state to create special cells, bureaus, departments and ministers within the state to focus on women.

Over the years, feminist engagement with different socio-political issues continued to gain momentum. Some of the actions were well planned, but many were reactive, somewhat like a fire-fighting response to immediate events, for example the anti-Sikh violence that overtook many parts of the country in the aftermath of the assassination of Indira Gandhi in 1984, or the disastrous gas leak at the Union Carbide factory in Bhopal in the same year,[9] both of which resulted in the deaths of thousands of people. Other pressing issues such as the increase in communal, identity-based violence, or the spread of a coercive family-planning programme also became major issues for feminist politics in India.

THE RESPONSE OF THE STATE

Initially, before the feminist movement emerged, there were other developments that helped maintain pressure on the state and paved the way for feminist groups to take the agenda of women's rights forward. In 1974, a report published on the Status of Women helped to bring the question of women's unequal status to public attention.[10] The mid-eighties was also a time when the presence of a strong women's movement pushed some states to initiate specific programmes for the development of women. The first one of such initiatives was put in place in 1984. Meant to address issues of rural women and develop their leadership, the Women's Development Programme (WDP)[11] was put in place in Rajasthan. In this programme, village level women, mostly without literacy skills, were selected as catalysts of change and were given the name sathins, (village level activists). This programme signalled a fundamental shift in the thinking of the state. Recognizing the need for bringing about change in the lives of poor, village women, the programme focused on building women's leadership. Soon there was a pool of nearly 800 village-level sathins and more than a hundred support women called prachetas. Feminist activists played an extremely important role in training village level women activists for building feminist perspectives and action plans for the sathins and prachetas.

Residential trainings, often a month long, provided women an opportunity to reflect on their own lives and investigate the patriarchal oppressive system that enforces their subordination.

The programme was successful in challenging the myth that women from oppressed communities were not capable of change as they were ignorant and uneducated.

Based on the success and potential of the WDP, the Department of Education, in the Ministry of Human Resource Development (HRD), initiated a large national educational programme for women called Mahila Samakhya[12] (Education for Women's Equality). The programme was piloted in four states of the country and has since been introduced in more than ten states. It was envisioned and architected in consultation with feminist activists and academics and was an excellent example of partnership as the programme design followed many principles of process-oriented feminist learning and training. During its initial phase, the entire training design was evolved and implemented by feminists with no targets set except self-awareness and empowerment of rural poor women. In addition, some of the feminist activist and senior scholars joined the programme as consultants and/or coordinators at state and national levels. A National Resource Group comprising of feminist trainers, educationists, scholars and subject experts worked with the education department and played the role of guiding and advising the programme. This was a significant experiment in collaboration between the women's movement and the state, recognizing the rich experience of the feminist movement. Some of the activists were of the view that feminists working with this programme had been co-opted by the state. However, the massive outreach of the programme that had no tangible targets, created space and time for women to articulate their concerns and build their determination to take action. The women's movement provided the political content to the programme implementation strategies.

Mahila Samakhya was founded on the understanding that any programme for women has to be relevant to their daily lives and issues. It was also an assertion by both the Department of Education and feminists that the lack of literacy did not mean that women were uneducated. It was successful in establishing that poor and marginalized women are knowledgeable and capable of learning and changing their destinies. According to Vimala Ramachandran, the state's acceptance of feminists as a resource for the programme brought feminist thought directly into the design and implementation of the programme. However, barring training and hand holding in the initial years, the programme had no real power to accept the recommendations of the National Resource Group. (Ramachandran and Jhandyala 2012)

ENSURING JUSTICE

In the feminist autonomous collectives that functioned as resource centres in metro cities, activists began to engage with local and national issues. Their day-to-day involvement on the ground, combined with larger issues was to become a characteristic of the feminist movement.

As far as accessing the legal justice mechanism was concerned, as early as the eighties, feminists had begun to challenge the state's lack of response and action, the non-recording of the First Information Report (FIR), particularly when it was marginalised women who attempted to file them, and other such biases. Women used many different strategies to create awareness and confront the state. These included street plays, pamphlets and posters, street writing and campaigns; many of the feminist platforms and collectives did consciousness raising and claiming public spaces, thereby creating visibility for issues of violence against women. This visibility often on the front pages of newspapers, especially to dowry-related cases initially in Delhi and later in many other cities, enabled women who had escaped extreme harassment and murder to continue to walk into the resource centres that were set up in the eighties to seek justice.

Women's groups combined legal remedies with 'extra-legal' – as in within the bounds of legitimacy, but not using the law as a means. The most common action was to go in a 'gang' with the woman to her marital home and ask her to identify all her belongings, put them in a pick-up truck and leave. En-route they would give a copy of the list of belongings that the woman had identified as hers to the police and move on. Often activists would go in a large group and help the woman to wrest her child free from the father's family. The system deemed such actions illegal. We were beginning to train ourselves in erasing the line between the legal and illegal.

Despite considerable evidence that the legal system was weighted against women, some of the women's groups chose to continue to pursue the legal option. Many groups took to court some landmark cases of women, thus challenging and changing the discourse within the four walls of the courts, and broadening the debate. However, by the early nineties, it was clear to activists and academics alike that unless there was a political commitment to address the structural barriers – economic, social, cultural and religious – women's position would continue to deteriorate, and violence against them would continue to rise.

The continuing engagement with issues of violence and the growing voices of women speaking against its pervasiveness provided the impetus for some feminist groups to seek alternative platforms for ensuring justice.

In this journey, challenges for feminists have been twofold: first, to imbibe the feminist perspective into the impermeable legal institutions and other justice seeking systems; and second, to search and seek alternative strategies to redefine jurisprudence based on a feminist understanding of the systemic nature of violence against women and its widespread acceptance.

The subversion of the system requires new strategies. In order for the alternatives to become political, feminist, community spaces, simply stating the case is not enough. The feminist movement began to look for alternatives to the formal justice system that could address women's specific experiences of violence and abuse.

There are innumerable reasons that deter women from approaching courts. Among them are: mistrust of the law, the fear of judges and lawyers, the lack of understanding of legal language, a lack of familiarity with formal procedures and the alienating and intimidating atmosphere of the courts. In addition, women's lack of mobility and freedom of movement makes it difficult for them to attempt to seek redressal. It is against these realities that women began to seek alternatives to the existing justice system. In addition to the age-old methods such as public hearings, rallies, demonstrations, protest songs, it became imperative to evolve some ways to address issues of domestic violence in a more women-sensitive way.

As the issue of violence against women gained importance within the women's movement in India, it found resonance in similar struggles in other parts of the world. At the Vienna Women's Tribunal held during the UN conference on human rights in 1993, women's groups resoundingly declared: 'Women's rights are human rights'. The determined declarations and the demand for inclusion of women's rights in the category of human rights irrevocably changed the definition of human rights. The international conference on human rights not only made violence against women a concern of the global state community, but also affirmed the rising concern of feminists the world over that the sanctum sanctorum, the home, was often the most unsafe space for women and girls.

Indeed, the home as a site of discrimination, of the denial of rights, the violation and often murder of women, was now brought squarely under the spotlight. Women's groups emphasized that safety inside the home is a state responsibility, and the global feminist movement demanded state accountability for crimes against women. It was evident that so long as the state and society continued to reinforce the public-private divide, the state would abdicate its responsibility towards women's safety inside the home. Women's groups asserted that violent men had enjoyed impunity for their actions inside the home because of the prevailing belief that what goes on inside the home is the private business of those who live there, and indeed the personal business of the man. Women did not really count other than as man's property.

The Genesis of Women's Justice Systems

The first state programme in the country that established the Nari Adalat or the women's court as an alternate system of justice was evolved in 1995 in Gujarat in the district of Baroda primarily to train rural women as barefoot lawyers. The idea emerged as a lot of women started approaching the Mahila Samakhya team with cases of violence against women. While women activists started to respond to some of these cases in an informal way, there was no training or a mechanism in place to address the issues of VAW inside or outside the home in a more systematic way. A three month long training course for Nyay Sakhis (friends of justice) was designed and initiated by Jagori, a feminist organization based in Delhi.

Simultaneously, in other states women's groups had begun the process of listening to stories of violence against women and reflcting on possible solutions, sometimes also helping to initiate action to resolve conflicts. Many of the women involved found themselves acting as counsellors, although without any formal training.

These informal groups and forums helped women to find a conducive environment to speak out. The collective nature of their experiences helped create both solidarity and strength. Visiting police stations in a group, going to the man's family, confronting a rapist, an employer, all this led to growing confidence to deal with those in power. This collective courage of the meek was a significant milestone in the process of regaining dignity.

The legal literacy training module covered an entire range of themes such as the constitutional framework, the definition of democracy and gender justice, the analysis of the family as a patriarchal institution, the difference between equality and equity, a critical understanding of all laws related to women, the structure of the state and its various institutions, the history of women's movements, the extent and the kinds of violence, women's rights over their body and sexuality, principles of feminist jurisprudence and so on. The training also included visits to police stations, prisons, village panchayats, courtrooms and government-run homes for destitute women. Women who participated in the course stayed together for three months, going home every weekend to see their families.

In the legal literacy classes, women were taught terms and words relevant to court language. They also learnt to read and write. The programme was ambitious and fulfilling for both the trainer and the trainees.

The women, who were trained as barefoot lawyers, were extremely proud of their status as 'vakil sahib' as they came to be known in their villages. They set up open courts under trees, in the compound of the panchayat, in the courtyards of homes, and put up banners announcing the Nari Adalat. They also carried a stamp in their bags which gave 'official' status to their work. Along with the young staff of the programme, they used legal, extra-legal and what could perhaps be named by the mainstream as 'illegal' measures to seek justice. They began investigating violations of women's rights, both hidden and obvious. Every now and then, they would hire a jeep, pile into it and take off to locate a violent husband and confront him. They did not succeed every single time, but they lost no opportunity to learn from their experiences and to develop their strategies.

What surprised the barefoot lawyers as well as the programme staff was the fact that the judgments they pronounced were accepted by both parties. The trainees working as barefoot lawyers sought help from their educated children and neighbours in getting them to write out agreements on stamp paper. Perhaps it was the fact of the 'official' look of the court paper that somehow provided the agreement legitimacy. Litigants paid the expenses as the amount was so minimal compared to lawyers' fees, and the time they would have spent at hearings, and on travel. I remember a very difficult case of the rape of a woman by one of the high caste villagers. The family was not willing to report the case to the police. The Nari Adalat succeeded in getting a part of the land of the rapist transferred in the name of the rape survivor and made him apologize in public and pay a fine. The case was dealt in an open court as the entire village knew about the incident.

The women's court, or Nari Adalat, is an umbrella term. A number of similar initiatives were set in place in different parts of the country at the time. Their basic premise was the swift delivery of justice, and an expanded definition of it, which worked at the community level. These women-led resistance and redressal mechanisms came to be known by different names, such as the Mahila Nyay Panchayat, the Mahila Nyay Samiti, the Jamaat. Their methods of functioning were broadly similar.

The Nari Adalat model is based on building the legal literacy capacity of Nyay Sakhis or women legal activists, in a planned manner, with support from feminist lawyers. The courts are held at regular intervals, there are follow up visits to homes and also to the courts, case studies are recorded and relief sought. All cases are not what we call successful, but even where the Adalats have not been helpful, women know they have support and access to a feminist space and that in itself helps to strengthen their position in the home. A great deal of work is put into keeping in touch with families and survivors, collecting accurate data and information from both families and continuing to support the woman or the man as the case may be. As one of the barefoot legal activists said, 'Now more than our families, it's the survivors who phone us.'

The Nari Adalats have used multiple strategies rather than a single practice. The informality of the community-based institution allows for flexibility and creativity. No claim is made to instant success; however the process is a transformative one for both the survivor and the legal activist. The objective is not to amplify success stories but to make a strategic intervention in the realities of women's lives.

Functioning since the early nineties the MNPs/ Nari Adalats are institutions that are symbolic of marginalized rural and urban women's leadership in the feminist movement and in the struggle for women's rights and justice. Over these two decades, mature community interventions and Nari Adalats have come a long way in terms of developing practices and curricula for training of rural and urban poor women and helping women in distress. They have carved out a new legitimate role for poor women as justice defenders. The women themselves have shown their keenness to learn and become capable. Their strong sense of justice combined with common sense based strategies have earned them community acceptance. This has also helped to begin the process of changing community perceptions about women. Women's courts are an excellent model because they interface with formal and informal systems.[13]

By and large the experiences of women within the alternative or parallel justice systems have been positive as these systems have gained tremendous acceptance within the community. However, it is evident that unless other institutions which impact on women's lives also become gender sensitive, 'project justice' remains an incomplete agenda. Further, if women's courts are to continue to hold their stake in the larger territory of claim for justice, for a national level feminist review of these small but significant spaces, that women's courts have opened up, can become a significant step in the future.

Coming Full Circle?

On 16 December 2012, a young woman, Jyoti Singh Pande, was brutally assaulted and gang raped in Delhi. A few days later, she died of extensive injuries a few days later.

The case was covered extensively in both the national and international media. In its aftermath, it became evident that the feminist movement was confronted with new challenges: these included engaging once again with the question of state irresponsibility and neglect, and dealing with an inadequate legal framework as well as the failure of various state institutions. Activists who gathered in Delhi and other parts of the country to protest the violence put pressure on the state to look afresh at the legislation on sexual violence. In response, the state set up a three-member committee, the Justice Verma Committee, to look into the question of amendments to the existing law. Public protests, as well as extensive and continuing coverage in the media, and the subsequent punishment meted out to the perpetrators of the assault, seem to have created a greater social awareness about sexual violence and there seems to be increased reporting of cases both from inside the family and in public spaces. Media coverage also kept the issue alive so that it no longer remained a taboo subject in discussions inside families and in the academy. The issue has since remained in the public arena with continuing mobilization of various stakeholders. Of course, this had negative consequences too – the insecurity of having young women out on the streets meant that many parents pulled their daughters out of jobs and even stopped them from studying. Equally, it was not surprising that very few parents thought of talking to their sons about the increasing crimes against girls and women and men's role as either perpetrators or spectators. However, while it is significant that the last decade has seen a slew of legislation that has to do with women,[14] it bears remembering that implementation still remains a major problem.

It is in these troubled times that the Nari Adalat model continues to find a niche space for women, sharpening the praxis of feminist justice and providing much needed support, legal and otherwise, to victims. Nari Adalats have moved far beyond the limited role of mediation and counselling. Some of the states have even used the model to set up women's Panchayats.

With strengthened legal provisions, women activists have to learn to face new challenges. In addition to providing relief, educating the judiciary on issues of laws for gender justice; exposing malpractices within the police and the judicial system; training police and protection officers, the family and the neighbourhood; as well as walking the difficult path of investigation in remote corners of villages and marginalized spaces in cities and towns, remain real challenges for women activists and practitioners.

The future is for us to make and see.

Notes

---

1. Saheli, one of the first feminist autonomous collectives, was set up in Delhi, India in 1981 by nine feminists. It was created as an autonomous organization independent of foreign funding and party politics. The collective continues to be a significant voice for political thought and action within the feminist movement.

2. Laxman Kumar and Mrs.Shakuntala Devi were found guilty in a case of dowry death. They were accused of killing Sudha Goel, who was in her ninth month of pregnancy, after she failed to meet their demands for extra dowry. Mother and son were sentenced to death by the trial court in May 1983, the only time an Indian court imposed capital punishment in a dowry killing. But they appealed and were acquitted by the New Delhi High Court. In 1985, the Supreme Court heard a second appeal by the wife's family and again convicted the two. But it reduced the death sentence to life imprisonment. The court order for their arrest never reached the police, said T.N. Mohan, assistant

commissioner of police. According to a police officer, they were never sent to prison to serve their life terms.

3. According to the National Crime Record Bureau, every 9 minutes, a case of cruelty is committed by either a husband or a relative of the husband. Indeed, violence against women is the greatest occurring crime against women. NCRB statistics tell us that from 2011 to 2012, there was a 7.5 per cent increase in cruelty by husbands and relatives against women. The volume of domestic violence referrals from the police rose to 103,569 in 2013-14, a rise of 17.5 per cent from 2012-13 and the highest level ever. 72,905 (70.4 per cent) of these referrals were charged, the highest volumes and proportions ever and a rise of 12,716 charged defendants (21.1 per cent) from 2012–13. The volume of prosecutions completed in 2013-14 rose to 78,071 – a rise of 7,369 prosecutions (10.4 per cent) from 2012-13, but not yet reaching the highest volume of 82,187 prosecuted in 2010-11. The caseload of DV cases 7 has risen since 2012-13 from 8.9 per cent to 10.7 per cent in 2013–14. The volume of convictions reached 58,276 – a rise of 5,727 convictions (10.9 per cent) since 2012-13.

4. Mathura, a minor and orphan Harijan girl, was raped by two policemen at a police station in Maharashtra in 1978. She filed a case against them. This was at a time when the rape laws in India were heavily skewed in favour of the rapist. The most controversial question related to the issue of consent. In most cases, the victim found it impossible to prove that she had not consented to the act. In Mathura's case, the district court believed her and awarded the death penalty to the accused while the high court acquitted them, and the Supreme Court upheld the acquittal. The Supreme Court ruled (Tukaram Vs. State of Maharashtra, AIR 1979 SC 185; (1979) 2SCC 143; 1978 CrLJ 1864; 1979 SCC 143), that there were no injuries on the person of the girl, which meant that she had not resisted and that the incidence was a 'peaceful affair'! The case stirred up a hornet's nest and the government was forced to wake up from its long slumber. In 1983, a comprehensive change was made in the rape laws. The Mathura judgment, as it came to be known, went largely unnoticed until September 1979, when law professors Upendra Baxi, Raghunath Kelkar and Lotika Sarkar of Delhi University and Vasudha Dhagamwar of Pune wrote an open letter to the Supreme Court, protesting the concept of consent in the judgment. 'Consent involves submission, but the converse is not necessarily true....From the facts of case, all that is established is submission, and not consent...Is the taboo against pre-marital sex so strong as to provide a license to Indian police to rape young girls?' Spontaneous widespread protests by women's organizations followed and activists demanded a review of this judgment. The protests received extensive media coverage.

5. Rameeza Bee, 26, accused four policemen in Hyderabad of gang raping her in 1978, and beating her husband, a rickshaw puller, to death. The rape and

murder sparked off riots in the twin cities of Hyderabad and Secunderabad and some other parts of the state. Women's groups across the country demanded an enquiry into the case.

6. Ibid.

7. The feminist groups that emerged included Vimochana, Bangalore 1979. Forum Against oppression of Women (FAOW) , Bombay, 1980, Stree Sakti Sangtana, Hyderabad 1989.

8. Passed by Indian Parliament in 1983, Indian Penal Code 498A, is a criminal law (not a civil law) which is defined as follows, "Whoever, being the husband or the relative of the husband of a woman, subjects such woman to cruelty shall be punished with imprisonment for a term which may extend to three years and shall also be liable to fine. The offence is cognizable, non-compoundable and non-bailable.

9. Over 500,000 people were exposed to methyl isocyanate (MIC) gas and other chemicals. The toxic substance made its way into and around the shanty towns located near the plant. Estimates vary on the death toll. The official immediate death toll was 2,259.

10. Towards Equality: The Report of the Committee on the Status of Women. 1974. Government of India, Ministry of Education and Social Justice.

11. WDP was started in Rajasthan in 1984 in six districts and later extended to nine. The programme was a departure from the old practice of seeing women as object of welfare to seeing them as active agents of change. WDP occupies a crucial place in a key aspect of empowerment i.e. enabling women to become active participants in the process of planning and decision making at the village and macro levels. These tangible service oriented programmes, importantly, cater to the needs of women and children within mainstream development processes. Taking a quick look at some of these, however, we can assess whether these interventions are also addressing the crucial dimension of the empowerment of women.

12. The Mahila Samakhya programme was launched in 1988 in pursuance of the goals of the New Education Policy (1986) and the Programme of Action as a concrete programme for the education and empowerment of women in rural areas, particularly of women from socially and economically marginalized groups.

13. Some excellent documentation of these practices are done by feminist film makers such as Deepa Dhanraj. Women's Courts – Blurring Lines of Legalities.

14. The Criminal Law (Amendment) Act 2013, the Protection of Women from Domestic Violence Act 2005, the Sexual Harassment at the Workplace Act & Rules 2013, the Pre-Conception and Pre-Natal Diagnostic Techniques (PCPNDT) Act, 1994, the Protection of Children from Sexual Offences Act (POCSO) 2012.

References

Rajan, Anuradha and Nandita Bhatla. 2002. *Women-Initiated Community Level Responses to Domestic Violence. Summary Report of Three Studies.* Washington, DC: International Center for Research on Women (ICRW).

Batliwala, S. 2014. *Carving A Space: Reflections On The 2nd MenEngage Symposium.* Association for Women's Rights in Development (AWID).

Gandhi, Nandita and Nandita Shah. 1992. *The Issues at Stake Theory Practice in the Contemporary Women's Movement in India.* New Delhi: Kali for Women.

Geetha, V. 2002. *Gender-Theorising Feminism.* Kolkata: Stree.

Government of India. 1974. *Report of the committees on the status of women India.* New Delhi: Government of India, Ministry of Education and Social Welfare, Department of Social Welfare.

Menon, N. 2012. *Seeing like a Feminist.* New Delhi: Zubaan-Penguin.

Ramachandran, Vimala, and Kameshwari Jandhyala (eds.) 2012. *Cartographies of Empowerment: The Mahila Samakhya Story* New Delhi: Zubaan.

Smart, C. 1989. *Feminism and the Power of Law.* London: Routledge.

Stubbs, J. 2002. 'Domestic violence and women's safety: Feminist challenges to restorative justice.' *Restorative justice and family violence,* 42–61.

FOUR

Challenging the Collusion of Caste, Class and Patriarchy Embodied in the State

Kanchan Mathur

No justice system in the world can match our strength. Our power is immense. If we unite who can put us down? Our struggle to stop violence against women must continue and I am committed to fighting for this cause no matter what.

Bhanwari Devi
December 10, 2012, Jaipur
(Human Rights Day and launch of One Billion Rising)

Introduction

The Bhanwari case in September 1992 became a rallying point for the women's movement in the state of Rajasthan and in India. The name of Bhanwari Devi, a *sathin* of the Women's Development Programme of the Government of Rajasthan, has since become synonymous with the arduous legal battles faced by women fighting against violence.[1] Bhanwari's struggle is a milestone for the Indian women's movement. The protracted struggle, the countrywide campaign led by feminist activists, attracted national and international attention, and resulted in the historic *Vishakha* judgment – wherein the Supreme Court used international framework/principles of CEDAW to formulate guidelines for the redressal of sexual harassment at the workplace.[2]

For the women's movement, it was important not only to provide support to Bhanwari but to maintain its united voice and to challenge the caste/class politics of those in power, especially when this power is used against a poor woman from a marginalized community in order to deny entitlements and rights. The state not only reneged on its responsibility towards a state employee who was entitled to state protection but also failed to understand the strength of character of the woman it was dealing with. Bhanwari refused to give up her struggle for justice for all women despite the fact that she lost her own legal battle. Support for her came from all over the country in the form of agitations/protests, *dharnas* and mass mobilizations. What happened to Bhanwari resonated with previous histories of rape around which there had been major struggles, such as that of Mathura and Rameeza Bee, which had created an alliance of women's movements across the country and which had also drawn in other progressive forces, primarily from the academic corridors of the law faculty in Delhi.[3]

This essay explores the intersectionalities of caste, class, gender and patriarchy, in an effort to highlight the factors that have enabled Bhanwari and subsequently many women like her to assert their right to live with dignity in the face of an indifferent and non-responsive state machinery. At another level it attempts to capture the series of events that shaped the struggle of the women's movement and the ensuing support which, in turn, helped redefine the understanding of rape, justice and injustice, and the success and failures thereof.

The Delhi rape case of 16 December 2012 and the subsequent death of the young victim gave rise to unprecedented outrage. There was also extensive coverage by the media, both local and global. The Bhanwari rape case provides many parallels as it inspired both urban and rural women to come out in large numbers and stage protests across the country. The lessons learnt during the campaign for justice for Bhanwari helped initiate a process to put in place many of the extra-legal strategies to fight violence against women that exist in the country today.

I have been witness to the public and private protests following Bhanwari Devi's rape case. In this essay I provide a brief backdrop to the Women's Development project of the Government of Rajasthan launched in 1984. Following this I attempt an analysis of the role of the patriarchal state and its collusion with caste and class and the campaigns initiated by the women's movement to attain justice for Bhanwari. The concluding section of the essay underscores both the gains garnered by the women's movement and the challenges confronting it.

The Women's Development Project

Bhanwari, an oppressed caste *Kumhar* (potter) woman from Bhateri village in Bassi tehsil, 45 kilometres from Jaipur, was around 40 years old when she was selected and trained as a sathin in the Women's Development Project (WDP) of the Government of Rajasthan in 1985.[4] The WDP was initiated in 1984 with financial support from United Nations fund for Children (UNICEF) in six districts of Rajasthan viz. Jaipur, Ajmer, Bhilwara, Banswara, Udaipur and Jodhpur.

The trainings in WDP, primarily conducted by feminist trainers, sought to demystify the process of women's subjugation by unpacking the multiple power relations that have a bearing on women's lives. They also aimed at strengthening the self-confidence of women and enhancing their collective capacities for the transformation of their own lives. WDP enabled rural women to translate and link their personal experiences of gender subordination to the larger systemic forces of gender inequality in society.

With the programme still awaiting a full-fledged take-off, a beginning was made with the first sathin training in August 1984 at Bada Padampura (Jaipur district). It gave centrality to the issue of violence. This was the first time that women who participated in the training recognized domestic violence as an act of violence per se, for they discovered that 20 out of the 22 sathins were victims of domestic violence (Banerji 1984). Such discussions helped to arrive at a clearer understanding on why violence against women is endemic in society and how it is sustained by patriarchal forces that subordinate women.

The programme functionaries subsequently took up several cases of extreme violence – rapes, domestic violence, dowry murders, incest, labelling of women as witches, compulsion to wear a chastity belt and forced incarceration – apart from the denial of rights to food, education, economic resources and healthcare. The forms of violence meted out to women in each of the cases discussed might have been different; however, the strongly embedded notions of 'honour' and 'shame' were central to them. In the context of the state, honour and shame have been highly effective tools for perpetrating the conspiracy of keeping women from speaking against different patriarchal forces and acts of outrage meted out to them (Mathur 2004). WDP used innovative strategies to reach out to women sufferers of violence by drawing on the strength of the collective.

Bhanwari's Story

Sathin Bhanwari's sensitivity to women's issues and her overall commitment to ensuring justice, made her especially respected in the WDP group. In May 1986, as part of project activities, the issue of child marriage and its implications were discussed in Bhateri village. Bhanwari and other sathins who had got their children married before they joined the programme agreed to postpone the *gauna*.[5] In 1987, Bhanwari took up a major issue of attempted rape of a woman from a neighbouring village and elicited substantial support.

Bhanwari's alienation in Bhateri began specifically with the issue of child marriage just before Akha Teej[6] in 1992. That year the state government had decided to observe the fortnight preceding Akha Teej as an anti-child marriage fortnight. The Chief Minister issued a public appeal, and the Chief Secretary wrote to all district collectors to conduct a campaign in this regard (Mathur 1992). The stopping of child marriage became a challenge for the programme. Bhanwari, along with the *pracheta* (block level worker) and Project Director of the District Women's Development Agency (DWDA)[7], tried to persuade people in the area against child marriages. It was clear that, along with some of the families belonging to different castes in the village, some influential Gurjar[8] families were also planning child marriages and were determined to perform them. Bhanwari visited Ram Karan Gurjar of Bhateri and tried to convince him not to get his one-year old daughter married; she met with a hostile and aggressive response. The *vidhayak* (Member of Legislative Assembly – MLA) of the area also strongly opposed Bhanwari. Perhaps he felt that since 40 of the 100 households in the village belonged to Gurjars, his support to the issue would have serious implications for him politically. Some of these families were financially well-off and had political connections.

In response to an appeal by the district collector, the sathins prepared a list of villages where child marriages were rampant in the district. The Sub-Divisional Officer (SDO), and the Deputy Superintendent of Police (DySP) started making rounds of the villages to prevent child marriages. This added to the tension. On May 5, 1992, the SDO and the DySP visited Bhateri to stop the marriage of the one-year old girl in Ram Karan Gurjar's family. The latter was also a ward panch.[9] As was the case with all the other marriages in the area, the state machinery only succeeded in preventing the marriage from taking place on the day of Akha Teej itself. The marriage, however, did take place at 2 am the next morning and no police action was taken against the family. People in the village, however, connected Bhanwari's efforts to convince them against child marriage with police intervention.

According to Bhanwari, around 6 pm on September 22, she and her husband, Mohan, were working in the fields. While Mohan had gone to relieve himself in the neighbouring field, five men – Ram Sukh Gurjar, Ram Karan Gurjar, Badri Gurjar (Ram Karan's uncle), Gyarsa Gurjar and Shravan Sharma – attacked him with *lathis* and beat him up. On hearing his screams, she rushed to the spot. Taking advantage of Mohan's temporary unconscious state, two men – Shravan and Ram Karan Gurjar – bodily held Mohan down. While Ram Sukh Gurjar caught hold of Bhanwari, Badri and

Gyarsa took turns to rape her. To prevent her from screaming her *odhni*[10] was stuffed into her mouth. Bhanwari was threatened with dire consequences were she to speak about the incident.

Despite being in a state of shock, Bhanwari drew on what she had learned in the WDP trainings she had attended and refrained from bathing, washing or changing her clothes. The next morning she and Mohan reached Patan, Krishna sathin's village, still in a somewhat dazed state. With her help they reached Bassi and contacted pracheta Rasila, a senior colleague. While Bhanwari and Mohan waited at Bassi, Krishna went on to Jaipur DWDA to mobilize support. On her return they all went to the Bassi police station to lodge a First Information Report (FIR). For the next hour, they had to argue with the DySP and *thanedar* (police officials) who were sceptical about the incident.

Caste, Gender and Patriarchy

When it came to the medical examination, the male doctor present at the Primary Health Centre (PHC) refused to conduct the examination and neither of the two woman doctors posted at the PHC was available. Bhanwari was referred to the Sawai Man Singh (SMS) hospital at Jaipur. Interestingly, it was later revealed that the the doctor at the PHC had requested the doctors at SMS through his prescription to conduct a medical examination for confirming the age of the 'victim' rather than rape.

The medical jurist at the SMS Medical Hospital, Jaipur refused to conduct a medical examination without orders from the magistrate. By the time the magistrate was contacted it was past five in the evening. The magistrate refused to give them any orders, saying that they should return the following morning and meet him in court. The police then left Bhanwari and Mohan at the women's police station (*mahila thana)* for the night. Finally, although the Indian law requires a medical examination to be conducted within 24 hours the vaginal swab was taken 52 hours after the incident. The trial in a lower court began only two years later.

From the moment Bhanwari went to lodge the FIR to the time the medical examination was conducted, the police subjected her to inhuman treatment. Even the MLA (Member of the Legislative Assembly) of that area made a statement in the state legislative assembly that Bhanwari was lying. It was very clear that the Gurjars had both political and financial backing. Bhateri had only three families who were Kumhars (potters) and hers was one of them. They were poor, dependent on others and could not be confident of receiving any support from the village community. Hence, poverty intersected with caste to render Bhanwari helpless at the hands of the legal and police system.

Both Bhanwari and the rapists belonged to a larger group defined as 'Other Backward Castes' (OBC). However, within this group too there are hierarchies and Bhanwari, as part of the minority potter caste, was at the bottom of this group. Thus, stringent intra-caste hierarchy colluded with patriarchy to become the single most important factor in denying justice to Bhanwari – something that is not uncommon where women belonging to lower castes are concerned. Within the OBCs, the rapists belonged to the majority dominant caste which was economically and politically sound. The village community who had decided to support the Gurjars because of their position felt angered that *'Bhanwari ne ganv ki izzat ko bahar ucchal diya'* (Bhanwari has shamed the village by making public a private matter of the village). This was the irony of caste hierarchies: the dominant Gurjars could rape a lower caste woman and get away scot free, but if the woman, in this case Bhanwari, made public her rape, she was seen as having betrayed the honour of the village community. The fact that Badri – one of the perpetrators – was a prominent local politician, and in Bassi block the Gurjars were extremely powerful, and the local MP, Rajesh Pilot, was not only a Gurjar but a cabinet minister in the central government, combined to work powerfully against Bhanwari. In 1993 a state election was due, and no party could win seats in the area if they alienated the Gurjar vote. It was evident that political pressure had been exerted on the police to delay Bhanwari's medical examination as well as to clear Badri.

The interplay of caste politics and patriarchy also became apparent when the then Chief Minister of Rajasthan not only failed to acknowledge state responsibility in the case but also refused to accept that Bhanwari had been gang raped. He made a public statement against Bhanwari: '*Dhaule baal wali mahila se kaun balatkar karega?*' (Who will rape a grey-haired woman?). He and other members of his cabinet – primarily upper caste and class males – tried their best to suppress the case.

It became apparent to the WDP functionaries and to all those associated with the case that there was a need to expose the nexus of intra-caste hierarchy and patriarchy. This was essential to gain a better understanding about the forces that were constantly confronting them, and if they were to counter the already fraught relationship with the state and its anti-women and casteist system that it implemented with its many institutional arms – the judiciary, the police, the executive, the medical and political systems.

The Quest for Justice

What followed was Bhanwari's long quest for justice, in which she was fully supported by the entire WDP machinery in various ways, as well as by local and national level women's groups. For them, it was no longer just a matter of removing the stigma from one woman's name: the stakes were much higher as the incident would deter all women workers from working in the state and no rape victim/survivor in Rajasthan or anywhere in the country would ever dare to come out in the open and seek justice. They decided to create a political lobby to rival the influence of the Gurjars by organizing a new wave of marches and petitions and to gain wide public attention on the issue by sending a series of articles in the press.

As a first step, the newly set-up National Commission for Women (NCW) was requested to intervene. The Commission conducted an independent enquiry and reached the conclusion that Bhanwari had indeed been raped. It recommended an immediate inquiry by the Central Bureau of Investigation (CBI), an interim relief payment of Rs. 50,000 to be sanctioned to her by the state government, immediate arrest of the accused and conferring on sathins the status of Special Police Officers (SPOs). The NCW also published its report and circulated it widely through the media. Medical experts in Delhi were highly critical of the 52 hour delay in getting Bhanwari medically examined and questioned the value of the evidence. All through this, the local police and state authorities remained unmoved.

A massive rally was organized in Jaipur on October 22, 1992. The sathins were joined by social action/feminist groups from within Rajasthan, Delhi, Gujarat, Himachal Pradesh, Uttar Pradesh, Maharashtra and several other parts of the country. Many *sakhis* and *sahyoginis* (women workers) of the Mahila Samakhaya (MS) programme from UP and Karnataka also participated in the rally. Over 1500 women marched through the streets of Jaipur to express solidarity with Bhanwari and against the issue of rape, demanding the arrest of the rapists. Numerous telegrams and letters of support were received by the organizers and there were a number of petitions and resolutions that were sent to the state government to build up pressure.

The Gurjars retaliated by alleging even more vociferously that Bhanwari had fabricated the story and shamed the entire village community of Bhateri by speaking about her rape at public forums, and therefore she should be condemned. In complete contrast, WDP functionaries and the women's groups who joined them felt that Bhanwari had shown tremendous courage by not remaining silent and speaking about the gruesome act. The larger issue for the women's groups linked with Bhanwari's case remained much the same as during Roop Kanwar's immolation, also in Rajasthan, some years earlier: *'Sawal hai naari ki pehchan ka, sawaal hai naari ke samman ka'* (The issue is one of a woman's identity, of her self respect).[11]

Some of the political statements and slogans used at the time were:

Jab tak suraj chand rahega
Bhanwari tera naam rahega
(Till the sun and moon light up the sky

Bhanwari you shall be remembered)
Naak kati kiski, kiski?
Bhateri ki, Bhateri ki
(Who's the one who has lost face? Bhateri not Bhanwari)

Naak kati kiski, kiski?
Police aur kacheri ki
(Who's the one who has lost face? The police and the courts, not Bhanwari)

Izzat barhi kiski, kiski?
Bhanwari ki, Bhanwari ki
Izzat ghati kiski kiski Badri aur Gyarsa ki
(Bhanwari has gained respect while Badri and Gyarsa have lost all dignity and respect)

These statements captured the essence of the struggle and succeeded, to some extent, in subverting the prevalent thinking in Rajasthan and all over the country that a woman can be battered, raped, molested but should not break the culture of silence – for that brings shame and dishonour to her family and community. The campaign strongly underscored the fact that the responsibility of rape and the *izzat* (respect) of Bhateri lay, not with Bhanwari but with the accused and all men who were party to such heinous crimes. Ideologically, the women's movement reiterated its demand that it was the rapist who was at fault, not the victim/survivor. Above all, the campaign asserted that the responsibility for the violence perpetrated on women lay with the state level bodies who needed to act to protect their citizens and guarantee them a secure environment within which to live.

The CBI harried Bhanwari into making her statements nine times. It was due to the continuous pressure of women's groups in Jaipur and Delhi that the top officials of CBI intervened. Bhanwari and her husband's statements were finally recorded by a magistrate under Section 164 and that ultimately became the basis for the CBI to charge sheet the accused after a full year.

The repercussions of the agitations impacted other mainstream programmes at the national level as well. In November 1992, a discussion note was prepared by the then National Project Director of Mahila Samakhaya[12] (MS) on the Bhanwari incident and its subsequent developments for the consideration of the District Implementation Units (DIU), State Office, Executive Committees and the National Resource Group of MS. It was subsequently widely circulated and discussed in all MS forums i.e. village, cluster and district level meetings in three different states of the country. The note highlighted the expectations from social change agents (particularly women) who are involved in community-based action and how this can often lead them to experience immense hostility from the powers that be. The note underpinned the difficulties faced by many of the grass root workers in remote areas i.e. women teachers, Adult Education supervisors, ICDS (Integrated Child Development Support) workers, especially the Auxiliary Nurse Midwives (ANMs) in travelling alone – especially at night – when they are expected to attend to women during childbirth. It stated that what happened to Bhanwari could happen to any of the workers in any of the states where Mahila Samakhya programmes were being run, or to any of the development workers. Debates and discussions within MS were thus initiated, reiterating the importance of building a support group in each district.[13]

In January 1993, the National Resource Group (NRG),[14] discussed Bhanwari's case in a meeting. They passed the following resolution:

> It is resolved that in the event of any worker – Sahyogini, Sakhi, Sahayki or Sangha member of MS programme – in any state being abused, threatened, molested, physically attacked or intimidated in any manner in the course of carrying out her responsibilities, the MS programme at the state and national levels will extend full assistance to them – be it physical, legal, emotional or financial – in their quest for justice and redressal.[15]

None of this, however – the massive protests, the condemnation of the police by the NCW, the various resolutions and considerable media attention – resulted in the arrest of the accused. Nevertheless, the campaign did ensure that the state was unable to remove Bhanwari from her post as sathin. Despite its considerable strength, pressure by feminist activists rendered the state helpless. A symbiotic relationship thus developed between WDP – a mainstream development programme – and the women's movement in India. Until then, feminist activists had tended to keep a distance from such programmes. Subsequently, the Mahila Samakhya programme was architected by feminists and the training and hand-holding of its workers was done by women's groups in many states. Mobilizing women on such a large scale for this programme was a heady and exciting experience and the synergy developed through this impacted programme functionaries as well as the large number of rural women's groups, activists and urban women, who came together for the first time to lend strength to the campaign.

It was at this moment, as part of the larger challenge to give visibility to sexual violence against women, that women's groups all over the country decided to conduct workshops on the crime of rape and all other forms of sexual violence faced by women in their daily life. It was as though a campaign had been launched, where feminist legal activists and others joined hands to conduct sessions with rural and urban poor women on the issue of rape and the inadequacy of rape law to ensure justice. It provided an opportunity for women to analyse the patriarchal bias within the law and to fully confront the complete apathy of the patriarchal state machinery in addressing the issue of violation, ensuring justice and yet using every opportunity to use the law to one's advantage. Through this process, many women learnt about the need to take precautions to save evidence, file an FIR as well as to gather courage to face and challenge the propaganda spread by the patriarchal family and society.

The First Legal Victory

On 27 September 1993 – a year and five months after Bhanwari's rape, the women's movement achieved its first victory when the CBI was finally forced to issue arrest warrants for the five accused. When Badri, Gyarasa and the others disappeared from the village, the CBI threatened to confiscate their property, and on 24 January 1994, all five men surrendered to the police. A fortnight later, a second and even more important victory was won when the bail application of the accused was rejected by Justice NM Tibrewal, the High Court judge who was hearing the case. His concluding statement made it apparent that he believed what had happened:

> From the above details it is quite clear to me that Bhanwari Devi was gang raped, and that despite her appeals for help the local villagers did not come to her aid for fear of the accused. Prima facie it is case of gang rape which was done to take revenge against Bhanwari for her success in preventing the child marriage.[16]

Justice Tibrewal was also highly critical of the police response to the case which he described as 'highly dubious'.

In April 1994, however, the Rajasthan High Court divided the accused as co-accused and main accused and granted bail to the three co-accused who had assisted the two main accused to perform the act of rape. Women's groups, mostly based in Jaipur and in other districts of Rajasthan, closely followed the court proceedings in all three courts. It is recorded that they attended more than 180 hearings in the sessions court.

Bhanwari was continuously under pressure to withdraw the court case. When a special leave application was filed in the Supreme Court for cancellation of the bail, the Gurjars were taken by surprise. Between the months of August to October 1994 the Gurjars, with other prominent people of Bhateri, made several efforts to convince Bhanwari to settle the case out of court. Some of the Gurjar men also approached her supporters and met representatives of women's groups who were active in the case, as well as the Project Director of WDP in Jaipur district. They invited Bhanwari to a meeting in the village in which the three accused (Ram Karan Gurjar, Ram Suhk Gurjar and Shravan Panda) laid their turbans at Bhanwari's feet begging her to 'compromise' on the case and declare in court that she had not been raped. Bhanwari maintained that she would do so provided they accepted their crime openly in a larger public meeting in the village. However, the accused refused this demand and became even more hostile towards her. Bhanwari's subsequent statement in the court that she was raped increased their rage and created tension in the village. At this point, the women's group decided to centrally send a regular bulletin from Delhi to all other NGOs and women's groups on the progress of the case and expose anti-Bhanwari arguments to keep up the momentum of the protest.

The Trial and its Aftermath

The trial in the lower courts commenced in the month of October 1994, and five judges were changed during the course of trial, the judgment being finally delivered by the sixth. Thus, each got only a partial picture of the case. The judge who had heard Bhanwari and her husband Mohan's case was not the one who finally delivered the judgment. Bhanwari's statements in court were recorded in-camera. However, 'in-camera' was a bit of a misnomer. Bhanwari had to narrate her story in the presence of 17 men. In an attempt to intimidate and humiliate her, she was continuously cross-examined about the position of her body during her alleged rape and who held her arms and legs during the act etc. Since Bhanwari described the act of rape explicitly in the presence of the accused, the matter was reported in the village and she had to suffer the abusive taunts of the villagers even for this.

On 21 February 1995, the newly elected panchayat met for the first time in Bhateri. On this day the panchayat meeting was open to all villagers and the group secretary was to hand over charge of the panchayat to the sarpanch and welcome all the members. Though no formal invitation was extended to the villagers, there was general enthusiasm about interacting with the newly elected members. Bhanwari, along with twelve women from Prempura, a neighbouring village, and Bhateri, also participated in the meeting to welcome the newly elected representatives, especially the women. She was taken by surprise when the sarpanch, after garlanding the elected members, garlanded her saying that she was a *mukhiya sadasya* (respected member) of the village.

In retaliation for the above, on 23 February 1995 the then Development Officer of Bassi Panchayat Samiti (PS), called a meeting of all 39 newly elected sarpanches at the PS headquarters. The meeting was also attended by the *pradhan* (local head), the Member of the Legislative Assembly (MLA), the Block Development Officer (BDO), the *tehsildar* (revenue administrative officer) and the Child Development Project Officer (CDPO). The MLA was an uninvited guest and came with several villagers who were not supposed to be there. Ram Sukh Gurjar, one of the accused in the case, hung around outside the meeting premises throughout. Since the main agenda of the meeting was ways of stopping child marriages, the concerned pracheta, Bhanwari and other sathins of the area were also invited. The sitting MLA of Bassi, Kanhaiya Lal Meena, chaired the meeting. He appealed to the sarpanches to involve WDP functionaries in their drive to stop child/early marriages. However, the sarpanches refused to do so, asserting that by lying about her rape, Bhanwari had shamed Bassi in the country as well as the world over. Despite loud protests from Bhanwari as well as from the samiti pradhan and BDO, a resolution was passed boycotting the sathins.[17]

Following this event, an urgent meeting of the civil society organizations and concerned citizens of Jaipur and Rajasthan[18] was held in Jaipur on 28 February 1995. The group discussed the humiliation and boycott suffered by Bhanwari and other sathins in detail. It concluded that the move was not only symbolic of an entrenched, stringent patriarchal and feudal mindset but also an aggressive step by the elected political representatives to usurp political power in their favour. This decision also reflected how the latter, rather than strengthening women and other marginalized sections of society, were using their power against them. The group said that the move to boycott and alienate the sathins was an attempt to pressurize and intimidate Bhanwari to withdraw the rape case and demoralize all the sathins of that area. A press note stating this was released in the local press and two prominent newspapers the *Rajasthan Patrika* and the *Navbharat Times* carried it in their edition of 2 March 1995.

The Judgment of the Session's Court

On 15 November 1995, the sessions and district court (rural) acquitted all the five accused, Gyarsa[4] Gurjar, Badri Gurjar, Ram Sukh Gurjar, Ram Karan Gurjar and Shravan Panda against the charge of gang rape, although they were sentenced to six months in prison on other minor charges such as conspiring and beating up Mohan and manhandling Bhanwari. Since Badri and Gyarsa had already spent about two years in jail, they were exempted from imprisonment.

The judgment, delivered by the sessions court judge Jagpal Singh on November 15 1995, ignored the testimony of Bhanwari and her husband, the prime witness. It revealed a patriarchal and prejudiced mindset that unquestioningly accepted the defence counsel's fanciful arguments that 'the case itself is against Indian culture and human psychology'. It observed that the alleged rapists were middle-aged and as such were 'respected persons'. The 26-page judgment further stated, 'It isn't possible in Indian culture that a man who has taken a vow to protect his wife, in front of the holy fire, just stands and watches his wife being raped, when only two men almost twice his age are holding him.' and that rape is 'usually committed by teenagers'. It was argued that, 'Since the offenders were upper caste men and included a brahmin, rape could not have taken place because Bhanwari belonged to a lower caste'.[19] The judgment was countered by prosecution lawyer Virender Godika and his assistant R.S. Chauhan.

The court, in its anxiety to acquit the alleged rapists, also cast aspersions on Bhanwari's husband Mohan by raising the question, 'In our society how can an Indian husband whose role is to protect his wife stand by and watch his wife being raped?' Nowhere in the judgement does it explain why Bhanwari should have fabricated this story and why a woman would trump up false charges against anyone. The court commented adversely on the inordinate delay caused by Bhanwari in recording her complaint against the rapists. It ignored Bhanwari's plea regarding bureaucratic and procedural barriers in getting herself medically examined. The most appalling aspect of the case was that whatever was recorded in the medical report needed scrutiny by medical experts, which was denied to the prosecution. The stained *ghagra* (skirt), produced in the court as an exhibit, was found to be too short to be Bhanwari's. It was also argued that the forensic report could not identify the alleged rapists. It was clear that the original skirt had been replaced by the investigating agencies in order to destroy evidence. Such manipulation and scuttling of procedures shielded the rapists. The court also obliquely cast aspersions on her character by suggesting the presence of a third man and implying that Bhanwari was an adulteress.

The judgment deterred many women in rural areas who were being encouraged by government to act as agents of change in a caste-ridden and male dominated society. WDP's statewide effort to bring down the number of child marriages also suffered a major blow. As an immediate effect, the verdict discouraged thousands of sufferers of sexual assault, who would think twice before speaking out, let alone fight a court case. The strong realization that emerged was that if feudal Rajasthan cruelly subordinated women, the modern nation state, with its organized legal, policing and political systems, under the garb of order and justice, subjugated them further. However, most significantly, the judgment undermined the spirit behind the changes in the rape law in the mid 1980s.

At the village level also, a large majority of people were surprised by the judgment. Bhanwari had never withdrawn support to the local community over issues of social justice despite her personal battle. She had also begun to symbolize the assertion of rights, hence, they felt she had been denied justice by the court.

Following the judgment a press conference was organized by several women's groups and organizations[20] in Delhi on 24 November 1995 in which Bhanwari announced her decision to fight on a criminal revision petition in the state High Court, challenging the lower court's decision. The organizations that joined hands to lend support to her viewed the matter as a 'test case' of a brave woman fighting for justice – one which would set the parameters for women's rights in the country. According to Delhi-based lawyers present at the press conference, the incident raised the issue of Bhanwari's credibility as a witness. They declared the judgment 'gender-biased, unethical and full of loopholes'.[21]

The Post-judgment Scenario

The appalling judgment by the session's court in Rajasthan came as no surprise as far as the low rate of conviction in rape cases goes but it came as a rude shock to Bhanwari and all who had supported her and been involved in her struggle. However, she was acknowledged for her courage and strength in many different ways: she visited Beijing for the Fourth World Women's Conference and received numerous awards including the Neerja Bhanot Bravery Award in November 1994 which carried a Rs 100,000 cash prize, for her 'extraordinary courage, conviction and commitment'. Bhanwari was also felicitated by a small group, the Stree Adhikar Samiti in North campus, Delhi University on December 27 2002 (*Stree Samman Divas* or Women's Dignity Day). Her courage in fighting her rapists for more than a decade was yet again recognized and applauded. She received Rs 10,000 from the then Prime Minister, Mr. Narasimha Rao. In 2002, with a change of political leadership and the coming of a new government, the then Chief Minister allotted a residential plot to Bhanwari and announced a grant of Rs 40,000 for construction of a house on the plot. He also sanctioned an additional amount Rs 10,000 for the education of her son.

Support continued to be mobilized in favour of Bhanwari, both at the national and international levels, and on a number of other fronts. WDP functionaries once again extended support to Bhanwari. The director of the state programme and the DWDA both wrote to the Collector to ensure Bhanwari's safety and security. A rally was organized to express solidarity with Bhanwari on December 15, 1995 – one month after the sessions judge acquitted the five accused in the case. Various women's organizations, social action groups, civil society organizations of Rajasthan as well as from different parts of the country participated in the rally. In an expression of solidarity with Bhanwari, about 5000 women and men from rural and urban areas came together to unleash their anger and anguish over the judgment. They marched through the streets of Jaipur with black arm bands, condemning state inaction over the case and demanding fair and fast justice.

Bhanwari's articulation of the issue on a public platform at the end of the march strengthened her as well as many other rural women who came forward and spoke about the violence and sexual harassment they had been facing for a long time. It was the first time in the history of Rajasthan that they spoke about balatkar (rape) openly, shared their anger and anguish but emerged emboldened for having spoken in public about it. Bhanwari's case led every woman to resolve that the issue of violence against women has to be kept alive and the struggle against patriarchal structures, be it the family, the workplaces, the community or the state, has to continue, thus breaking the silence around sexual violence.

Similar protests were organized in different part of the country. In Raipur, the Chhatisgarh Mahila Jagriti Sangthan staged a three hour long dharna in the campus of Raipur district headquarters in support of the rally in Jaipur. A street play based on Bhanwari's case was organized by them. Besides, they also wrote a letter to the Chief Minister of Rajasthan through the district Collector of Raipur, condemning Bhanwari's rape and demanding justice for her.

In 1995 the seventh Indian Association of Women's Studies Conference on the theme 'Looking Forward, Looking Back: In Search of Feminist Visions, Alternatives, Paradigms and Practices' was held in Jaipur. The conference saw a mix of grassroots women's organizations along with women's groups and academics. Several rounds of discussion were held on Bhanwari's case and the judgment pronounced by the lower court, leading to the passing of a resolution where the participants stated that they have been deeply disturbed by the decision of the Sessions Court in Bhanwari's case. 'Physical and mental violence against women is on the increase because the present systems have failed in providing justice to women. It is time to start a nationwide movement against violence against women, to create public pressure against it through mass media. To attract the attention of the judiciary towards it in order to make the desired change and so we resolve to run a campaign against it through the following:

- To provide forums to rape victims and their families to articulate the violence done to them.
- Hold discussions on physical violence at various levels and help rehabilitate the victims and to create a consensus that sharing one's violation does not tarnish one's image.
- To collect extensive information about the barriers that prevent their access to justice
- Record extensive case studies of rape victims.
- Share experiences through interstate meetings.
- Prepare a code of conduct for the investigator and for judges dealing with rape cases.
- Recommend changes if required to make the judicial process more sensitive to women.'[22]

A special event was organized by some of the feminist activists to honour Bhanwari where she pledged the prize money that she had received in various awards to a fund that would be used to take up such cases in the future. Justice V. R. Krishna Iyer (former Supreme Court Chief Justice) participated and condemned the judgment of the Court, and said that it was a black day in the history of Indian courts and the Constitution. He added that, 'I have nothing personal against the judge himself – he is ignorant of the law as well, unfortunately' (Ghosh and Srivastava, 1995)

The Vishakha Guidelines

The appalling injustice in Bhanwari's case, together with her fighting spirit, prompted several women's groups to file a Public Interest Litigation (PIL) in the Supreme Court of India, under the collective platform of Vishakha.[23] The petition was filed by four women's groups. However, it came to be called Vishakha judgment as Vishakha's name was first in the list of petitioners.[24] They demanded justice for Bhanwari Devi and urged action against sexual harassment at the workplace. In 1997, the apex court took cognizance of the case and delivered a historic judgment.[25] It used international principles to formulate guidelines to address sexual harassment at the workplace and recognized such incidents as violations of the fundamental rights as guaranteed in the Constitution. It defined sexual harassment as any one or more unwelcome acts or behaviour like physical contact and advances, a demand or request for sexual favours or making sexually coloured remarks or showing pornography. The acts whether directly, or by implication, include any other unwelcome physical, verbal or non-verbal conduct of a sexual nature. The court, for the first time, drew upon an international human rights law instrument, the Convention on the Elimination of All forms of Discrimination against Women (CEDAW), to pass a set of guidelines known as the Vishakha guidelines. In the prefatory comments as part of the judgment, the Supreme Court stated:

> The immediate cause for the filing of this writ petition is an incident of alleged brutal gang rape of a social worker in a village of Rajasthan. That incident is the subject matter of a separate criminal action and no further mention of it, by us, is necessary. The incident (rape of Bhanwari Devi) reveals the hazards to which working women may be exposed and the depravity to which sexual harassment can degenerate; and the urgency for safeguards by an alternative mechanism in the absence of legislative measures.[26]

Anti-woman and Casteist Reactions

As a result of the agitation/protest by the women's movement over the Bhanwari case, the environment in the state became blatantly anti-woman and casteist, as it had done several years ago at the time of the widow immolation case of Roop Kanwar in 1987. Male brotherhood, which is validated only by the suppression of women and revitalized as long as it can assert its superiority, was not prepared for a rational debate; instead, it indulged in a show of strength. Many politicians had vociferously supported the right to worship sati and glorify the immolation of Roop Kanwar in Deorala, Rajasthan. In a similar turn of events, the Bhartiya Janta Party (BJP) openly supported a rally organized by the five accused in Jaipur on 18 January 1996. The key person involved in organizing the rally was the then BJP MLA from Bassi (Jaipur district). He chaired the meeting after the rally and women from the BJP's women's wing – which was in the forefront of mobilizing women – addressed the rally. This was an attempt to put pressure on Bhanwari to not file an appeal against the judgment of the session's court acquitting the accused of the charge of gang rape. It was also an attempt to discredit Bhanwari and mobilize public opinion against her. The rally was vicious and aggressive. The mood was one of rabble-rousing, with the organizers asking for Bhanwari to be hanged and burnt alive. A number of inflammatory speeches were made. The speakers vented their anger against Justice Krishna Iyer and the National Commission for Women. The rapists were sitting on stage throughout the meeting and were garlanded. As a consequence there was fear for the life and security of Bhanwari and it was not unfounded. She was attacked and beaten up by a few villagers at the behest of these powerful men. Despite these pressures Bhanwari refused to leave her village.

Soon after the BJP rally, a number of Delhi-based organizations[27] working on women's rights issues sent a press release on January 21 1996, strongly condemning the rally organized against Bhanwari and the aggressive and violent manner in which elected representatives, together with the five accused, had used their power to intimidate and obstruct one of the most significant struggles against sexual violence. They:

- Condemned the BJP's tactics to use the issue of caste to obstruct, influence and bias the judicial process against Bhanwari;
- Demanded that the leadership of the BJP and the Congress curb the activities of their party members;
- Called upon all political parties to denounce the BJP for using this issue to capture votes and the manner in which it used the Panchayati Raj institutions to this end; and

- Asserted that the BJP and Congress need to affirm their commitment towards the fight against sexual violence on women. This is due to the fact that Bhanwari's case was no longer one individual's fight but had become a rallying point for a much larger struggle against violence experienced by women.

The press release at the event said that if the women's movement were to allow the misguided and vicious politics of the rapists and the BJP to snuff out women's voices, it would be a sad day for the women's movement and other democratic voices of this country.

In 1999, Director Jugmohan Mundra made a film named *Bawandar* (Sandstorm) based on Bhanwari's story. The film was released in different parts of Europe in the year 2000 and women's groups in London collected approximately 3000 pounds (valued at approx. Rs 210, 000) for Bhanwari after the film and sent it to Jaipur. The women's groups in Jaipur held several meetings over the issue and finally Bhanwari did not accept the money but donated it to the fund set up earlier. The movie was released in Jaipur in the year 2001 and Bhanwari and her family faced further repercussions post its screening. Her son, a college student, had to face taunts like 'Kumhari raand ka beta' (potter whore's son) and subsequently left the college where he was studying.

What We Gained and What We Lost

Looking back at this historic campaign one realizes that it had its contradictions and the victories did not come without a price, especially for Bhanwari. Despite all efforts to gather support, Bhanwari felt alienated at times. She won many monetary awards like the Neerja Bhanot Bravery Award and received benefits from the film *Bawandar*. In July 2016 she also received the Ambedkar award of Rs 50,000 by FFEI.[28] This caused differences amongst the sathins. She increasingly began to feel the loss of the collective.

While Mohan, her husband, stood by her side throughout, unfortunately, both her sons. Satyanarayan and Mukesh, and their wives stopped interacting with her, as they felt that Bhanwari had shamed them overtly and covertly. Probably their anger was also due to the fact that she was not keen on spending the award money for personal use. Satyanarayan does not live with her while Mukesh lives with her but refuses to communicate with her. At times Bhanwari feels she should not have raised her own issue though her commitment to the cause, she feels, was right.

It is a matter of pride that Bhanwari has remained strong throughout and never surrendered to the adverse publicity. Her commitment is so genuine that no matter what her personal sufferings have been, she has not withdrawn from the cause of supporting every single individual woman who is victimized or faces violence. She expresses deep gratitude for the support she has received throughout from her husband and daughters on the one hand, and the women's groups and several feminist activists within Rajasthan and at the national level on the other.

Despite the groundswell of support, justice still eludes her. The Rajasthan High Court refused to transfer the case to the fast track court and till 2012, twenty years after the incident, it had held only one hearing on the case, by which time, one of the five accused had died.

On another front, the state could not shut down WDP; it could not expel the sathins from the programme. Presently Bhanwari continues to live in Bhateri and work on women's empowerment issues. She refused to move out of her village despite the land allotted to her by the state government. Her struggle for gender justice goes on unabated, as does her determination to counter the forces of women's oppression and exploitation. She has systematically reclaimed her dignity and respect within the village community and neighbouring villages and many women cutting across caste lines approach her when they need advice, especially over issues of domestic violence. Women and men of her village and nearby villages have benefitted from her information levels regarding how to deal with the police and forensic reports when a rape takes place.

There are several answers to the central question: What did Bhanwari and the women's movement achieve through the campaign around Bhanwari's struggle?

Bhanwari's case became a catalyst in strengthening the movement and creating large scale awareness around issues of sexual violence. Ironically, the failure of the state to provide justice to Bhanwari through its legal mechanisms led to a renewed outrage within the feminist movement and thus resulted in further nation-wide debates and protests. A national solidarity was built and the campaign succeeded in drawing global attention to the issue of violence against women/girls. The movement also succeeded in subverting the stereotypical understanding by asserting that a woman who is raped or physically assaulted does not lose her self-respect and dignity, but it is the accused who loses his dignity and self-respect.

The campaign helped the women's movement evolve feminist methodologies and feminist rethinking on the definition of rape. Three clear strategies have emerged:

1. Protesting against the state to demand justice for Bhanwari and all women who had faced similar harassment and violation;
2. Negotiating and creating spaces by working with the system, e.g. a monthly/bi-monthly coordination mechanism was set-up with the home secretary and the police department which succeeded in reopening many cases; and
3. Putting pressure on the existing system to fulfil the demands of women's groups. Owing to constant pressure, the police was forced to deal with some cases differently. For example, the infamous *JC Bose case*[29] came under scrutiny after fifteen years. The justice delivery system was compelled to relook at the case by opening the case files and punishing some of the perpetrators.[30]

To some extent, the campaign also helped break the silence around rape and masculinity. By refusing to feel either defiled or ashamed by the act and by continuing to speak about it, Bhanwari has essentially recast the discourse on the self and identity, and shifted it away from shame, which is central to a survivor's self definition. The most important message was that unless women come out and speak about their violation, there can be no change. The campaign following Bhanwari's rape played a crucial role in creating that strength and sustaining it. The Bhanwari case became a beacon of the women's movement and helped to strengthen the network of feminist activists and academics.

The campaign also helped focus attention on the processes through which men are conditioned to believe that they must express their power through aggressive and violent behaviour (rape) and succeeded in establishing that it is not a 'natural' inclination that makes them violent, but a flawed construction of masculinity that thrives due to the way society promotes patriarchy. It highlighted the need to address issues around women's entry into the workforce and the public arena. It also led to the realization that there was a need to put in place mechanisms for the protection of women and girls in the state. An informal network of more than 40 organizations under the Mahila Atyachar Virodhi Jan Andolan (MAVJA) banner was formed in Rajasthan in June 1996. They have since been working on several rape cases and other cases of atrocities against women. In January 2002 eight[31] women's and human rights organizations of Jaipur collaborated with the Rajasthan police and established the Mahila Salah Evam Suraksha Kendra (MSSK) to help and support women sufferers of violence. It is located at the Gandhi Nagar Mahila Thana in Jaipur. The venture was the first ever example of the Rajasthan police accepting the challenge of new experiments to provide assistance to women facing violence. It has opened spaces for the incorporation of women's experiences in police work with violated women. Later a second MSSK was established within the walled city of Jaipur.

As an offshoot of the campaign following Bhanwari's rape, there was tremendous pressure from women's groups to expand the network of the MSSKs. In February 2003 the Rajasthan police issued a state-wide circular acknowledging that women's access to justice, security and relief is significantly enhanced when there is a coordinated effort in this regard on the part of the police, NGOs and the community. In response to this order, the organization Vishakha, inspired by the Special Cells for Women and Children model initiated by Tata Institute of Social Sciences (TISS), Mumbai, took up the responsibility of setting up MSSKs in ten districts of Rajasthan.[33] The MSSKs thus initiated aimed to evolve processes for women facing violence to negotiate their lives in a non-threatening and non-judgmental space.

However, in tangible terms, the prime achievement of the campaign following Bhanwari's rape has, been the Sexual Harassment of Women at Workplace (Prevention, Prohibition and Redressal) Act 2013, which has given more teeth to the Supreme Court directives in Vishaka's judgment of 1997. The passage of the Act is an admission of state responsibility for preventing and prohibiting sexual harassment at the workplace, and providing legal redress for the same – a core issue in Bhanwari's rape.

Notes

1. 'Sathin' literally means 'friend'; the word was used to describe women workers at the grassroot level appointed by the Rajasthan government under its Women's Development Programme (WDP). For more details, see note 5 below.
2. *Vishakha & Others vs State of Rajasthan* AIR 1997 SC 3011.
3. The rape incidents of Mathura and Rameeza Bi, the Open Letter to the Chief Justice of the Supreme Court written by four law professors, and the manner in which protests around the incidents galvanized the women's movement are discussed in greater detail in the paper by Madhu Mehra in this volume.
4. The sathin or the village level active change agent was the key player in the struggle against patriarchy, class and caste inequalities around whom all the WDP activities evolved. She was responsible for forming women's forums at the village level and discussing issues related to their development. She was supported in all such activities by the block level worker i.e. prachetas, and functionaries of IDARA (Information Development and Resource Agency) and Project Directors of the District Women's Development Agency (DWDA).
5. Formal send off of the bride,
6. A day considered auspicious for marriages according to the Hindu calendar.
7. The District Women's Development Agency (DWDA) was a body set up under the chairpersonship of the Collector at the district level.

8. The Gurjars are an ethnic group, classified under the Other Backward Class (OBC) category in Rajasthan and some other states in India. Gujarat state took its name from the Gujara, the land of the Gurjars, who ruled the area during the 700s and 800s. http://www.gujaratindia.com/about-gujarat/history-1.htm

9. 'Ward panch' is an elected member of the gram panchayat – the local self-government body at the village level.

10. Odhni, also called 'duppata' – a stole/shawl worn by women in India, often to cover their chests and/or head.

11. Roop Kanwar, an 18 year old girl, was murdered on her husband's funeral pyre on 4 September 1987 in Deorala village, Sikar district of Rajasthan. This was based on sati – the practice of a widow burning herself or being burnt on the funeral pyre of her dead husband, largely prevalent in Rajasthan. The incident was a reflection of social oppression of women and led to public protests all over the country.

12. Mahila Samakhya is a programme initiated by the Ministry of Human Resource Development in 1988 under its Department of Education; it emphasized the need for achieving gender equality through women's education, and has sought to pursue the objectives of the National Policy on Education 1986. More information on the programme is available at http://mhrd.gov.in/mahila, accessed on 8 November 2013

13. (GoI 4/11/1992 No. F.1–91/92–PN (V).

14. The National Resource Group has been constituted under the Mahila Samakhya programme and plays an advisory role, to look at larger programme processes, interventions, directions and trends.

15. Ramachandran V., and K. Jhandhalaya.2012.*Cartographies of Empowerment – The Mahila Samakhaya Story.* New Delhi: Zubaan.

16. William Dalrymple.1998. *The Age of Kali – Indian Travels and Encounters*, New Delhi: Penguin.

17. *The Indian Express.* 1995. 'Saathins Kept Out of Panchayat Affairs'. 28 December.

18. IDSJ Women's Studies Unit, PUCL, RUWA, Bodh Shikshan Samiti, BGVS, Mahila Punarvas Samooh, Muslim Women's Welfare Society, Samagra Sewa Sansthan, Ujala Chadi, Sankalp, Vihaan, Urmul Trust Bikaner, Charkha, New Delhi.

19. Kang, B. 1995. 'Controversial Verdict: The ruling on the Bhanwari case raises the hackles of activists'. *Outlook Magazine*, December 6, 1995; State Vs Ramkaran and Others, Nov 15, 1995

20. Some of these groups were Sakshi, Forum on Violence Against Women, Nirantar, Kali, Action India, Shakti Shalini, Media Storm, Jagori and Centre for Feminist Research.

21. *The Indian Express.* 1995. 'Why did Justice Favour the Culprits: Bhanwari'. 25 November.

22. Indian Association for Women's Studies. 1995. 30 December. Jaipur.

23. Vishakha (Group for Women's Education and Research) came into being on January 28 1991. The group came together due to the events that followed the Roop Kanwar incident detailed above in this paper, which gave an impetus to the women's movement in Rajasthan. In the initial years the group was intensively involved in working towards empowerment of women with an emphasis on building, sustaining and strengthening links among rural women. Many of the members were earlier working in the WDP but became disillusioned due to the discrepancies that crept into the programme structure.

24. *Vishakha and Others V. State of Rajasthan and others* AIR 1997 SC 2011.

25. Ibid

26. Ibid

27. This included the National Commission for Women, All India Democratic Women's Association (AIDWA), National Federation of Indian Women (NFIW), Joint Women's Programme, All India Government Nurses Federation, Progressive Students Union Delhi University, Nirantar, Jagori, Sakshi, Alarippu, Purogami Mahila Sangathan, Shakti Shalini, All India Progressive Women's Association, Charkha, Women's Political Watch, Kali for Women, Indian Institute of Social Studies Trust, Action India, Ankur, Centre for Social Research, Indian Social Institute and the YWCA.

28. FFEI is a small organization running with the support of a few concerned individuals in Andhra Pradesh.

29. In September of 1997, 25-year-old Pragati revealed how she had been gang-raped, coerced and blackmailed into sexual bondage over the past few years. The last act of sexual exploitation took place in the J.C. Bose boys' hostel of the University of Rajasthan, Jaipur. As a result of appeals and protests by women's and other social groups in the state and exposure in the media, public pressure was built to keep the case alive (Ujala Chhadi, Dec. 1997).

30. The final judgment of the fast track (sessions) court was delivered on 26 October 2012 by Judge Nepal Singh.

31. RUWA, AIDWA, AIPWA, NFIW, PUCL, Vividha, Mahila Punarwas Kendra and the National Muslim Women's Welfare Society.

32. Ajmer, Alwar, Bharatpur, Bhilwara, Bikaner, Barmer, Chittorgarh, Jaipur (Rural), Jodhpur and Udaipur.

References

Banerjee, S. 1984. 'Sathin Training: Report on Training Programme Conducted in Padampura', IDS Training Report 4, Jaipur: Institute of Development Studies

Dalrymple, William, 1998. *The Age of Kali: Indian Travels and Encounters*, New Delhi: Penguin India.

Institute of Development Studies. 1991. WDP: Emerging Challenges. Jaipur: Institute of Development Studies.

Mathur, K., 1992. 'Bhateri Rape Case: Backlash and Protest', *Economic and Political Weekly,* Vol. XX No 41, October 10

————. 2004. *Countering Gender Violence: Initiatives Towards Collective Action in Rajasthan.* New Delhi: Sage India Private Limited.

Mathur, K., and S. Rajagopal. 1999. 'Will the Law Dispense Justice?' *The Hindu,* March 14.

Srivastava, K., and S. Ghose. 1996. 'The Battle for Justice Continues' *Hindustan Times,* February 4.

Ramachandran V. and K. Jhandyala. 2012. *Cartographies of Empowerment – The Mahila Samakhaya Story.* New Delhi: Zubaan.

The Indian Express. 1995. 'Why did Justice Favour the Culprits: Bhanwari', 25 November.

The Indian Express. 1995. 'Sathins Kept Out of Panchayat Affairs'. 1995. 28 December.

FIVE

The Women's Movement and Legislative Reform on Violence Against Women

Madhu Mehra[1]

Introduction

Issues of violence against women and the law have been of continuing concern over decades for the contemporary women's movement in India. Soon after independence, it became clear that the constitutionally guaranteed equality and affirmative action were not shaping the law, policy or development programmes; and that systemic forms of violence against women would remain mere 'social evils' that attracted no legal consequences. In fact, the law's blindness towards gender-specific violence, in public and private domains, was striking in the face of increasing reports of dowry deaths and custodial rapes in the 1970s, around which the initial campaigns for law reform began. These campaigns set off the first phase of legislative reform, that began with a focus on specific forms of violence to grow into broader movements – from rape to sexual violence and from dowry to domestic violence. Both campaigns gained momentum from public outrage against cases that became symbolic of blatant impunity, institutional bias and apathy in their time. The movements for law reform focussed for the most part on criminal law remedies, dedicated courts and special mechanisms in the quest for creating women-friendly institutional spaces, moving on eventually from 2005 onwards, to include in their demands, victim-centric reliefs as part of the legal redress. Over time, reasons for engagement with law reform changed – the idealism and belief in gender justice through the law became tempered with realism that the structures of caste, sexuality, class amongst others intersect and result in differential legal access as well as differential outcomes for women. Despite this, engagement with the law has been necessary for altering and challenging social norms, and creating possibilities to pursue accountability at individual and collective levels.

From Rape to a Gradation of Sexual Offences

Sexual violence in the legal discourse, as in society, is replete with gender stereotyping that blames the victim for provoking violence, sustaining as a result, *de facto* impunity for perpetrators. This is only one aspect of the many ways in which patriarchal attitudes and practices adversely influence the law on sexual violence. Until recently, the law did not recognize any serious sexual offence other than a narrowly defined provision on rape – collapsing the spectrum of sexual violence as it exists in society under a trivial, problematically worded, generic offence of 'outraging the modesty of woman.'[2] Legal prosecutions therefore have been more about interrogating the victim's chastity rather than about the violation of her bodily integrity and sexual autonomy. In this way, the legal process has been demeaning for rape survivors, reproducing and exacerbating the cultural shame, victim-blaming and stigma, while letting off perpetrators in most cases, or according sentences less than the minimum prescribed in cases of conviction.[3] The law reform movement on sexual violence converged around cases that foregrounded key limitations of the law, around which more complex critiques and suggestions were pegged. The pivotal concerns that triggered these debates at different points in time were consent, custodial rape, narrow definition of rape and the gender neutral vs. gender specific framing of rape, although each of these debates combined more complex concerns of procedural justice, forensic procedures and impunity. The debates surrounding law reform in 2013 involved a wider participation of civil society than ever before, were considerably dominated by calls for deterrent punishment, through castration and death penalty. The focus on resisting the calls for retributive justice, did not allow attention towards discussing the value of proportionality and judicial discretion in sentencing for rape, and indeed to justice, both of which were compromised in the 2013 amendment.[4]

In the post-emergency period of the late 1970s, when the nation's memory of state authoritarianism and impunity was still fresh, three cases of custodial rape became flashpoints, highlighting police impunity. The case of Rameeza Bee in 1978, in Hyderabad, involved rape by several policemen inside the police station, accompanied by beating her protesting husband to death. The public protests in the city, resulted in police firing and death of some protestors, leading to the appointment of the Justice Muktadar Commission. The Commission found the policemen guilty of rape and murder, and recommended that they be prosecuted. However, the police were subsequently acquitted by the session's court in the neighbouring state of Karnataka, to where the case was transferred, on the ground that evidence recorded before a Commission of Inquiry was inadmissable.[5]

In 1979, the nation was shocked with the Supreme Court's views on custodial rape in the Mathura case. A minor tribal girl was raped by two constables while in police custody, but the policemen were acquitted by the sessions court on the grounds that the girl, who had a lover, was 'of loose morals' and must have consented to the sexual intercourse. The High Court on appeal, distinguished submission from consent, noting that the young girl had little option in the custody of two policemen in the police station, thus reversing the acquittal. In contrast, the Supreme Court rejected Mathura's contention that she had not consented, and had in fact resisted the rape, on the ground that medical evidence did not record any injury on her body. The Supreme Court reversed the High Court's conviction, concluding that Mathura was a 'shocking liar' and the alleged rape was in reality a consensual sexual intercourse and a 'peaceful affair'.[6] Outraged by the reasoning of the Supreme Court, four law professors from Delhi University wrote an open letter to the Chief Justice of India in protest – pointing out that it was unfair to expect a tribal girl in custody of two policemen, in circumstances relating to a criminal complaint, to raise an alarm or attempt to resist rape without endangering herself. It was pointed out that passive submission was not the same as consent.[7] Even as the definition of consent was at the heart of the concern expressed in the open letter, the letter also questioned the legitimacy of placing the burden of proving rape on victims in custodial settings, and drew attention to the differential access to legal redress and justice for the poor and the underprivileged. The letter contrasted the Supreme Court's stand in 'civil liberties cases involving affluent women' like Nandini Satpathy, that condemned the practice of calling women to police stations to participate in police investigation in their cases,[8] while saying nothing about the vulnerability of poor tribal girls. The review petition moved by the women's organizations against the said judgment was rejected at the time, as the Supreme Court was yet to fully relax the requirement of *locus standi* (according to which only the person harmed/affected could approach the court for relief, and not anyone on his/her behalf), that paved the way for Public Interest Litigation.[9]

Even as debates arising from Mathura's case continued, another case stunned the nation, and the Parliament. On June 16, 1980, Maya Tyagi's husband retaliated against a policeman who molested her when their car broke down in Bhagpat in the state of U.P. In response, the policeman returned with their colleagues, shot her husband dead, forcibly disrobed Maya, inserted a stick inside her body and paraded her naked on the streets. As a cover up, she and her husband were charged with being dacoits.[10] The findings of the P.N. Roy Commission appointed by the U.P. government reflected the extent to which patriarchal values shape interpretation of law. Despite holding that the cases against the Tyagi couple were trumped up to cover police atrocities, the Commission rejected the contention that insertion of a stick amounted to rape, suggesting instead, that such police violence was provoked by Maya Tyagi's protest, resistance and her husband's retaliation.[11] As noted by a

PUCL report: 'the truth is that it was not only rape, but the real form of rape where the desire to exhibit force was more marked than the sexual act.'[12]

Rape law reform became the rallying point for the progressive voices, civil liberties groups and the women's movement. There were public protests in several cities across the country and animated discussions in the Parliament. The main concerns related to the manner in which consent and its absence were linked to notions of chastity, the victim's 'character', her social location, and marks of injury/physical resistance. In the words of the open letter to the Supreme Court: 'Is the taboo against pre-marital sex so strong as to provide a licence to Indian police to rape young girls?' Further, in view of the difficulty of proving an absence of consent in custodial situations, where submission was inevitable to persons in authority, who exercised power and control over the victim in the precincts of an institution, the demand grew for shifting the onus of proof from the victim to the perpetrator; the demand was however divided on whether the onus of dis-proving rape (by proving that the woman consented to sexual intercourse) be shifted on the accused in all situations, or only in custodial situations. Some within the women's movement maintained that fair trial principle of treating the accused as innocent until proven guilty, be disturbed only in exceptional cases of custodial rape, where power of the accused combined with control and custody over the victim, placed upon the accused an additional onus to protect the victim, and answer for any breach of that protection.

The Law Commission of India's 84th Report in 1980, reiterated a number of recommendations that were part of the above debates, including that consent must be explicitly defined as being free and voluntary. Further it recommended that once sexual intercourse was proved and the woman stated it was without her consent, then it should be presumed that there was no consent. The Law Commission suggested that this be introduced as a presumption in law that the accused could rebut by evidence to the contrary. This was recommended as a general rule and not an exceptional one operative in cases of custodial rape alone, although the subsequent amendment limited this presumption to situations of custodial rape. In 1983 the government brought several amendments to the law on rape for the first time since its enactment in 1860. A new set of offences involving rape in the custody of police, hospitals, remand homes and rape against minors and pregnant women was created. A minimum mandatory punishment of seven years imprisonment for non-custodial rape and ten years for custodial rape, was laid down, to be reduced with judicial discretion in exceptional cases. Additionally, the shift in the onus of proof, as suggested by the Law Commission, was introduced with respect to custodial rape. The issue of consent and the woman's word, though central to the preceding debate and the Law Commission report, remained untouched.

After a long gap, attention turned to the definition of rape and the desirability of gender neutrality, particularly in the context of the difficulties posed by the definition of rape for prosecuting child sexual offences. The Supreme Court directed the Law Commission in *Sakshi vs Union of India*,[13] to reconsider the rape law in light of increasingly reported cases of child sexual abuse, following which the Law Commission submitted its 172nd report.[14] The report suggested that the offence of 'rape' be redefined as 'sexual assault' to cover within its scope a number of sexually violent penetrative acts apart from penile-vaginal penetration; that the offence of rape be made gender neutral, so that cases of sexual assault on young boys could also be brought within the scope of the law; and accordingly, Section 377 be deleted.[15]

The Law Commission reports generated substantial debate within women's groups, as well as child rights, sexuality rights and lesbian, gay, bisexual, transgender and inter-sex (LGBT+) groups, that had emerged by that time. While there was consensus on the need for an inclusive definition of rape, the debate on gender neutrality has been an evolving one, with positions getting nuanced with the changing context and the growing visibility of the queer movement. In the backdrop of the Law Commission report, the consensus veered against a blanket gender neutral rape provision. There was agreement that a gender neutral victim and perpetrator ought to be limited to custodial situations and for child victims only, since at that time, it was envisaged that child sexual offences would be addressed through the general criminal laws. Subsequently however, with the move towards enacting a separate and distinct law on child sexual offences, the discussions on gender neutrality in respect of rape law reform revived.

Queer feminist groups evaluated both positions of gender neutrality and gender specificity of victims and perpetrators, to agree that although theoretically, a gender neutral definition of rape might appear to make legal redress available to men and transgender victims, which was desirable, it was realistically impossible to do so in the context of stigma and criminalization of homosexuality; a gender neutral rape law would only fuel a backlash of counter charges against women exercising rights.[16] It was also agreed that since rape was a gendered crime used primarily against women, any attempt to address it in gender neutral terms would obscure the brutal ways in which patriarchal control over women's sexuality is manifested. Conversations on gender neutrality revisited yet again later in the context of the Criminal Law Amendment Bill of 2010, after the Delhi High Court's judgment decriminalising homosexuality.[17] Although there was agreement that the perpetrator be gender specific, while victim be gender neutral, differences persisted broadly, between gay groups and women's groups, including queer feminist collectives, in the formulations for giving effect to gender neutrality of the victim in law reform proposals.

More amendments were carried out in the intervening years. In 2003, the Indian Evidence Act was amended to remove the clauses pertaining to the 'immoral character' and the past sexual history of the victim.[18] Amendments were introduced to the Criminal Procedure Code in 2005 pertaining to the medical examination of accused, medical examination of victim and the requirement of an inquiry by the magistrate in cases of custodial rape.[19] In 2008, additional amendments to the Criminal Procedure Code introduced procedures for recording the victim's statement; investigation in the case of child rape; completion of inquiry/trial in cases under 376 IPC and notably, a victim compensation scheme.[20]

The push for law reform arose once again in 2010, in the backdrop of the Ruchika Girhotra case,[21] leading the government to propose the Sexual Offences Special Courts Bill, 2010. The Bill proposed to set up special courts for trying sexual offences and dispose of them within six months, and introduce provisions regarding sexual offences against 'young persons'. Women's groups rejected piecemeal proposals, demanding, instead, comprehensive law reforms, in response to which the Bill was shelved. The Criminal Law Amendment Bill (2010) followed, proposing substantive and procedural changes in the criminal laws with respect to rape, in response to which autonomous women's groups submitted a memorandum for comprehensive reforms relating to rape and other acts of sexual violence, including during communal and sectarian conflict. This proposal included a section on sexual offences relating to minors and persons other than women.

Discussions on law reform stalled again for two years until the appearance of the Criminal Law Amendment Bill 2012,[22] which replaced the term rape with sexual assault that encompassed all forms of penetrative sexual contact, framed for the first time, in wholly gender neutral terms; it also included offences against public servants for disobeying the law in relation to recording of complaint or carrying out investigation; and included the offence of acid attack. The concerns flagged by autonomous women's groups in relation to this bill included objections in respect of making both the victim and the perpetrator gender neutral, emphasizing that the existing evidence of sexual violence reflected a gender specific and not a gender-neutral reality. The absence of an affirmative definition of 'consent' was another gap that needed attention, to counter moralistic inferences of consent/non-consent based on the victim's clothes, conduct, hymen tears etc to her detriment. The Bill retained the provision of 'outraging the modesty' of women which was based on patriarchal notions of honour and chastity, and ironically retained Section 377 despite the fact that the Delhi High Court had in a historic judgment delivered on 2nd July 2009, read down the provision to de-criminalise consensual homosexual activities between adults and a specific law on sexual offences against children had been enacted, making S. 377 redundant.[23]

Soon after the 2012 Bill was placed before the Parliament, the December 16, 2012 homicidal gang rape unleashed public outrage, and in response to which a high level committee headed by retired Supreme Court judge, Justice J.S. Verma, was constituted to recommend steps to address sexual violence.[24] Following extensive consultations with women's groups, legal academics, civil society organizations and victims, the Committee submitted its recommendations in January 2013. The most significant recommendation was a rejection of moral protectionism in law in favour of Constitutional protection of sexual autonomy and bodily integrity of victims of sexual violence. For the first time, a spectrum of graded sexual offences was introduced, which included stalking, voyuerism, acid attacks and forced disrobing, amongst others; and notably, an expanded definition of rape, and a holistic legal redress that included medical treatment and compensation to the victim-survivor. Further, accountability of state mechanisms and procedural changes geared towards making the justice system sensitive to the needs of victim-survivors of sexual violence were introduced.

The Verma Committee recommendations did get partially enacted into law through the Criminal Law Amendment Act 2013, but not without dilutions and reversals. On 3 February 2013, a few weeks before the parliamentary session, the central government introduced a hastily drafted Ordinance. The Ordinance introduced the blanket gender neutral definition of sexual harassment, assault and rape (from the 2012 Bill), and selectively incorporated the recommendations of the Committee. The Ordinance was rejected by women's groups for its failure to implement the Verma Committee recommendations and for circumventing the parliamentary process. After much public criticism it was replaced by the Criminal Law Amendment Act 2013, which was enacted on 21 March 2013. Some salient features of the amendment were as follows:

- It retained the term 'rape', defined in gender-specific terms with regard to both the victim and the perpetrator, and expanding the scope to include penetrative acts beyond penile-vaginal.
- Consent was clearly defined to mean an unequivocal agreement to consent to the sexual act in question. Further,

physical resistance by the victim was immaterial to the determination of consent.

- Acts such as forced disrobing, stalking, voyeurism and acid attacks were criminalized.
- Provisions were introduced for free and immediate treatment for the victims of sexual violence and acid attack, by all healthcare facilities, with penalties for refusal to provide such treatment.
- It strengthened penal accountability of public servants for disobeying the law to the detriment of the victim.
- The requirement of prior sanction of the government for prosecuting public servants was dispensed with in cases of sexual offences.
- Provisions were made for the first time with regard to physically and mentally challenged victim-survivors of sexual violence. These included interpreters and special educators, for assisting disabled victims of sexual violence, while registering complaints, recording their evidence and during the trial.

Despite these significant changes in law, other longstanding demands made by the women's movement and the queer movement, which were endorsed by the Justice Verma committee, were excluded in the 2013 amendment. These continuing concerns are as follows:

- The amendment failed to extend protection to male and transgender victims; it also failed to repeal Section 377. It also failed to mention systemic sexual violence against Dalit and adivasi women by non-Dalit/non-adivasi as aggravated sexual offences.
- The marital rape exemption was retained, although rape during de facto separation has been recognized.
- The legal age for sexual consent (below which age, consent to sexual intercourse is not recognized in law as a minor is deemed to lack the capacity to consent) was 16 since 1983, it was raised to 18 in 2012. The 2013 amendment affirmed the increase in legal age of consent to 18 years, thus criminalizing

consensual sex between young adults in the age group of 16 to 18 years, a move that has only strengthened control and policing of relationships between young people by the parents, community and religious leaders.

The focus of the campaign for reform of rape law began with custodial rape, which highlighted the problematic interpretations of consent/non-consent that blamed victims while exonerating the accused. Despite this, law reforms over successive years until the 2013 amendment did not introduce a definition of 'consent'. The campaign grew to address an expanded definition of rape, taking on new challenges relating to gender neutrality, and more recently, witnessed reversals such as with the enhancement of the legal age of sexual consent. Definitional issues have been more central to law reform campaigns on rape, with concerns relating to caste, communalism and the accountability of security forces in conflict zones, being included much later, once these concerns developed within the intersecting movements in respect of the existing and proposed special laws relating to caste atrocities, communal violence and sexual violence by the armed forces.[25] The 2013 amendment significantly incorporated the concerns of the disability rights movement for the first time. This journey speaks of the inevitability of an evolving law reform agenda that has grown with, and will continue to grow, with the inter-sectionality of new movements and concerns, such as those relating to caste, communalism, sexuality, child rights and disability.

From Dowry to Domestic Violence and Beyond

The dowry campaign was the starting point of the journey to bring violence inside the private domain of the 'family' within the public discourses of law and rights. Initially framed as a 'social ill' instead of violence, dowry was one of the first women-specific issues debated in the Parliament in post-independence India. In 1953 Uma Nehru introduced a private member's Bill in the Parliament on the prohibition of dowry, which was deferred in the hope that rights granted to women under the Hindu Code Bill which was being discussed in the Parliament, would render the dowry law unnecessary. When the Dowry Prohibition Act was passed in 1961, one of the major concerns of the lawmakers was whether all giving of gifts and money could be viewed as a problem, the potential harassment posed by such a law and whether at all a law was necessary to deal with a 'social problem.' There was also ambivalence regarding the effectiveness of such a law, given the wide cultural sanction given to the practice of giving and taking dowry.[26]

The 1961 legislation made it an offence to give, take, agree to give or demand dowry, but the limited definition of dowry, wide social sanction and a lack of political will made for an unenforceable law.[27] The 1970s saw a spurt in news reports of 'unnatural deaths' of young wives, typically by burns caused by the bursting of cooking stoves leading to their clothes catching fire. Each case revealed some history of dowry demands, driving home the point that in addition to dowry demands, there were taunts, violence, murder and suicide in the matrimonial home. Women's groups such as Mahila Dakshata Samiti and Stree Sangharsh organized demonstrations against such deaths, targeting the marital families of the deceased women for the crime as well as the state for its inaction. It was due to their active mobilization on the issue, that the discourse began to shift from one of 'social ills' to 'criminal offences' such as extortion and murder.

The campaigns also highlighted the problems with the law and the legal system. Disinclined to interfere in what is, till date, viewed as a private matter, the police registered cases as accidents or suicides. The judiciary too grappled with having to treat a socially sanctioned practice, and violence arising from that as offences. The case of Tarvinder Kaur in 1979 is a case in point. Tarvinder, a young newly-wed, left death-bed statements alleging that her in-laws had set her alight because her parents failed to fulfil their ever-increasing dowry demands. This relevant piece of evidence was disregarded by police who registered her death as a suicide. In protest, Stri Sangharsh's mobilization around Tarvinder's death, public protests spread around Delhi and beyond, sparking public debate on dowry-related crimes.[28] Dying declarations were seldom seen as convincing evidence, resulting in the acquittal of the husband and the in-laws. In response to the ineffectiveness of the law and the ever-rising incidents of 'bride burning' and pressure from the women's movement, the Dowry Prohibition Act was amended first in 1984 and then again in 1986. Dowry defined narrowly as given 'in consideration of marriage' was redefined to include, 'Any property or valuable security...given or agreed to be given....at or before or any time after the marriage... or in connection with the marriage.' Nonetheless, presents given without demand, that were customary in nature and not excessive in comparison to the financial status of the giver, remained exempt. Dowry advertisements were banned although these remained integral to almost all matrimonial columns in the newspapers and a new mechanism of the Dowry Prohibition Officers was created for investigation of cases, since police intervention was deemed ineffective. These posts, however, remained vacant for decades.

Alongside, amendments were introduced in the criminal laws to address violence, cruelty, unnatural deaths and suicides within marriage. The social and historical context of dowry, the distinct patterns of violence, its occurrence within the privacy of the home by persons in whose care and custody the bride lived, called for a distinct set of offences based on the presumption that unnatural deaths were related to dowry violence and cruelty. In 1983, Section 498A was inserted in the Indian Penal Code, making the infliction of physical or mental 'cruelty' upon a wife by her husband or in-laws, a criminal offence. Even as this provision on 'cruelty' included dowry harassment, its ambit was much broader than that. Thus cruelty to a wife was made a cognizable, non-bailable offence punishable with a maximum of three years imprisonment with fine. At the same time Section 113A to the Indian Evidence Act was also introduced, allowing the court to draw an inference of abetment to suicide if cruelty was proven in a case of unnatural death within seven years of marriage. In 1986, a new offence of 'dowry death' was created through the insertion of Section 304B of the IPC, along with Section 113B in the Indian Evidence Act that invoked presumption of dowry death, if a woman died within seven years of marriage, under suspicious circumstances and if it was shown that the woman or her family was being harassed for dowry by the husband or his family prior to her death. Despite these amendments in law, a weak investigation machinery, poor evidence collection and prosecution, the institutional bias of the police and the patriarchal attitude of the judiciary combined to reproduce prevailing social values and gender stereotypes, posing obstacles to gender justice. The judiciary, in its reasoning, often normalised some violence as the 'wear and tear' of ordinary married life, and exempted the giving of considerable amount of gifts from the purview of the law, by stating that they were given out of free will, or that this was not unreasonable in view of the status of the bride's parents. In fact, judicial reasoning and responses to dowry-related violence against women often varied with class, caste, motherhood, educational status of the women.[29]

While S. 498A criminalized cruelty within marriage, being a criminal law, it came to be used for grave and overt (physical) forms of domestic violence. This meant that legal redress was difficult for routine harassment, which comprised largely of economic and psychological violence, including acts such as taunts, verbal abuse, denial of food, taking away of *streedhan* (economic resources provided to a bride for her personal use at the time of her wedding) and other economic resources belonging to the woman, that were often independent of dowry. Further, it was extremely challenging for women to prove violence by the husband and his family members 'beyond reasonable doubt' as warranted by criminal law, particularly due to a lack of witnesses to corroborate (substantiate) the woman's testimony of violence that was inflicted on her in a private space. The institutional bias of the police, which considered domestic violence to be a private matter unworthy of legal intervention, and condoned the same, often pushed women back into violent homes after 'counselling'. Women too, were reluctant to take recourse to criminal proceedings, as they often sought legal intervention to stop the violence, negotiate better terms without threatening the marriage or sending the husband and his family members to jail. It became evident that a criminal remedy did not allow that – for the prospect of arrest and imprisonment foreclosed the possibility of reconciliation and resumption of marital life. In fact, a large number of women who were successful in registering complaints of cruelty against their husbands under Section 498A, would fail to pursue the criminal proceedings later either due to pressure from family members, due to the fear of losing an earning member of the family, or indeed, the fear of breaking the marriage. Women also failed to participate and testify in court in the criminal proceedings in contexts where a settlement had been negotiated with the husband, and non-pursuance of a complaint under S. 498A was part of the settlement.

With experience, the limitations in relying solely upon criminal remedies became apparent. At best, criminal remedies could result in conviction of the accused. It could not offer specific reliefs to the victim-survivor, such as security against eviction from home, freedom from violence within the home, medical assistance, monetary help or a short stay home. Moreover, criminal complaints could be registered only after an offence had been committed. To the contrary, in a context of domestic violence, the woman required protection orders against her perpetrator when she apprehended violence or danger to her life. There was a need for law that offered something different, and equally, a need to define domestic violence in terms unconnected with dowry or grave cruelty. Legal protections to 'wives' alone were also not adequate, with evidence that daughters, single women in the family, as well as women in relationships akin to marriage experienced similar forms of violence.

Taking into account the above learning, the discourse gradually shifted from dowry violence to a broader category of domestic violence; and correspondingly, to civil law remedies that could respond effectively to the diverse reliefs that women needed. After more than a decade of campaigning, the Protection of Women Against Domestic Violence Act (PWDVA) was enacted in 2005. The statute considerably transformed the manner in which domestic violence and its remedies were understood. It defines domestic violence broadly to include physical, emotional, economic and sexual abuse against women; it offers remedies that focus on protecting women's rights and enabling their recovery, rather than punishment of the perpetrator; it extends legal protection to women in the household and not just wives, covering within its scope, mothers, sisters, daughters and women in relationships akin to marriage; being a civil law, it created a cadre of Protection Officers and Service Providers, minimizing the dependency on the police for redress. The remedies include protection orders that prohibit further violence, protection of the right of a woman to reside in the shared household irrespective of formal ownership of the house, obtain temporary custody of children, maintenance and compensation. That the implementation of these legal provisions continues to be poor, is another story.[30]

Despite successes in securing laws to address dowry and domestic violence, legal redress in reality is primarily available to wives. The stereotype of the chaste 'good woman' colours all laws that seek to protect women. Even though theoretically, the Protection of Women Against Domestic Violence Act (PWDVA) widens the scope of 'rights holders' to include women in relationships akin to marriage, and offers diverse kinds of reliefs and interventions, in practice, it is primarily used for wives to secure maintenance or economic support.[31]

A range of non-marital intimate relationships make for diverse family forms in India, many of which have historically had social approval and recognition at local levels. In fact, conjugality has historically been shaped by the relationship with land, modes of production, geography, sexuality, caste and custom, amongst others, making for a diverse landscape of family forms. Yet, the focus of the activism for legal protections to women within the domestic sphere has largely been in relation to married women and marriage. Growing initially from a concern for the vulnerability of brides in the context of dowry, it evolved more broadly to wives within the context of the matrimonial home. The marriage-centric legal framework, leaves women in de facto common law marriages, second wives, women in same sex relationships – broadly, women in non-normative conjugal relationships - bereft of legal protection.[32] Despite the PWDVA's notional protection to women in relationships akin to marriage within it, there have been renewed efforts towards making 'proof of' marriage a pre-condition for legal protection, through support for compulsory registration for marriage, being presented as it has been, as a panacea for multiple matrimonial wrongs. This push came from the National Women's Commission and several women's groups, and was endorsed subsequently by the Supreme Court directing states to establish a legislative framework to secure compulsory registration,[33] with very few voices protesting this.[34] Not only does such a move undermine the principle that legal protection to women in all family forms is necessary; it also privileges and promotes marriage as a safer/better institution, along with its notions of normal-deviant sexuality for women.

With women's increasing assertion of agency with respect to sexuality and marriage, there was growing evidence of parental as well as community policing, control and retribution against young women and couples. Law became a ready instrumentality of parental control and vengeance with false complaints of kidnapping lodged against the intimate partners of daughters. This has resulted in the use of law to forcibly wrest 'custody' of daughters who exercise agency with respect to sexuality and marriage, through the use of *habeas corpus* and the manipulation of law enforcement agencies to destroy/obscure evidence related to the same.[35] While most such cases that gained attention have been in the context of elopement and choice, marriages of heterosexual couples, controls and retribution, have also been used against same sex-desiring daughters. Violence by the natal family in contexts of gender non-conformity, forced marriage, forced psychiatric treatment, as well as false kidnapping charges and *habeas corpus* petitions have also been used against women in same sex relationships; and documentation shows the extent to which coercion, stigma and repression have resulted in suicides.[36]

The feminist queer movement and disability movement have helped bring to light the violence against women in the natal family. The campaign against dowry in the 1970s, argued for excluding the natal family from the purview of criminalisation in order to encourage reporting of dowry-related offences. The work of women's groups, crisis intervention groups and Nari Adalts[37] (women's courts) has focussed primarily on the matrimonial home and legally valid wives, as has the PWDVA, despite extending protection to daughters and women in relationships akin to marriage. The struggle for legal protection and non-discrimination in the family, is one where implementation remains a serious concern, as does the inclusivity of a broader range of women as rights holders.

In retrospect, the law reform campaigns also tell a story of exclusions and the continuous efforts towards inclusion and expansion – in terms of rights holders and types of remedies. If anything, this calls for continuing efforts to re-visit legal frameworks to examine how these re-constitute privilege and disadvantage. The rights framework in the family has for instance, been based on rights claims against husbands as male providers, particularly in the contexts of maintenance, matrimonial property and the right to residence. Even as these are necessary steps forward for those with property and financial resources, they make rights contingent on economic status. An inclusive rights framework compels us to explore social security frameworks that entitle single women and women without economic resources, to live with dignity and security. Such a framework also opens possibilities for breaking out of essentially patriarchal frameworks premised on lineage and male providers, while also de-centring marriage as a privileged family model.[38]

Women's Access to Law, the Legal System and Justice

The major focus of the women's movement in the seventies and eighties was to secure legal recognition for specific forms of gender-based violence. Creating new offences opened possibilities for individual legal redress. However it became clear soon that ensuring implementation of the law was an impossibly uphill struggle that required investment of substantial energy and resources. In the period following legislative reforms, it became apparent that the statutory framework on its own did not ensure legal redress. Access to the legal system was impossible for a vast majority of women, due to economic, social and cultural barriers. The language of the law and its individual rights-based adversarial framework were alienating; the requirement of financial and social capacity to navigate the system was a barrier. Women's groups across the country responded to this in different ways – some engaging with formal institutional reform, and others focussing on community-based alternative mechanisms at the local level; still others questioned law's capacity to transform or even alter the status quo. This section looks at the institutional responses and alternative mechanisms that incorporated law with gender justice at the community level, to primarily address concerns within the matrimonial home.

INSTITUTIONAL REFORMS

Two primary institutional reforms were recommended to overcome the insensitivity of legal structures – the first, through demands for separate spaces for women seeking matrimonial remedies and the second, by increasing women personnel in these institutions. This was based on the assumption that institutions staffed by women would be empathetic and sensitive to women's concerns. Two examples of special institutional arrangements are women's police stations and family courts.

(a) *Women's Police Stations:* As part of its engagement with law reform, the women's movement demanded the formation of separate, women-only police cells for women pursuing reliefs for dowry-related harassment/violence and domestic violence. It was argued that victims would feel more comfortable talking about intimate matters to women police personnel, who by virtue of being women, would also be gender sensitive.

An anti-dowry cell was set up in Delhi in 1983 to enforce the Dowry Prohibition Act. In 1986, the Anti Dowry Cell was renamed the Crimes against Women (CAW) Cell, and separate CAW cells were established in each of the nine districts of Delhi. Over the years, the use of CAW cells has also expanded to other Indian states. Although these cells and the additional resources made available for women were welcomed, it gradually became clear that the fundamental purpose of the CAW was family counselling, rather than investigation. Counselling is the 'first response' of CAW cells in 'domestic matters,' and its use was endorsed as recently as 2006 in the Delhi High Court.[39] Counselling is seen by many as the 'most suitable way of dealing with domestic discord' in the Indian context, ensuring the protection of marriage, avoiding a lengthy litigation in court and ensuring the participation of the husband and his family in a manner that ordinary counselling services would be unable to do.

This police-initiated family counselling has been critiqued, on the ground that the *dual* aim of protecting the victim-survivor and protecting the institution of marriage leads to advice that reinforces patriarchal conceptions of marriage, which are not in her best interests. The cell personnel receive no specific training for working with dowry harassment or domestic violence victim-survivors, and often seek to solve disputes by encouraging the woman to return home, failing to appreciate the dangers facing her. Counselling is also rarely accompanied by post-settlement follow-up to ascertain whether the violence has actually stopped. As a result, there is a risk that the cells function as little more than 'marriage counselling bureaus', that privilege marriage over a woman's security and dignity, and result in a failure to register cases of domestic violence because they are 'private matters', as was reported by Human Rights Watch.[40]

(b) *Family Courts:* The *Towards Equality* report (1974), by the Committee on the Status of Women in India, had recommended that issues pertaining to the family must be dealt with by separate courts designated for that purpose. A similar suggestion was also made by the Law Commission in its 59th Report, which resulted in an amendment to the Code of Civil Procedure in 1976, to provide for family courts. These state-initiated developments were boosted further by the women's movement in the following decade. What began as a campaign for the laws on dowry and matrimonial cruelty, also drew attention to the manner in which women were treated in the adversarial trial process. This led to the demand for a separate institution, free from legal technicalities and rigid rules of procedure, evidence or limitation, for handling family matters. As a consequence, the Family Courts Act was enacted in 1984, with the goal of facilitating women's access to speedy and effective justice.

Although conceptualised to expressly facilitate gender justice, this did not get reflected in the legislation that gave effect to those demands. 'Preservation of family' was the primary concern of the Act, on the assumption that the rights of women and children were synonymous with the preservation of the family. The judicial discourse in the area of matrimonial law also reveals the extent to which the ideology of 'family' is used to undermine women's equal rights in the family. Apart from the problematic ideological design of the family courts, their functioning has been compromised by technical questions of territorial jurisdiction, subject matter jurisdiction, personal appearance of parties and so on.[41] The wide discretionary power granted to family court judges by the Act has not been adequately and creatively used. At the same time, the role played by the government in setting up family courts and providing adequate infrastructural support, also leaves much to be desired. In order for family courts to protect women's rights, there must be a concerted effort to provide continuing training and re-orientation of judges in constitutional and international standards on gender justice.

MAHILA NYAYA PANCHAYATS/SHALISH/NARI ADALATS/ WOMEN'S JAMAAT – ALTERNATIVE FORA FOR DISPUTE RESOLUTION

Women's groups have also been instrumental in setting up community-based, women-led platforms/structures of justice redressal, outside the mainstream justice system, such as women's panchayats or Nari Adalats or shalish. Established largely as a response to economic and cultural alienation of the formal justice system and in rejection of the patriarchal justice doled out by the caste panchayats, these mechanisms seek to provide effective alternatives that use a combination of mediation counselling, informal and formal strategies to provide access to remedies and justice to women. By focussing on remedial justice rather than punitive action, such mechanisms have been effective in positively impacting the power equations between the parties. Although these are informal women led adjudication/mediation mechanisms at the community level, they are fairly heterogenous in their approaches and ideologies, varying with the extent of feminist consciousness and linkages with women's movements and feminist groups. So for instance, there are examples of positions as diverse as that of rapists being forced to marry the rape victim, supposedly to save her 'honour', in contrast with a case where a women's panchayat in Arkonam, Tamil Nadu ruled that instead of beating or lashing a rapist, he should be made to give his share of land to the victim and her child.[42] The latter approach is undoubtedly derived from an ideological position based on responsibility and entitlement rather than honour, while also ensuring a concrete benefit to the victim.[43]

The all women's *jamaat* movement of Tamil Nadu, with their over 25,000 strong membership across 15 out of 31 districts of Tamil Nadu, are a symbol of women's empowerment and quest for equality. The very existence of women's jamaats challenges the monopoly of the conservative male elite over community mediation and leadership. Beyond that, it has succeeded in re-defining adjudication processes as being accessible, inclusive, transparent, fair which are not exclusive of, but linked to formal systems of justice. Unlike the traditional male jamaats, they abjure parallel justice, and where necessary, refer the cases to the legal system, acting as a bridge between the informal and the formal.[44]

The informal setting of the women's panchayats, the practical conciliatory approach of the proceedings, a built-in process of enforcement of the decisions and the shared gender identity of the 'client' and the 'judges' are in themselves viewed as facilitating gender justice. As with all non-formal mechanisms, the informality of its processes and the fluidity of its normative framework poses challenges. Formal legal rights are often more progressive than what is offered to the women by way of a mediated resolution. A study of Gujarat initiatives notes that the alternative courts are managed and presided by lay women, untrained in law, and this often results in their being unable to comprehend the complexities of legal or revenue documents presented by the clients in support of their claims.[45] Being a community-based initiative, the fear of sanctions also may not be as strong as compared to judgments and orders passed by the formal courts. The Gujarat study further notes that

'Their relatively low understanding of the laws, legal provisions and procedures, coupled with unconscious slips into patriarchal ways of judging and seeing – both of which were evident during the study – can make them vulnerable to the same faults as both the Gynati Panchayat and the formal justice system.'[46]

Another study of the shalish in rural West Bengal shows that women's groups intervene in and influence the community shalish led by influential men, that commands considerable social sanction. Women's groups use this mechanism strategically to further gender justice, although the composition of the shalish is subject to the influence of local power politics and political affiliations. Nonetheless, women's groups have used these mechanisms to resolve women's cases effectively, valuing the mechanism for its flexible remedies and injunctions, its power of social sanction and the practicality of enforcement.[47]

Conclusion

The campaigns for legislative reform from the 1980s to 2013 reflect an evolving reform agenda, shaped by emerging perspectives and movements. They highlight the need to constantly reflect upon and re-examine legal frameworks for their limitations, partiality and to be in conversation with emerging emancipatory movements that throw light on bias and exclusions within the law reform agenda. A continuing reform agenda requires a greater investment than there has been so far, on policy-oriented socio-legal studies to create evidence of law's interface with structures of caste, gender, class and sexuality, as well as evidence of its differential impact on marginalized constituencies amongst women. There is equally a need to evaluate the assumptions underlying over-reliance on criminal law and stringent penal frameworks for addressing violence against women. To what extent do punitive responses assist the victim-survivor's need for healing and recovery; and indeed, to what extent does legal justice recognize and address the needs of the victim-survivor are necessary questions to ask. The trend towards demanding support services to women in the PWDVA, 2005 and more recently, in the inclusion of duty to provide medical treatment under the CLAA, 2013 marks a normative shift in the demands by the women's movement and its expectations of legal justice, even if the mechanisms for operationalising these remedies are severely inadequate, and non-existent in many parts of the country. The discomfort and reluctance of women's groups to proactively push for or endorse compensation as part of legal redress, calls for introspection, although the law has now been amended to provide compensation to victims of sexual and acid violence. The reliance on penal remedies arises from an excessive focus on wrongs and victimisation which in the context of sexuality has resulted in 'systematis[ing] sexuality within a marital, heterosexist paradigm' that has created a 'narrow…and rigid view of sexuality' steeped in 'negative' aspects of a woman's sexuality in rape and violent contexts.[48] In the absence of policy debates on sexual rights, sexuality in law has become limited to sexual wrongs and victimisation, played out through the stereotypes that are used in legal discourse to determine 'consent' and 'non-consent'. These are likely to persist, even if re-configured somewhat, despite the introduction of a statutory definition of consent in the 2013 amendment.

The engagement with the law, despite this rich history, has been accompanied by critical debates questioning the over-reliance on law and also, its relevance in the struggle for social transformation. As part of this critique is the questioning of the relevance of rights language to the emancipatory agenda since the articulation of rights in law delinks it from the political ideology or the structural critique they originate from. Rights claims, it is asserted, tend to get fixed in terms of identities – of woman, caste, disability and so on, rather than the normative frameworks that are radical and transformative, irrespective of identities. This has been critiqued particularly in relation to sexuality, where the rights activism has been fixed on categories: woman, sex worker and LGBT+, that add to the list of rights holders, without transforming the violation-centred, heteronormative framework of the law. Once codified into law, rights have limited potential to disturb the social values from which inequalities and hierarchies emanate.[49] Another criticism has been that rights and claims in law flatten and universalise the category of woman, creating the foundation for stereotypes of good and bad women, selectivity, and the inevitable othering of the subaltern categories.[50] Law reform activism with its focus on state and the law, tends to get lawyer-led, and may get monopolised by a few professionals, without the participatory processes or consultations necessary for strategic framing of the reform agenda.[51] Once enacted, these reconfigure and reproduce the status quo. And further, that rights and laws are problematic pathways to radical transformation as they rely upon the primary state as the agent of social transformation and emancipation, which is a contradiction. This is why law, regardless of the intention with which it is framed, reinforces the dominant interests the state embodies – rather than its subversion. While seeming to be women- friendly, the law co-opts the language of women's rights without transforming the very norms that underpin gender, social, sexual, caste and class heirarchies.[52]

Even as many share the view of law's tendency to reconstitute the status quo, the women's movement's engagement with law reform has been premised broadly on the fundamental necessity of negotiating de jure equality for women and for engendering the law, to make it cognisant of, if not uniformly responsive to socially sanctioned injusitce. If one views law, both in terms of being a necessary tool to contest power, and a site of power itself, the legal terrain is an unavoidable arena of struggle. The contradictory and heterogenous nature of law in fact, holds possibilities of contestation through litigation. There has not been enough of discussions however, on the limitations of pursing a reform agenda that gives greater controls to the state, and indeed, to the police, rather than to women. That while the women's movement has been pacified with new laws, the levels of violence against women and its legitimization continued to increase, and the public-private divide remains.[53] Further, that even as public outrages and media attention that seem to be forthcoming in recent times for select cases, little attention is paid to the structural nature of violence, particularly for the marginalized. The call for greater critical reflection however, is not to argue against a robust engagement with the law, but to emphasize greater need for tracking the impact of law, to create evidence for informing future law reform; and indeed, for a stronger emphasis on parallel political and creative strategies that challenge normative frameworks that entrench the status quo, while simultaneously being transformative.

Notes

1. Research assistance for this paper was provided by Claire McEvilly and Saptarshi Mandal from PLD.
2. It was not until February 2013, that the definition of rape was expanded to include other forms of penetrative sexual assault. Until then, the only serious sexual offence was that of rape; with a trivial offence of 'outraging the modesty of a woman' as a secondary catch-all offence to cover everything other than narrowly defined rape.
3. Mrinal Satish (2013, January 4), 'Chastity, Virginity, Marriageabilty and Rape Sentencing', available at http://lawandotherthings.blogspot.in/2013/01/chastity-virginity-marriageability-and.html accessed on 5 October 2013
4. In the period post December 16, 2012 homicidal gang rape in Delhi that evoked widespread public outrage, the demand for retribution and deterrence coloured all debates, including to some extent the Criminal Law Amendment Act, 2013, that introduced a high minimum sentencing for rape, without judicial discretion to reduce sentence for adequate and special reasons. In fact, the sentencing structure brought in by this amendment was higher than that in the Protection of Children from Sexual Offences Act, 2012 for similar offences against children.
5. For more details on the case, see, Kalpana Kannabiran. 1996. 'Rape and the Construction of Communal Identity' in Kumari Jayawardena and Malathi de Alwis (eds.), *Embodied Violence: Communalising Women's Bodies in South Asia.* New Delhi: Kali for Women, pp. 32–41.
6. *Tukaram vs. State of Maharashtra* AIR 1979 SC 185.
7. Upendra Baxi, Lotika Sarkar, Raghunath Kelkar and Vasudha Dhagamwar. 1979. 'An Open Letter to the Chief Justice of India', *SCC Journal*, Vol 4, 17.
8. 1978. 2 *SCC* 424.
9. The pioneering case in this regard, was *Hussainara Khatoon vs Home Secy., State of Bihar* AIR 1979 SC 1979.
10. For more on this case, see Baghpat Report Supports Oppression, *PUCL Bulletin*, May 1981 available at http://www.pucl.org/from-archives/may81/baghpat.htm, accessed on 5 November 2013.
11. 'Bhagpat report Supports Oppression', *PUCL Bulletin*, May 1981.
12. Ibid.
13. Writ Petition (Criminal) no. 33 of 1997.

14. The Law Commission submitted two reports – the 156th Law Commission Report submitted in 1997 did not address the concerns adequately, so the Supreme Court directed the Commission to re-consider the precise issues posed, which it did in the 172nd Report that was submitted in 2000.

15. S. 377 of the Indian Penal Code titled 'unnatural offences' is based on a colonial notion of that any form of sexual relationship other than penile-vaginal intercourse is 'against the order of nature' and deserves to be severely punished, even if it is between two consenting adults. While this provision serves to criminalize homosexuality (and has been the subject of constitutional challenges in the Delhi High Court and subsequently the Supreme Court), the provision was used to prosecute child sexual abuse, particularly those perpetrated on boys, till the enactment of Protection of Child Sexual Offences (POCSO) Act 2012.

16. Naisargi N. Dave (2012), *Queer Activism in India: A Story in the Anthropology of Ethics* (London: Duke University Press, and New Delhi: Zubaan, pp. 167–204.

17. *Naz Foundation vs NCT of Delhi* 160 *Delhi Law Times* 277.

18. See sections 155(4) and 146 of the Indian Evidence Act.

19. See sections 53A, 164A and 176 respectively.

20. See sections 157, 173, 309. The victim compensation scheme under section 357A went unnoticed for the most part by the women's groups, and came to be debated much later in 2011, with the framing of a financial assistance scheme for rape victims by the government.

21. The molestation of a 14 year old girl by the Inspector General of Police (Haryana), S.P.S. Rathore, in 1990 took 19 years to secure a conviction. In the course of this period, the persistent harassment by the influential accused unleashed continuing violence against the victim, causing her to commit suicide and her family to re-locate. The victim's expulsion by her school, the loss of job by her father, and a false case against her brother led to the suicide.

22. The text of the Bill is available at http://pldindia.org/wp-content/uploads/2013/04/Criminal-Law-Amendment-Bill-20121.pdf, accessed on 4 October 2013.

23. The Protection of Children from Sexual Offences (POCSO) Act, 2012.

24. The terms of reference constituting the committee were limited to speedy justice and punishment with respect to aggravated rape, but the committee expanded its scope of inquiry to address all aspects necessary for addressing sexual violence.

25. Many of these concerns were part of special laws rather than the criminal law reform debates. The repeal of the Armed Forces Special Powers Act in relation to the conflict areas of the Northeastern states, and later Kashmir; the Prevention of Atrocities Act in relation to caste-based sexual violence; and the debates on recognition of mass sexual violence, witness and victim protection as well as culpability arising from command responsibility developed post

Gujarat carnage in 2002, and became part of the campaign for the Communal Violence Bill from 2005 onwards.

26. See Lotika Sarkar, Usha Ramanathan, Madhu Mehra. 1994. 'Gender Bias in Law: Dowry' (Karmika), available at http://pldindia.org/wp-content/uploads/2013/04/Gender-Bias-in-Law.pdf, accessed on 6 November 2013.

27. The Committee on the Status of Women in India, set up by the government in 1975 found only one case filed under this law.

28. Radha Kumar. 1993. *The History of Doing: An illustrated Account of Movements for Women's Rights and Feminism in India, 1800–1900.* New Delhi: Kali for Women, pp. 115–26.

29. For a detailed discussion on this differentiation, see Madhu Mehra. 1998. 'Exploring the Boundaries of Law, Gender and Social Reform', *Feminist Legal Studies,* Vol. VI, No.1.

30. Reports show that the appointment of Protection Officers across states is far from adequate, and that most appointments are in fact additional charge handed over to existing local level officers, who besides being overburdened, have not received adequate orientation to enable them to carry out their tasks. The Service Providers envisaged under law remain largely on paper.

31. Lawyers Collective Women's Rights Initiative. 2013. *Staying Alive: 6th Monitoring and Evaluation Report 2013 on the Protection of Women From Domestic Violence Act, 2005.* New Delhi: Lawyers Collective, at p. ix.

32. For discussions, research and documentation on why for legal protection of women in all family forms is necessary, including for women in non-normative intimacies, see Madhu Mehra (2010), *Rights in Intimate Relationships: Towards An Inclusive and Just Framework of Women's Rights and the Family,* New Delhi: Partners for Law in Development.

33. *Seema vs Ashwini Kumar,* (2005) 4 SCC 443: (2006) 2 SCC 578: (2008) 1 SCC 180.

34. Partners for Law in Development submitted a memorandum, endorsed by several community organizations and women's rights activists, to the government and the National Women's Commission arguing against compulsory registration of marriage, in light of the resultant rollback on women's rights. http://pldindia.org/wp-content/uploads/2013/10/Petition-against-registration-of-marriages-and-definition-of-wife.pdf.

35. A writ of *habeas corpus* is a legal action that requires a person who has restrained another to produce the person in court, in order that the court may determine the legality of the 'custody' and restraint.

36. Ponni Arasu and Priya Thangaraja, 'Queer Women and Habeas Corpus in India: The Love that Blinds the Law', *Indian Journal of Gender Studies* 19, 3 (2012) 413–435. See also, *Rights in Intimate Relationships: Towards An Inclusive and Just Framework of Women's Rights and the Family* (2010) Supra note 32.

37. Feminist organizing of women at the community level, amongst urban poor and in rural contexts, has often led to the formation of collectives assuming

leadership to address cases of violence, harassment and matrimonial wrongs faced by women in the community. Women's courts as they are informally called, intervene, counsel, mediate, initiate compromise and where appropriate, report the matter to the police.

38. For an exploration of a transformatory framework of rights in the family, see ibid.

39. 'In a 2006 judgment, the Delhi High Court's Justice Aggarwal explained: '[T]he CAW Cells have been constituted with a social purpose so that the crimes relating to women are dealt with sensitivity [sic].... Firstly an attempt is made to bring about unity between the two spouses so as to make the marriage a success.... This cell is meant to safeguard the marriage and not to ruin it by registering case immediately on the asking of the complainant.' *Jasbir Kaur vs State (Govt. of NCT Delhi)* WP (Crl) No. 134/2006 & CM No. 545/2006, 27 July 2006. See Human Rights Watch (2009), *Broken System: Dysfunction, Abuse and Impunity in the Indian Police* New York: Human Rights Watch, p. 52.

40. Broken System, ibid. p. 52.

41. For a critique of family courts, see Flavia Agnes. 1991, 'A Toothless Tiger: A Critique of Family Courts', *Manushi*, No. 66, pp. 9–17.

42. Nandita Gandhi & Nandita Shah. 1992. *The Issues At Stake: Theory and Practice in the Contemporary Indian Women's Movement.* New Delhi: Kali for Women p. 269.

43. The Mahila Nyaya Panchayats and the Tamil Nadu Women's Jamaat, two examples of women's alternative dispute resolution, are discussed in greater detail by Poonam Kathuria and V. Geetha in their respective articles in this publication.

44. For more discussion on their ideological framework and strategic positioning, see Madhu Mehra and Gayatri Sharma. 2010. *Negotiating Gender Justice, Contesting Discrimination: Mapping Strategies that Intersect Culture, Women and Human Rights'* New Delhi: Partners for Law in Developmentt pp. 124–32.

45. Sushma Iyengar 2005. *A Study of Nari Adalats and Caste Panchayats in Gujarat,* Bangkok: United Nations Development Programme. p. 15.

46. Ibid.

47. International Centre for Research on Women. 2002. 'Women-Initiated Community Level Responses to Domestic Violence: Summary of Three Studies', Washington D.C.: International Centre for Research on Women.

48. Geetanjali Gangoli. 2007. *Indian Feminisms: Law, Patriarchies and Violence in India* Hampshire: Ashgate Publishing Ltd, p. 57.

49. Jaya Sharma. 2007. 'The Language of Rights, Development with a Body: Sexuality, Rights and Development', in Andrea Cornwall, Sonia Correa and Susie Jolly (eds.), Zed Books p.67–76.

50. Nivedita Menon. 2004. *Recovering Subversion: Feminist Politics Beyond the Law* New Delhi: Permanent Black.

51. Nivedita Menon (ibid), in chapter 5 refers to the law reform proposed in relation to sexual assault in 2000 by the Law Commission of India based on consultations with select professionals, that was later critiqued by the autonomous women's groups for not being inclusive, participatory or reflective of serious concerns of the women's movement on the subject of gender neutrality.
52. Ratna Kapur. 2005. *Erotic Justice: Law and New Politics of Postcolonialism*, New Delhi: Permanent Black.
53. Flavia Agnes. 1992. 'Protecting Women Against Violence – a decade of legislation, 1980–89', *Economic and Political Weekly*, Vol XXVII, No. 17, April 25.

References

Flavia Agnes. 1991. 'A Toothless Tiger: A Critique of Family Courts', *Manushi*, No 66, 9–37.
———. 1992. 'Protecting Women Against Violence – A Decade of Legislation, 1980-87, *Economic and Political Weekly*, Vol XXVII, No 17, April.
Geetanjali Gogoi. 2007. *Indian Feminisms: Law, Patriarchies and Violence in India.* Hampshire: Ashgate Publishing Ltd.
Human Rights Watch. 2009. *Broken System. Dysfunction, Abuse and Impunity in the Indian Police.* New York: Human Rights Watch.
International Centre for Research on Women. 2007. 'Women Initiated Community Level Responses on Domestic Violence: Summary of Three Studies'. Washington DC: International Centre for Research on Women.
Kalpana Kannabiran. 1996. 'Rape and the Constructin of Communal Identity' in Kumari Jayawardena and Malathi de Alwis (eds.), *Embodied Violence: Communalising Women's Bodies in South Asia.* New Delhi: Kali for Women.
Lawyers Collective Women's Rights Initiative. 2013. Staying Alive. 6th Monitoring and Evaluation Report on the Protection of Women from Domestic Violence Act, 2005. New Delhi: Lawyers Collective.
Lotika Sarkar, Usha Ramanathan, Madhu Mehra. 1994. 'Gender Bias in Law: Dowry'. New Delhi: Karmika. Available at http://pldindia.org/wp-contents/uploads/2013/04/Gender-Bias-in-Law.pdf, accessed on 6 November 2013.
Madhu Mehra. 1998. 'Exploring the Boundaries of Law, Gender and Social Reform', *Feminist Legal Studies*, Vol VI, No 1.
Mrinal Satish. 2013. 'Charity, Virginity, Marriageability and Rape Sentencing' available at http://lawandotherthings.blogspot.in/2013/01/charity-virginity-marriageability-and.html.accessed on 5 October 2013.
Naisargi N. Dave. 2013. *Queer Activism in india: A Story in the Anthropology of Ethics.* London: Duke University Press and New Delhi: Zubaan.

Nandita Gandhi and Nandita Shah. 1992. *The Issues at Stake: Theory and Practice in the Contemporary Indian Women's Movement*. New Delhi: Kali for Women.

Madhu Mehra. 2010. 'Rights in Intimate Relationships: Towards and Inclusive and Just Framework for Women's Rights and the Family'. New Delhi: Partners for Law in Development.

Madhu Mehra and Gayatri Sharma. 2010. 'Negotiating Gender Justice, Contesting Discrimination' Mapping Strategies that Intersect Culture, Women and Human Rights'. New Delhi: Partners for Law in Development.

Radha Kumar. 1993. *The History of Doing: An Illustrated Account of Movements for Women's Rights and Feminisms in India, 1800–1990*. New Delhi: Kali for Women and Zubaan.

Sushma Iyengar. 2005. 'A Study of Nari Adalats and Caste Panchayats in Gujarat'. Bankgok: United Nations Development Programme.

Upendra Baxi, Lotika Sarkar, Raghunath Kelkar and Vasudha Dhagamwar. 1979. 'An Open Letter to the Chief Justice of India', SCc Journal, Vol 4. 17.

Ponni Arasu and Priya Thangaraja. 2012. 'Queer Women and Habeas Corpus in India: The Love that Blinds the Law'. *Indian Journal of Gender Studies*, 19. 3. 413–45.

Ratna Kapur. 2005. *Erotic Justice: Law and New Politics of Postcolonialism*. New Delhi: Permanent Black.

SIX

Courts of Women

Re-Imagining Justice

Corinne Kumar

We have entered the night to tell our tale
to listen to those who have not spoken
we who have seen our children die in the morning deserve
to be listened to:
we have looked on blankly as they have opened their wounds.
Nothing really matters except, the grief of the children
their tears must be revered
their inner silence speaks louder than the spoken word
and all being and all life shouts out in outrage
we must not be rushed to our truths
whatever we failed to say is stored secretly in our minds
and all those processions of embittered crowds
have seen us lead them a thousand times
we can hear the story over and over and over again
our minds are muted beyond the sadness
there is nothing more we can fear.[1]

Context

We live in violent times:

> times in which our community and collective memories are dying;
> times in which the many dreams are turning into never-ending
nightmares,

of violence, of power, of profit, of patriarchy,
while the future is increasingly fragmenting;
times that are collapsing the many life visions into a *single cosmology*
that has
created its own *universal truths* - equality, development, freedom;
truths that are inherently discriminatory, even violent.
times that are creating the globalized world order that dispossesses
the majority,
desacralizes nature, destroys cultures and civilizations, denigrates
the women;

times in which the war on terrorism brings
a time of violent uncertainty, brutal wars:
wars for resources- oil, land, diamonds, minerals: wars of
occupation,
times that are giving us new words;
pre-emptive strike, collateral damage, embedded journalism, enemy
combatants,
unmanned drones, military tribunals, rendition:
new words

words soaked in blood.

times in which the dominant political thinking, institutions and
instruments of
justice are hardly able to redress the *violence* that is escalating and
intensifying,
times in which *progress* presupposes the *genocide* of the many; the
gendercide of the women;
the violence taking newer and more contemporary forms,
denying the women, disappearing the women, destroying the
women
times in which human rights have come to mean the rights of the
privileged, the
rights of the powerful and for the masses to have their freedoms,
their human rights, they must surrender their most fundamental
right of all, *the right to be human*
times in which the *political space* for the other is diminishing, even
closing.

The world, it would seem, is at the end of its imagination.

Perhaps it is in this moment when existing systems of meaning
are fragmenting
that we may search for new meanings;
who will deny that we need another imaginary?

The Courts of Women as a New Imaginary

It was a dream-journey that began many years ago in Asia and the
Pacific with the Asian Women's Human Rights Council, and
Vimochana, India. It then moved with El Taller International, and
supporting and collaborating organizations to other regions of the
world including Africa, the Arab world, Central and Latin America.
Gathering momentum and meaning as it grew into a movement of
hope for women in the global south, even while taking root in the
specificity of the regions where the Courts have been held, offering
new notions, new ways to justice. The courts of women is the dream
of trespass, a dream to reclaim our memories, to rewrite women's
histories, to find new visions for our times, offering another way
of knowing.

Our Imaginaries Must be Different

The new imaginary cannot have its moorings in the dominant
discourse (for instance, women's rights are human rights) but must
seek to locate itself in a *discourse of dissent* that comes from a deep
critique of the different forms of domination and violence in our
times: any new imaginary cannot be tied to the dominant discourse
and systems of violence and exclusion.

The Courts of Women, draws its philosophical moorings from *A
South Wind: Towards a New Political Imaginary* located as it is in a
discourse of dissent and imbued with *a new vision of human rights*.
It is a journey away from the centre to the peripheries of power,
where power itself is being rewoven from the fabric of powerlessness.
Courts of Women as a global movement seeks to relook at rights
and other notions of justice from the lives of women and life visions

of women – particularly from the global South. People's Tribunals, Truth commissions, Public hearings, are expressions of people's resistance.

It is not difficult to see that we are at the end of an era, when every old category begins to have a hollow sound, and when we are groping in the dark to discover the new. Can we find new words, search for new ways, create out of the material of the human spirit *possibilities* to transform the existing exploitative social order, to discern a greater human potential? We need to imagine alternative perspectives for change: to craft visions that will evolve out of conversations across cultures and other traditions; conversations between cultures that challenge and transcend the totalitarianism of the western patriarchal logos; conversations that are not mediated by the hegemony of the universal discourse.

The new imaginary invites us to another human rights discourse; one that will not be trapped either in the *universalisms* of the dominant thinking tied as it is to a market economy, a monoculturalism, a materialistic ethic and the politics and polity of the nation state; neither must it be caught in the discourse of the *culture specific* but one that will proffer universalisms that have been born out of a *dialogue of civilizations,* of cultures. And this will mean another *ethic of dialogue.* We need to find new perspectives on the universality of human rights, *in dialogue with other cultural perspectives of reality,* other notions of development, democracy, even dissent; other concepts of power (not power to control, power to hegemonise, but power to facilitate, to enhance) and governance; other notions of equality. Equality makes us flat and faceless citizens of the nation state, perhaps the notion of *dignity* which comes from depth, from *roots,* could change the discourse.

Through its very diverse voices, the Courts of Women speak of equality not in terms of *sameness,* but in terms of *difference,* a difference that is rooted in dignity, from the roots of peoples, of women who have been excluded, erased; other concepts of justice – *justice without revenge,* justice with truth and reconciliation, justice with healing of individuals, of communities, because humankind proffers many horizons of discourse and because our eyes do not as yet behold those horizons, it does not mean that those horizons do not exist.

Take the universal discourse on *democracy*: the new magical word to *reform* the world. The dominant understanding of democracy is tied to the notion of individual rights, private property, patriarchy, profit, the market economy; we are all equal we are told but the market works as the *guarantor of inequality*, of unequal distribution, of how only a few will have and how the many must not have. What shall we do with the rhetoric of political equality on which this democracy is built, while the majority are increasingly dispossessed, living below poverty lines? We must seek new understandings of democracy that will include a concept of freedom that is different from that which is enshrined in the Enlightenment and its Market. There is an urgent need to reinvent the political; to *infuse the political with the ethical*.

In its expression of a new imaginary the Courts are finding different ways of speaking *truth to power;* of challenging power, recognizing that the concepts and categories enshrined in the ideas and institutions of our times are unable to grasp the violence. The Courts of Women are more than speaking truth to power, more than being a critic of power; they are about *creating another authority*. The Courts of Women also speak *truth to the powerless*, seeking the conscience of the world, creating reference points other than that of the rule of law, returning *ethics to politics*. They invite us to the *decolonization* of our structures, our minds and our imaginations; moving away from the master imaginary, finding worlds, as the Zapatista say, that *embrace many worlds*. The Courts of Women are about subsumed cultures, subjugated peoples, silenced women *reclaiming their political* voice and in breaking the silence and refusing the conditions by which power maintains its patriarchal control.

The Courts of Women are Public Hearings

The Court is used in a symbolic way. In the Courts, the voices of the survivors are listened to; women bring their personal testimonies of violence, transforming private individual memory into shared public knowledge, giving what is seen as personal violence *a public face*, a political significance. The Courts are *sacred spaces* where women speak in a language of suffering, name the crime, seek redress, even reparation and healing.

The issues that have been focused at the over forty Courts held so far since the first Court held in Lahore, Pakistan in 1992, have been varied. They have ranged from violence against women within the home, acid and dowry burnings, wife battering, sexual assault and female infanticide to community-based violence like forced feeding and honour crimes and direct state based violations like displacement and migration, trafficking, rape in times of war and peace. The Courts have also provided the perspectives of women on issues such as war, racism, development, nuclearisation and militarisation and communalisation of faiths.

The Courts of Women are assemblies of peoples in resistance. Yet the point of departure they signify is the denial of violence as a means of justice even when fully pitted against the myriad state/civil society violations of women's rights to be and to remain human. The courts of women do not proselytize violent social transformation as a justifiable response to atrocious forms of lynch justice of the caste Biradri and the Hadood-based frameworks justifying violence against women. Rather, they represent fresh starts in critical solidarity.

The Courts of Women inaugurate the art and craft of the three 'Rs': rethinking, re-imagining, recrafting the practices of new points of departure. Thus, the metaphor of the court stands divested of the signature of the sovereign power of the state. In this imaginary practice, the idea of the court emerges as a theatre of the voices of suffering.

In their vision and methodology, the Courts of Women challenge the dominant ways to knowledge, seek to weave together the *objective* reality with the *subjective* testimonies/voices of the women; the personal *text* with the political *context*; the *logical* with the *lyrical*; the rational with the intuitive; *reason with compassion*; moving to deeper layers of knowing; offering the pain, the politics, the poetry; urging us to discern fresh insights, seeking other ways of knowings, listening to other tellings, inviting us to create a new imaginary.

Lawrence Liang[2] in his essay on the Courts of Women tells us that the Courts consciously adopt vulnerability in their imagination[2] and the women bringing testimony in bearing witness to their experience also bear witness to the fragility of life as it encounters the brutality of violence and power. The Courts offer the spaces for that which is vulnerable and fragile, and from this is the beginning of drawing the contours of another imaginary that must bring us to *re-imagine justice.*

What is unique to the Courts of Women is their feminist methodology that is rooted in a *discourse of dissent;* a methodology that revolves around weaving together the personal testimony with the political analysis, the affective sensibility with the aesthetic expression. It seeks to invite the audience to relook at these issues not as experts but as witness to the violence of our times.

In the experience of a feminist organization Vimochana, the Courts of Women brought together diverse women and organizations from a range of cultural and political realities reflecting an intense diversity of ideologies and perspectives. And yet they have been transformed into collective spaces of healing and resistance, articulating, rooted in diverse visions of transformation, justice and peace that transcend the divisive and violent nature of contemporary politics. And that is also because the Courts have evolved another ethic of working together in which *differences enrich and not fragment the dialogue.*

Perhaps, it is in the expressions of *resistance* seeking legitimacy not by the dominant standards, not from a dominant paradigm of jurisprudence, not by the *rule of law,* that begin to draw the contours of a new political imaginary: the Truth Commissions, the Public Hearings, the Peoples' Tribunals, the Courts of Women are all expressions of a new imaginary refusing/refuting that human rights be defined and confined by the dominant hegemonic paradigm.

The Courts of Women are a New Articulation of a Political Imaginary Speaking of Ethics of Care

While the Courts of Women listen to the voices of the survivors, they also listen to the voices of women who resist, who rebel, who refuse to turn against their dreams. They hear of survival in the *dailyness of life*; they hear of women and movements resisting violence in its myriad forms. In its search towards a new political imaginary, the Courts of Women work towards a politics with an *ethic of care*; for any theory of poverty (poverty lines, the World Bank one-dollar-a day, millennium development goals, poverty reduction strategies etc.) that is disconnected from a theory of care will not listen to the voice of the Other, and simply leave the poor out! The new political imaginary speaks to an ethic of care, affirming one's responsibility to the other, an ethic that will include compassion, connectedness, community, *conviviality* (that wonderful word of Ivan Illich[3]). The discourse and praxis of rights cannot mean only economic and political emancipation, but must challenge the current paradigms of knowledge, thought and politics.

The Courts of Women are a horizon that invites us to think, to feel, to challenge, to connect, to dare; they are an attempt to define a new space for women, and infuse this space with a new vision, a new politics; they are a gathering of voices and visions of the *global south*, locating themselves in a discourse of dissent, in itself a dislocating practice, challenging the new world order of globalization, crossing lines, breaking new ground; listening to the voices and movements from the margins; conversing with the diverse visions and cosmologies of cultures and civilizations in the Global South.

Vimochana: a feminist organization, together with partner organizations in India and other countries in Asia, held the Asia Court of Women on Crimes Against Women related to the Violence of Development.[4] In the words of Vimochana team,

> The Court was a turning point for us in Vimochana and indeed many other groups in the movement working on issues related to violence

against women. Primarily because in its narrative unfolding at the multi-layered realms of the emotional, rational and the intuitive, the Court so clearly revealed for us the deeper connections between the increasing incidence and forms of violence against women in the *personal* sphere that we work with like the violence of dowry burnings, wife battering, female infanticide, trafficking, migration, displacement etc. and the genocidal development paradigm of growth and progress that we see today as globalization. Some of these forms of violence perhaps may be rooted in local *customs* and therefore speak of the violence of cultures. But they speak also of fractured life patterns and cultural cosmologies that had their own inherent wisdoms and strengths with which they recognized and responded to injustice and misery within; wisdoms and strengths that have been eroded, cannibalized and commodified by the one universal world view of modernization and the market.

Development, the Court very clearly revealed, had brought with it a world view that forced a divide between the hitherto complementary and interdependent spheres of the public and the personal. What has become premium and mainstream today in the *public* sphere is the market, money, man and management; while home, household, women and labour that have become personal and *private* and therefore devalued. The devaluation of this sphere precipitated a devaluation of the woman and her role: Violence like dowry and female infanticide and female sex-selective abortions or even witch hunting became a product of this *devaluation* of the female sphere and the brutalized patriarchies resulting from the overvaluation of the male and the masculine.

Vimochana more specifically articulated how the Court of Women was a point of praxis, both personally for the organization and individuals within it as also politically in terms of a search for a new ethic and language of transformation. While Vimochana had been organizing public hearings that provided an open forum for the *victims* to directly speak, it was the first time in the Courts that the powerful impact of a *personal testimony was visible.* It is when it is woven together with the *political analyses,* both of which are then gently embedded in the subversive power of the poetic image that is able to hold and honour the pain of the individual even while intensifying the power of collective anger and resistance rooted in a reflective and intuitive analyses. They went on to say: 'We hope that the Courts, its vision, methodology and processes will strengthen our constant search for a new civilizational idiom of politics that connect ancient wisdoms, women's wisdoms with new visions; individual transformations rooted in collective justice.'[5]

The Courts of Women return through testimony, the voices of the dispossessed to political discourse. There are moments, as Audre Lorde once said of *bursts of light:*

The Courts of Women, as someone described the experience, are bursts of light

In the aftermath of all the violence
light remembers

light searches out the hidden places
fills every crevice

light slips into every place
where the women were killed

the houses, the streets, the doorways
light traces the blood stains

light pours into the wells
where they threw the bodies

light seeks out the places where sound
was silenced.[6]

Transformatory Jurisprudence

The Courts of Women speak too of another notion of justice; of a jurisprudence, which bringing individual and collective justice and reparation will also be transformatory for all. A jurisprudence that is able to *contextualize* and *historicize* the crimes, moving away from a justice with punishment, a justice of revenge, a *retributive justice,* to a justice seeking redress, even reparation; a justice with truth and reconciliation, a *restorative justice,* a *justice with healing,* healing individuals and communities. Can the Courts of Women, can the tears and narratives of the women, these sites of pain, and these sites of devastation and destitution lead us to re-thinking and *re-imagining another way to justice*? What ideas and sensibilities do we need to explore to expand the imagination of justice? The Courts refusing to separate the affective from the rational (juridical) creates a space in which emotive demands are allowed to be voiced and collective trauma is understood. The Courts of Women are a step towards re-imagining this jurisprudence from within civil society in which we are able to creatively connect and deepen our collective insights and understanding of the *context* in which the *text* of our everyday realities is being written.

We need to imagine justice, differently.

The Courts of Women invite us to write another history, to *re-tell* history, to re-claim the power of memory: a *counter hegemonic history*, a history of the margins. The Courts of Women are a journey of the margins, a journey rather than an imagined destination; a journey in which the dailyness of our lives proffer possibilities for our imaginary, for survival and sustenance, for connectedness and community. For the idea of imaginary is inextricably linked to the personal, political and historical dimensions of community and identity. It is the dislocation expressed by particular social groups that makes possible the articulation of new imaginaries. These social groups, the margins, the homeless, the social movements, the occupy movements, the Arab spring, the indigenous, the women, are beginning to articulate these new imaginaries. Women, through the Counts are writing another history, giving private, individual memory its *public face*, its political significance; transforming memory and experience into political discourse. The Courts of Women are communities of the suffering, communities of the violated but they are also communities of survivors, of knowers, of healers, of seed keepers, of storytellers, of people telling history as a way of reclaiming memory and voice.

There is an urgent need to challenge the centralizing logic of the master narrative implicit in the dominant discourse – of class, of caste, of gender, of race. This dominant logic is a logic of violence and exclusion, a logic of superior and inferior, a logic of civilized and uncivilized.

This *centralizing logic must be decentred, must be interrupted, even disrupted.*

The Courts of Women interrupt; they speak to this disruption; to this trespass. The Courts of Women are finding new paradigms of knowledge and new paradigms of politics; a politics with care, concern, community, connectedness: a *politics with ethics*; a political vision that can be transformatory for all.

The Courts of Women are a tribute to the human spirit; in which testimonies are not only heard but also legitimized. It invites the subjugated and the silenced, to articulate the crimes against them; it is a taking away of the legitimizing dominant ideologies and returning their *life-worlds* into their own hands. The Courts of Women celebrate the subversive voices, voices that disobey and disrupt the master narrative of war and occupation, of violence, of patriarchy, of poverty.

We need to find new spaces for our imaginations: gathering the subjugated knowledge, seeking ancient wisdoms with new visions, listening to the many voices speaking, but listening too to the many voices, unspoken.

The Courts of Women offer another lyric, another logic,
lifting the human spirit, creating a new imaginary,
offering another dream.

I remember a story, from another time, another place, another logic.
Let me tell you the story; a story of timeless care, a story of another imaginary.
It is a story that draws upon Verse XXXI of Tagore's Fruit Gathering, on the *Riches of the Poor*.

Once upon a long ago and of yesterday,
it was a *time of darkness*;

it was also a time of famine that was devastating the land of *Shravasti*.
People gathered; poor people, hungry people.
Lord Buddha looking at everybody asked his disciples,
'Who will feed these people? Who will care for them? Who will feed
these hungry people?'
He looked at Ratnakar the banker, waiting for an answer. Ratnakar,
looked down and said,
'My Lord but much more than all the wealth I have would be needed
to feed these hungry people.'
Buddha then turned to Jaysen, who was the Chief of the King's army.
Jaysen said very quickly,
'Of course, my Lord, I would give you my life but there is not enough
food in my house.'
Then, it was the turn of Dharampal who possessed large pastures. He
sighed and said,
'The God of the Wind has dried out our fields and I do not know
how I shall even pay the king's taxes.'

The people listened, and were so hungry.
Supriya, the beggar's daughter, was in the gathering, listening too.
As she raised her hand, she stood up and said,
'I will nourish these people, I will care for the people.'
Everybody turned to look at Supriya.

How would she, they thought, do this?
How will she, a beggar's daughter with no material wealth,
how would she accomplish her wish?
'But how will you do this?', they chorused
Supriya, gentle and strong, looked at the gathering and said,
'It is true that I am the poorest among you,
but therein is my strength, my treasure, my affluence,
because I will find all this at each of your doors.'

Supriya's words and actions come from *another logic*.
She refuses the logic of property, profit, patriarchy;
inviting us to another *ethic of care*.
She sees the poor as *a community of people with dignity* in a relational
way; not as individual separate units.
She speaks for the many all over the world who are challenging the
logic of the master imaginary;

and trying to re-find and re-build communities, regenerating
women's knowledge and wisdoms;
re-finding the dream for us all.

Perhaps, as the poet says we *should now break the routine, do
extravagant actions that would change the course of history.* What is
essential is to go beyond the politics of violence and exclusion of our
times and to find *new political imaginations.*
An imaginary where women are subjects of our own history, writing
our own cultural narratives, offering new universals, imagining a
world in more life enhancing terms, constructing a new subversive
imaginary.
Can we return the ethical to the political?
Can we re-find the feminine in the increasingly violent, male
civilizational ethos?
Can we bring back the sacred to the earth?

We need a different dream.
Violence against Women in all its myriad forms must be made,
unthinkable!
We need to invite each other to this different dream.
The Courts of Women ask us to re-imagine other ways to justice,
subverting patriarchal discourse,
trespassing untread terrain,
weaving subjective text with objective context,
moving us to deeper layers of knowings, of tellings,
refusing to separate the dancer from the dance.
Knowing that we are the dancers, and
knowing that we are also the dance!

Notes

1. *Congregation of the Storytellers at the Festival of the Children of Soweto Mazise
    Kunene, Ancestors and the Sacred Mountains.*
2. Lawrence Liang. 2013. 'The Threshold of Justice: From the Courts of Women
    to Antigone and Back' in Corinne Kumar (ed.), *In the Time of the Spring,
    Book 4 of Asking, We Walk: The South as New Political Imaginary,* Bangalore:
    Streelekha Publications

3. Ivan Illich 1973. *Tools for Conviviality* London/New York: Marion
    Boyars. He wrote that '[e]lite professional groups… have come to exert a
    "radical monopoly" on such basic human activities as health, agriculture,
    home-building, and learning, leading to a "war on subsistence" that robs
    peasant societies of their vital skills and know-how. The result of much
    economic development is very often not human flourishing but "modernized
    poverty", dependency, and an out-of-control system in which the humans
    become worn-down mechanical parts.' Illich proposed that we should 'invert
    the present deep structure of tools' in order to 'give people tools that guarantee
    their right to work with independent efficiency.' The book's vision of tools
    that would be developed and maintained by a community of users had a
    significant influence on the first developers of the personal computer, notably
    Lee Felsenstein.
4. Corinne Kumar et al.1995. *Speaking Tree, Womenspeak: Asia Pacific Public
    Hearing on Crimes Against Women Related to the Violence of Development,
    28 January 1995,* Bangalore: Asian Women's Human Rights Council and
    Vimochana
5. Corinne Kumar (ed.). 2007/9. *In the Time of the Wind, Book 2 of Asking, We
    Walk: The South as New Political Imaginary,* Bengaluru: Streelekha Publications
6. Lisa Suhair Majaj. 2009. Excerpts from *Fifty years On, Stories in a Unfinished
    Wall, Geographic of Light,* Palestine: Del Sol Press

Bibliography

Corinne Kumar et al. 1995. *Speaking Tree, Womenspeak: Asia Pacific Public Hearing
    on Crimes Against Women Related to the Violence of Development,* 28 January
    1995, Bangalore: Asian Women's Human Rights Council and Vimochana.
Corinne Kumar (ed.). 2007/9. *Asking, We Walk: In the Time of the Earth, Book 1 of
    Asking, We Walk: The South as New Political Imaginary,* Bangalore: Streelekha
    Publications.
———. 2007/9. *In the Time of the Wind, Book 2 of Asking, We Walk: The South as
    New Political Imaginary,* Bangalore: Streelekha Publications.
———. 2012.*In the Time of the Fire, Book 3 of Asking, We Walk: The South as New
    Political Imaginary,* Bangalore: Streelekha Publications.
———. 2013. *In the Time of the Spring, Book 4 of Asking, We Walk: The South as
    New Political Imaginary,* Bangalore: Streelekha Publications.
Lawrence Liang. 2013. 'The Threshold of Justice: From the Courts of Women
    to Antigone and Back' in Corinne Kumar (ed.), *In the Time of the Spring,
    Book 4 of Asking, We Walk: The South as New Political Imaginary,* Bangalore:
    Streelekha Publications.
Lisa Suhair Majaj. 2009. Excerpts from *Fifty years On, Stories in a Unfinished Wall,
    Geographic of Light,* Palestine: Del Sol Press.

SEVEN

Justice in the Name of God
Organizing Muslim Women in Tamil Nadu

V. Geetha

Women's movements in India have been concerned about the relationship between women and religion, and more specifically, women and the religious communities of which they are a part and whose customs, norms and laws are central to the way in which women's lives are structured and negotiated. Over the last two decades, issues concerning women, religious identity, the community and the State have emerged as focal points of both popular and critical debate. With the rise of the Hindu Right, religious identity has been made central to citizenship – increasingly, Muslims and, to a lesser extent, Christians are exhorted to 'prove' their inexorable 'Indianness' or face outright discrimination, humiliation and intimidation. In 2002, Gujarat witnessed extreme acts of abusive violence against Muslims, especially Muslim women, which have been rightly termed genocidal. The violence, distressing in itself, was even more horrifying since it was mandated and encouraged by the democratically elected government of Gujarat. The violent attacks against Christians in Kandhamal in Orissa (2007–8) and against Muslims in Muzaffarnagar in U.P. (2013) have equally tried to strip members of such religious minorities of their citizenship rights.

In this context, women's rights activists working with the Muslim community – in Gujarat and elsewhere – find themselves battling several odds. Firstly, there is the undeniable fact that Muslims, as a community, feel vulnerable. To raise questions on matters such as women's rights therefore becomes a delicate task: how does one do this without pushing the community into a protective defensiveness? Secondly, Muslim women themselves are caught between their sense of what they owe themselves as dignified, self-respecting women and their felt responsibility towards the community, whose very existence appears imperilled. Thirdly, the Hindu Right's politics of hatred has pushed a section of Muslim youth to profess their faith in radical ways – aggressive assertions of identity, accompanied by a call to adhere to Quranic norms have, in some instances, led to a tightening of community boundaries, and often, injunctions to preserve community honour and faith devolve on women – who have to 'voluntarily' submit to laws that restrain them. To organise Muslim women therefore has become a very complex task, requiring great courage, tact, intelligence, strategy and sensitivity.

To understand the issues at stake for activists working with Muslim women, and to comprehend the manner in which they work, I have chosen to look at the work of STEPS, a group in Pudukkotai, in the state of Tamil Nadu. This group has been active since 1988 on issues pertaining to gender-based violence. Since 1997, it has developed close links with Muslim communities in various parts of eastern and southern Tamil Nadu. From 2000–01, the group has successfully organized Muslim women's groups in over 15 districts in Tamil Nadu and has a programme that links issues of poverty, survival, community welfare and rights. Through its work, this group has elucidated what it understands by justice, faith and dignity from the experiences of the women that it works with.

It seems to me that the complex and imaginative manner in which the group has posed the question of rights within and outside the community provides a novel gloss on how identities are and can be fruitfully negotiated to serve the ends of justice and equality. In this essay, I examine the making of this group and the ideas that animated its members in its early days, that is, in the first few years of the twenty-first century.

Introduction: Another Islam

A dusty hot morning in August. At a busy intersection in Madurai city, under a hurriedly constructed cloth canopy, sit over 250 women. Their ages vary – some are clearly young, in their late teens, but a substantial number are older, anywhere between 30 and 70 years of age. The backing that holds the canopy in place is festooned with posters announcing that women are not going to give in to, or put up with abuse, humiliation and violence, as they have all these years, but will, instead, resist. A few posters bear verses which suggest that women expect men to be gracious partners in this struggle, rather than hecklers and tormentors.

In itself this scene is not unusual. One is bound to witness many such sit-ins across India – protestors of diverse sorts, demanding an end to one form of inequity or another. It is also not rare to find as many women doing this as men. But what distinguished the Madurai gathering was that almost all the women who sat under a sky turning blue-white with heat were Muslims. Their heads covered with an assortment of headgear – ranging from the full black *burqa* that falls as a robe from head to toe, leaving only the woman's face uncovered, to modest white scarves that some wore lightly on their heads – these women remained on the streets for the better part of the day, chanting slogans, singing songs, listening to speeches made by their comrades in the sit-in and by visitors who had chanced to look in or come to lend support to their cause.

Their demands were straightforward and concrete: (1) the compulsory registration of the Muslim *nikah namah*, or wedding contract, at an office of local government; (2) the repeal of the provision of 'triple *talaq*' (the thrice-uttered term meaning divorce/) which men in the Muslim community often use at will to abandon and get rid of wives they do not like or want anymore; (3) an equal representation for women in local community organizations, or the jamaats[1] that control all aspects of social life in the Muslim community in Tamil Nadu; (4) the abjuration by Muslims of the 'un-Islamic' practice of demanding dowry from the bride and the further demand that those who endorse the giving or taking of dowry be immediately barred from the jamaat. However, the sit-in was more than a protest against specific injustices. The very air that day was alert with the women's gaiety, anger and resolve, and resonant with their insistence that their Islam required women be treated with dignity, equally and granted the freedom that was theirs. It was as if a quiet but determined passion for justice and for being heard held these women together. It is not that they were agreed on matters of doctrine, or even strategy, but they wished to demonstrate their will to collective visibility, to standing up for each other.

How did this spirit of comradeship come about? What defined it? To understand the making of such a protest, we need to locate it within the broader history of the women's movements as it evolved in post-1970s India, and equally within the specific history of a women's group in Tamil Nadu that enabled this collective gathering.

In what follows, I shall examine the many contexts of STEPS – the organization that has advanced the question of gender justice in Muslim communities across Tamil Nadu.

STEPS: Inside the Women's Movement

STEPS was formed in 1987 by D. Sharifa Khanam, a 24-year old Muslim woman. She was living at that time in Pudukkottai (where she continues to live till date), a modest but old city in the southern Indian state of Tamil Nadu.

The decade of the 1980s had witnessed the emergence of the 'second wave' of the Indian women's movements – that is, if we consider the organising around issues of sexual injustice and for freedom from colonial rule as constituting a 'first wave'. The late 1960s and early 70s were turbulent years in India, as they were in the rest of the world. Left-wing militancy was on the rise and attracted several young people to its camp. The Vietnam War gave an impetus to a simmering anti-imperialist rhetoric, which, in turn, rendered the Communist cause even more urgent and attractive. Women, as well as men, joined or constituted various left groups, with some of them taking to arms – especially in the jungles of eastern and central India, where social and economic injustice defined everyday existence for millions of people. The imposition of the 'Emergency' – the declaration of authoritarian rule by Prime Minister Indira Gandhi in 1975 – lent the events of those years a local colour and demanded a re-statement of political and social objectives. Women, especially those associated with left-wing groups, and involved with trade-union work, found themselves in jail or made victims of state terror in different ways. As the Emergency came to an end, and a democratic government returned to power in 1979, radicalised young women began to re-examine their lives – both in a personal and a social sense.

Other developments too enabled women to claim rights which they realized had been habitually denied to them. These included the declaration of 1975 as the International Year of Women, the first conference to commemorate the occasion which took place in Nairobi and the Government of India's admission – in 1974 – in a searching policy appraisal document (The Status of Women report) that the lives of Indian women, with regard to health, survival, work and a life lived in dignity and freedom, were difficult and oppressive.[2] These events constellated into a moment of historical recognition of women's rights that spurred women to think and articulate their concerns. They were, of course, mostly middle class educated women, but given the general militancy of the times, their words commanded attention even from those women from the working classes, whenever they had an opportunity to hear such views being expressed.

What really catalysed a historically distinctive second wave into existence though were two gruesome acts of sexual assault: in the one case, against Mathura – an *adivasi* (Indian name for indigenous communities) girl[3] and the other – Rameeza Bee – a Muslim woman.[4] These instances of rape were reported but the attitude of the police, the judiciary and the general public as far as these women were concerned was so appallingly misogynistic that women – and a few men, especially lawyers – were moved to protest them. And as the protests unfolded, there began a widespread public debate on sexual violence, which soon transformed itself into a new discourse on rights, gender and patriarchal power. 'The personal is political' became a rallying cry for those involved in these debates and led to the forming of several women's groups, which announced their explicit commitment to challenging sexual violence and the economies and cultures which produced it. The immediate result of these deliberations were two conferences held in 1981 and 1982 in the city of Bombay (now Mumbai) where women from different parts of the country met and exchanged views and discovered how much they had in common. Many amongst these were from left-wing groups, who were appalled by the groups' unrelenting male biases. Some were from voluntary development groups that were committed to consciousness-raising and mobilising the poor around existential issues of poverty and economic discrimination in rural India.

When Sharifa started STEPS along with others, she had this history to turn to, and she became a part of it, even as it unfolded. How did this happen? To quote her:

I come from a fairly conventional, lower middle class Muslim family in Southern India. After I finished high school I was sent away to Aligarh Muslim University in Northern India. I got involved in a ragging (hazing) incident which resulted in the principal complaining to my brother. He grew suspicious and accused me of wanting to hang around boys all the time. I was heartbroken and tried to leave the university. But I was forcibly returned to it. I left again, but eventually came back to study a secretarial course. This time, I felt bolder and actually enjoyed not being at home, not being ordered about by my brother. I returned home, I think in 1987.

During this period, I met a woman who worked in a 'development' organization. She appeared to have been impressed by my knowledge of languages – in addition to my mother tongue, Tamil, I knew Hindi and English – and asked me if I would be interested in accompanying her and a group of women for a conference of women's organizations in Patna, Northern India as a professional translator (Hindi is spoken widely in the north but not the south of India). This was in 1987. I agreed. The conference – the third national conference of women's movements – proved to be a turning point in my life. I was overwhelmed by the stories I heard at Patna – stories of hurt, pain, humiliation, but also of resistance, courage and humour. I saw how women from different contexts and backgrounds could actually sit and talk to each other and discover comradeship. Most of all I was impressed that women could hold meetings, discuss their concerns with intelligence and protest instances of injustice. I liked the manner in which they communicated; their approach was so appealing. I also understood instinctively what they were saying about violence – after all, I had seen my mother suffer and my sister persist in a bad marriage. I also understood why my brother had been so unpleasant – not only to me, but my poor mother....

Back home, I started giving Hindi lessons – this gave me a chance to interact with a range of women, whose homes I would visit to teach Hindi. I also started to help them in different ways – write a letter, accompany them on a mission outside home – since I was a 'teacher', I was trusted! Soon I began to wonder why can't some of us begin a group that would assist women – we had no clear idea as to what form this assistance would take, but we knew that we wanted to be involved with women's issues. We enrolled girls for karate classes, organised a poster exhibition on the problems faced by women ... We called our group, 'STEPS', meaning literally steps to women's empowerment. And so it grew ....

The Consolidation of STEPS' Work in the 1990s

1990 proved to be a catalytic year for STEPS – for the fourth conference of women's groups was held that year in Calicut in southern India. Developmental groups in Tamil Nadu, individual women, and women's groups that had been formed in the 1980s came together to plan for their participation in the conference. At the conference and afterwards, the question of violence against women was eagerly discussed amongst the Tamil groups. STEPS found itself in the thick of these debates, for, now it had to learn to act – as various instances of sexual and domestic violence against women were being brought to the STEPS office. One such case of violence, of child sexual abuse, proved significant: it brought home the realities of fighting a culture of sexual secrecy, voyeurism and brute power. As Sharifa remarked on the details of the case:

The child's parents were extremely poor and were, initially, reluctant to make the matter public. We spoke to them and convinced them that we would make sure that the child was not harmed, or put through the trauma of a re-telling. We registered a case with the local police station, where our complaint was met with much jeering and contempt – how would anyone do this to a child? Surely we were not serious? Perhaps the child had invited this, in some way? It took us hours to even file a First Information Report and ask for an investigation. Meanwhile, we contacted local newspapers hoping media pressure would make the police act. To our horror, we found the media's interest in the case extremely voyeuristic. After several fights with the police, and interventions with the media, we managed to bring the case to court. This was the first of many cases that we would handle – cases of unimaginable violence and abuse, assault and hurt, sometimes leading to death. In each instance, we found out the hard way, that the police, the courts and the media are all equally susceptible to patriarchal and misogynistic biases. But in almost every instance, we were able to garner the support of other women's groups, and even if we did not successfully prosecute the case, we could at least bring into the open instances of sexual assault that most people were determined not to see for what they are.

By this time STEPS was working on a range of gender issues. The local government allotted land to the group, with which it constructed a shelter home (which doubled up as Sharifa's residence). This place became a general clearing house for people who wished to report many forms of gender discrimination and was sought out by women in distress or crisis. To quote Sharifa again:

By the early 1990s we were sort of viewed as a general all-purpose women's rights centre and sometimes the police, rather than enquire into cases that came to them, re-directed these, especially if the complainants were women, to our office. Thus we found ourselves dealing with issues of not only sexual violence, but also domestic abuse, inter-caste marriages contracted without the prior sanction of families, which usually ended in the bride and groom being harassed, unwed mothers seeking help, love struck teenagers who had nowhere to go, issues that had to do with customary and ritual prostitution. Sometimes other issues came up as well: unequal pay, especially for female manual labour, on construction sites; water and sanitary deprivation in villages, which women felt were their responsibility; the rights of women to participate in public bids for government contracts; women wanting loans under various government sponsored schemes, women demanding that a certain piece of land in the family be registered in their names. In most of these cases, we spoke to women, directed them to, or ourselves networked with, organizations that worked with particular issues to assist them. Many times, we accompanied women to local administrative offices, helped them fill forms, write out complaints, constantly kept in touch with local government officials so that we could call on them for help. In cases of sexual or criminal assault of women, we had to necessarily work with the police, accompany them in their investigation, expedite post-mortem reports, and network with higher police officers in the State capital. Sometimes, we held public meetings and protests, organized sit-ins, especially if the issues involved had to do with land or pay.

For Sharifa, though, it was not only her group's success – or failure, as the case may be – in addressing these issues that proved enabling and educative. She was, by this time, a member of a collective of feminists, rights activists and women thinkers that had been formed in Tamil Nadu after the Calicut Conference – this was the Tamil Nadu Women's Coordination Committee, constituted in 1991. It recognized the right of individuals, but not groups, to membership in what was conceived as a genuine, independent feminist collective. The Committee organised several meetings and at one such meeting it was decided to host a state-level conference on violence against women in 1992.

The 1992 Conference on Violence Against Women disseminated new definitions of violence in the Tamil context – it called upon women to examine their lives, recount to themselves the times that they had been abused, sexually humiliated, hurt, and urged them to see violence as an informing principle, which underwrote female existence and organised gender relationships, rather than as comprising accidental, random acts, provoked by specific circumstances. Further, the idea of violence as an experience shared by all women, in greater or smaller measure, invoked a sisterhood bound by vulnerability, creating a powerful secular rhetoric of suffering and anger. This enabled all women, irrespective of their social classes and contexts, to lay claims to a political notion of rights and justice – and enabled them to comprehend their personal and existential concerns within a logic of power and authority that held together both intimate and social worlds and structures.

For Sharifa and STEPS, as for several others, the Conference provided a forum to realise female comradeship and solidarity – and taught them the value of women forming strong public links with each other.

Two events proved decisive during the late 1990s, both for the kind of initiatives STEPS would undertake in the future, and for the nature of the issues that they would have to confront.

The first such instance was the Hindu-Muslim communal violence of the early 1990s – following the destruction of the Babri Masjid by Hindu Right-wing groups. This forced Sharifa to negotiate the consequences of being a 'Muslim' woman, though, until then, she had hardly regarded herself as that. But as riot victims came to her for assistance, she was forced to confront the fact that Muslim women faced problems that were distinctively their own. As she explained:

> I saw how Muslim women, already oppressed and unfree, were now rendered additionally vulnerable. Not only were they easy targets of Hindu hooligan sexual violence, but also if the men in their families died or disappeared or were arrested, they had to take on familial and public responsibilities – matters for which they are usually little equipped. Besides, given the endemic poverty in which most working class Muslims live, these responsibilities translate into financial burdens as well

The second instance was the Swami Premananda case.[5] The goings-on at his ashram came to light, when one of the Swami's victims fled to a police station and registered a complaint. Soon after, the place was raided, the Swami arrested and 14 young women enlisted as witnesses for the prosecution. STEPS came forward to shelter these women for the period of the case – for there were great fears that the Swami, who enjoyed political and monetary support, would try and harm them. STEPS and Sharifa were now accused by Hindu right wing groups of being part of a conspiracy to destroy the integrity of the Hindu faith. This experience brought home to the group the manner in which gender issues could be wilfully subsumed in religious rhetoric. As Sharifa noted:

> This incident made me think long and hard about religion, gender and women's rights. I had been thinking on and off on this matter, especially after we had done that survey (see above). After Premananda, I felt that I had to look at the links between women, sexuality and religious laws. That was also the time when I seriously began to think of working closely and in a focussed manner with Muslim women, in whose lives these matters were so closely linked. I asked myself: why not use my position as an 'insider' to gain their confidence, set up consciousness-raising groups, organize economic programmes, and workshops on law and rights.

The Tamil Nadu Women's Coordination Committee (hereinafter referred to as the Committee) became, over the years, a mainstay, a moral and emotional anchor for women like Sharifa. As Sharifa started working with Muslim women, her association with the Committee enabled her to preserve a sense of herself as a civic person in her own right, bound to the world and those around her through her commitment to a just cause. She was uneasy with being called a Muslim woman, – not because she did not want to own up to being one, but because she considered herself a feminist, first and foremost. Further, she did not want the effort and labour she and her group had invested to articulate this sense of themselves to be subsumed within a narrow politics of identity.

To get a sense of the issues at stake, STEPS commissioned a survey of around 1000 households. The survey was to document problems that Muslim women faced in an everyday sense, and inquire into their knowledge of the rights guaranteed them by their faith as well as by the laws of the land. The findings shocked Sharifa. She knew that Muslims were, by and large, very poor and women duped into unhappy marriages but she was not prepared for the findings that her survey brought to the fore: of very young girls being married to older men; of unspeakable sexual violence that women endured in marriage; of the pervasive presence of the triple talaq; of marriages that merely shackled women to their marital homes as unpaid household workers. And most of these women were unaware of the Quran's pronouncements on women, on its radical position on equality and the very distinctive rights it guaranteed women.

Feminist and Muslim

Sharifa's and STEPS' decision to work with Muslim women did not mean that they stopped working on the issues they had been working on, until then. But it did mean that they adopt a focused and sustained approach to the specific concerns they now wished to address.

The question of Islam, gender and women's rights had not really been contentiously debated in the Tamil context. However, for at least two decades, there had been isolated attempts to address the anomalous nature of the Shariat,[6] as it existed in practice, and to bring some of the strictures based on it, in line with the Quran's more expansive definition of women's rights. Bader Sayeed, a lawyer and Nazneen Barkat, head of a Muslim women's college, had been urging a reform of certain practices within Muslim communities, including the taking of dowry from a bride, the frequent recourse to triple talaq by men wanting to end their marriages and the wilful disregarding of the *mehr* or bridal settlement, usually bestowed on the bride at the time of the marriage – and which often served as her financial guarantee against destitution. Bader Sayeed tried to build a group – Roshni – that would address these issues, but unfortunately it could not acquire the public standing required to lobby and mobilise women and the general public on issues that are not usually deemed pertinent. (A reason could be that the group was not representative of the diverse Muslim communities of Tamil Nadu and reflected the concerns of urban-based, educated Muslim women, belonging to a particular sect.)

Nazneen Barkat too has been a persistent advocate of Muslim women's rights, and a passionate defender of the Quran's promises in this regard. She had carried the women's question forward into various all-India Muslim forums, and insisted on her right to be heard. But she too had not found it easy to mobilise women around issues affecting them, which included dowry and the triple talaq, and retain them in an organization that she formed – AWAZ. She engaged in a debate with reformist men interested in the cause of Muslim women's rights, on 'un-Islamic' practices that denied women equality and dignity. In the late 1990s, both Nazneen Barkat and Bader Sayeed, spoke in feminist forums in Tamil Nadu.[7]

By 2000, Sharifa and STEPS began to work closely with Nazneen Barkat and AWAZ. The group was linked to disparate non-governmental groups (NGOs) that desired to address Muslim community and gender concerns. Members of these groups had been part of larger rights efforts or development initiatives and had come away from these to form their own organizations. Together, these groups, including AWAZ, formed a collective – called SAYA, meaning shade or refuge. STEPS enrolled itself as a member of this collective network. SAYA organised workshops for Muslim women on questions of health, legal concerns. As the network grew, its members felt emboldened enough to call for a state-level conference. This took place in August 2003 in the city of Ramanathapuram in Tamil Nadu, with a large Muslim population. The conference provided a platform to women who had probably never spoken in public, for expressing their grief and anger at the manner in which the men in their communities projected the Quran as a document advancing equal rights to women, and yet, hypocritically, continued to suppress women's rights in practice.

At this conference, women were explicit in their criticisms of not merely individual men who disobeyed Quranic injunctions, but also of the jamaat or the common body, which represented Muslim concerns within a defined congregational location, based on attendance at a particular mosque. Jamaats are usually all-male groups that meet in mosques and arbitrate on community matters, including domestic concerns, and pronounce on marriage, divorce and property arrangements. Women are not allowed to sit in on jamaat meetings or granted membership in the jamaat – ostensibly on the ground that the jamaat meets in the mosque and women do not usually enter a mosque when men are present. But for the women who spoke out in Ramanathanpuram this seemed a specious argument – and some wondered angrily if women should not then have their own mosque – a space to get together and pray, to share experiences and thoughts. Further they suggested the establishment of their own jamaat, where they would be assured of a just and fair hearing. 'At least, we would be present when our lives are being discussed', quipped a young woman.

Sharifa and others from STEPS were serious about this demand for a mosque for women, and raised it as a point of discussion. Opinions were varied: While some women supported the demand for a separate mosque, others argued that the Quran did not forbid women from praying in mosques and therefore was no question of women not being allowed into mosques.

In some Islamic countries there did exist mosques where both men and women prayed in segregated spaces. Not all were sure, though, whether women should have the right to a common mosque space – they felt that they would hardly go there, if there was such a space, since their domestic duties would not leave them much time to do so; and in any case, they would be a heedless distraction for the praying men who would therefore be inclined to be less pious.

What emerged at this conference was a unanimous anger and resentment at being denied rights in the name of Islam by men who were themselves guilty of 'un-Islamic' practices – such as the taking of dowry, drinking, charging interest on loans. Dowry appeared as a major concern, as did triple talaq. The denial of education was another issue that was passionately discussed. Clearly women who spoke out were actually challenging what were, in reality, patriarchal practices, being defended in the name of Islam. For these women, such practices were indefensible and not part of what their faith mandated. Balkies, a 32 year-old woman, made a forceful case for a women's right to demanding equality, and also questioned the right that men exercised to sexuality, sexual freedom and pleasure, while the same was denied to women. She asserted as follows:

> It is thought that it is only men who can make decisions, that they are the ones who can love, have the right to love and desire – if a man is promiscuous, this society considers it alright, but if a woman is so, it decries her. We must ask where this double standard comes from.

We must ask why is it that just being a man gives a person the right
to do anything. We must question this and do away with this. We
must ask why is it that only men have the right to pleasure and not
women. We must be able to claim our equality ...

Interestingly, this conference unintentionally failed to discuss larger
debates on religious laws and citizenship in India. Women's groups in
India had, by and large, always been in favour of gender-just secular
laws and critical of the personal laws of religious communities which
denied women justice and equality. But in the late 1990s, it was no
longer possible to maintain such a position, without one's arguments
being co-opted into the Hindu Right demand on a 'uniform civil
code', that would apply to all communities, irrespective of the fact
that some of them might prefer to abide by their personal laws – a
preference guaranteed to them by the Constitution of India. So some
women's groups wondered if it was better to insist on reforms within
personal laws, rather than ask for a common gender-just legal code,
that risked an imposition of Hindu law on all religious communities.
These debates were conducted within a discursive rather than a
historical context, and defined by theoretical concerns about equal
citizenship in a diverse society. Even when it was argued that to ask
for a common civil code would feed into the Hindu Right's strident
rhetoric and render minority communities, especially Muslims,
vulnerable, the argument passed off as the opinion of the Muslim
community was, in most instances, expressive male opinion.

The Ramanthapuram conference however demonstrated that for
Muslim women the issue was not one of seeking secular or religious
solutions – what they understood as injustice was patently wrong
by the measure that they lived by, which, for them, was defined by
the Quran. Often, when they declared themselves as seeking justice,
they marvellously combined modern notions of rights with what the
Quran had defined as worthy of the faithful, both men and women.
And such justice and rights that they sought were being denied
them, not by abstract religious principles or passive secular options,
but by specific individuals in defined situations – individuals who
were mostly men and who used the prerogatives assumed by them
as aspects of their masculine existence to deny women what was due

to them. The Muslim women of Ramanathapuram had thus drawn attention to the issue of access to justice in a patriarchal society – an age-old feminist claim that was being voiced with renewed vigour in a new historical context.

A Mosque for Women

In the days following the Ramanathapuram conference, STEPS found itself busy attending to complaints and petitions brought by Muslim women from all over Tamil Nadu. Many of those who came seeking help were clearly surprised that such a forum for considering their claims existed – and that a Muslim woman had actually dared to take on customary practices and male-headed community organizations. They had been refused a fair hearing in their respective jamaats and sometimes turned away from police stations, with the ostensible explanation that 'you have your own laws, go to your own forums'.[8]

Meanwhile, Sharifa re-worked the demand for a woman's mosque, raised at the Ramanathapuram conference – she and her comrades argued that if women were to realize for themselves the rights granted to them by their faith they needed forums that would grant them a just hearing. A Muslim women's jamaat, which met in its own mosque appeared to be the solution. In her view, a woman's mosque would be a place where women prayed, talked, shared their personal and familial concerns, discussed community matters, and planned for women's education, childcare and work. After all, the Quran did not have anything against women praying in public and besides, had not the Prophet commandeered women to know the details and logic of their faith?

The ideology of the jamaat was succinctly expressed by a woman, Nisha, who said:

> All of us in the jamaat are of one kin, one family, and our men here are our dear brothers, this entire society is one huge community. So our jamaat is everyone's. There are bound to be protests. Your husband says, don't go. Your son says, why do you have to go? Why do you women want this separate place? Why? In the future we men

will have to walk with our heads down. But our God has enjoined us to be brave – Islamic women are brave women, we wear this burqa to affirm our modesty, our morality. But if someone was to harass us, it will not help if we draw the burqa tightly around our shoulders. Do you think such a man will let us be, simply because we are Muslim women. This burqa is there to state our ethics, not to prevent us from being brave.

Sharifa's feminist friends in the Tamil Nadu Women's Coordination Committee were both aghast and sceptical of her desire to build a mosque. The year was 2003 – a year after the communal carnage in Gujarat in which over 2000 Muslims, men, women and children, had been killed, tortured and humiliated by Hindu right-wing militants. The party of the Hindu Right had returned to rule in the state of Gujarat. Muslims everywhere were still in a state of shock and fear and continued to be vulnerable to popular hatred and violence in parts of the country. Given this context, Sharifa's friends in the Committee argued that it would not be prudent to raise demands – such as the one for a mosque for women – since this would provide the Hindu Right with an occasion and argument to further spread hate propaganda against Islam and Muslims. The Committee suggested that Sharifa could start a dialogue within the community before she launched a public campaign for a women's mosque.

There were others who felt uneasy with this development – for instance, Nazneen Barkat decided to distance herself from this demand for a mosque. She continued to endorse women's rights to equality and justice, within the terms outlined in the Quran, but did not consider it opportune or right that they demand a place of worship that was all their own. A section of progressive Muslim women backed Nazneen's approach.

As soon as Sharifa and STEPS put forth their demand for a mosque for women, a local jamaat came forward to support their claim and even offered land for the mosque. But widespread clerical uproar, which resonated across the country, held the jamaat's members back and the support quickly died down. Besides, around this time, sections of the Tamil Muslim media wrote extremely hostile stories on Muslim women who had dared to come to the streets – they were depicted as shameless and wanton women who would only bring dishonour on Islam and Muslims. While glad that the cry for a mosque had caused sections of the Muslim communities to face up to the question of women's rights, Sharifa did not imagine that progressive Muslim men would prove to be consistent in their support of Muslim women's demand. She had good reasons for her scepticism and would not go so far as to grant the community's largely male leadership the credibility that it so anxiously sought.

Sharifa had found her constituency – angry, indignant Muslim wives and widows who were determined to wield their faith in a manner that ratified its deepest truths. The old feminist slogan – the personal is political – stood to be reinterpreted by these intrepid women. For them, questions of desire, loyalty and conjugal comradeship appeared also to be questions of faith that ought to be discussed and debated within the terms outlined in the Quran. Sharifa is, of course, aware that a single mosque in an obscure South Indian town would not really challenge the spiritual and temporal authority vested in male clerics and community leaders. But, for her and others who supported her demand, the fact of women wanting and building their own house of prayer, worship and justice possessed a significance that went beyond a lone building. The mosque represented both religious faith and social desire. It constituted a radical claim on Islam, on the promise it offered them and others in search of justice, the promise of equality mandated by the Holy Book. The thinking of Sharifa and her small group of women was captured well in what 50 year-old Akhtar Biwi said:

> I want to ask why must there be one justice for men, and another for women, why is that men go on talking, whereas a woman has to only open her mouth and she is shushed up. Why? Did our mothers not bear us too for nine months, just as they bore these men? And they say they can enter mosques and we cannot. Though we may know our prayers and though they may be drunk, drugged and whatnot. Where does it say in the holy book that we cannot enter mosques. But because we are submissive and go further down with every blow,

because we have not spoken up, these men feel that there is no one to hold them accountable.

Where will women go with their case for justice except to a women's jamaat? The moment we talk to a man, our character is maligned. What about the men and how they sleep around? They think they can get away with everything because they are men, because they earn money.

We have remained silent, because we wish to retain our dignity and our self-respect, because we are raised modest, because we have children. But no, we will not, cannot remain silent any longer. I will not, for I have been so for all these years. So let us now talk back, and to this end, I call upon Allah to be with us, to guide us and grant longevity, good will and luck to all of us.

Akhtar Biwi's expression of anger was directed at the double standards practised by men, echoed at the Ramanathapuram conference, as well as at women's passive and subservient status within the family and community.

STEPS soon worked out an agenda that would bring Muslim women together into small and large forums where they could debate their common concerns and plan for their mosque. This agenda has, since, been put to work – several protracted meetings at various towns and villages, the forming of small self-help groups, the identifying of articulate and fearless women who advocated for the issue of equality and justice. These developments led to the forming of what has since become the Tamil Nadu Muslim Women's Jamaat Committee.

The Prophet's Promises

The Tamil Nadu Muslim Women's Jamaat Committee, set up in 2003, comprises of a cluster of women's jamaats from over 15 of the 31 districts of Tamil Nadu. These women's jamaats have more than 25,000 members. Each district has its coordinators, most of whom are voluntary workers. They encourage a liberal interpretation of Shariat law devoid of a patriarchal bias. They take up disputes, intervening to try and negotiate rights of women within unequal marriages. The women's jamaat members meet every month, usually at its headquarters in Pudukottai.

The women's jamaat members do not necessarily have a homogenous viewpoint or approach. For example, members often differ with respect to the approach they, as a group, desire to adopt with respect to a particular dispute: should they be confrontational or conciliatory? How should they engage with local jamaats (run by men, hereinafter referred to as mainstream jamaats) that direct disputants to them, or are themselves the disputants in many instances? Arguments are vociferously made, publicly argued and contested and decisions are taken only if there is a general consensus.

Sanma, one of the more active members of the Committee notes:

> We're like a court of law. But in a court, there is only a single judge and everything depends on him, his moods, attitudes. And there is no one to check him, hold him back if he makes a mistake. But here there are over twenty of us. Even if one of us errs with respect to a problem, you can be sure that there are others who see the thing clearly for what it is. So, you see, we are even better than a court.

In practice, the women's jamaat functions like a tribunal. A petitioner brings a dispute – this could be either a matter of domestic abuse and violence, or a betrayal of good faith which the wife and her family have reposed in her husband; the giving of dowry, or falsely contracted marriages or hastily undertaken ones, which serve to hide a man's defects (such as male infertility or impotence). The Committee members hear the petitioner out, closely question her, her family, ask after her children, if any, and then discuss how they might hold the man accountable. Sometimes, a counter-petition is made out and sent to the mainstream jamaat where the woman's family might have taken her case previously; or if the woman has been subjected to gross violence and cruelty, a petition is sent to the police station. In certain instances, a mainstream jamaat which had received a petition involving domestic violence visits the women's jamaat on its own accord and seeks to settle the matter through discussion and debate. Very rarely is a petitioner despatched to the courts of law. Each case is addressed and decided on its own merits – the woman's needs are heard out, her children's future discussed and the women's jamaat attempts to balance what is owed to her with what is possible to obtain from her husband. The women's jamaat, with support from STEPS, also offers other options to women who are not likely to obtain monetary support from estranged husbands, and who cannot expect their labour to pay for the children's education and well-being. Women are found jobs, are referred to various social service organizations that might support their case for childcare and employment. STEPS has, itself, begun a girls' hostel – an impromptu home for girls whose mothers have been abandoned by their marital families, or who are from single parent homes (the parent in question being a woman).

In much of its work, the Committee is directed as much by its understanding of specific Quranic injunctions, as by the details of the case at hand. Its members are convinced that the giving and taking of dowry is un-Islamic, that the word 'talaq' cannot be uttered lightly, and that women and men both have equal rights to a happy and companionable conjugality. But while all members look to the Quran for guidance, they do not always concur in their understanding of it. Of the many positions that are likely to emerge on any matter of common concern, two might be considered pertinent.

Many members of women's jamaats believe that the Quran is a transparent text, whose meanings are clear and coherent. They assert that the Prophet is unequivocally on the side of women, and in fact, favours their cause, for had he not, himself, chosen to take an older woman as his wife and respected her counsel throughout his life? As a member explained:

Our Prophet did not marry for lust. He wanted a companion, a woman who could help him in his work. You might ask, then why did he marry so many times – each time he did this, he set out to prove a moral. And did he not say that he wanted both men and women to observe the faith? He did not think women should not read scripture. He has given us an open book that we might benefit from it. We women should not remain ignorant.

Another member stated:

> ...the Prophet enjoined men to be just towards women... The Quran does not anywhere forbid women from learning – 'He wanted us to know the faith, as well as know what is required to live in today's world' – nor does it ask them to desist from going to work, or from making marriages of their choice. Further, both men and women are called upon to lead a sexually fulfilling life, and desire is licit for both. Marriage is an active social contract and men and women must strive to fulfil its terms by being companionable, supportive and respectful of each other.

The other position, which also draws its discursive energy from the Quran, asserts that women ought to realise the immense responsibility vested in them by their faith and live up to it. That is, they ought not to be slaves to petty desires, nor covet jewellery or finery. Instead, they ought to realise that this mortal body is always already in a state of decay and not strive to satisfy its appetites. Rather they should set their minds on being independent, dignified and look to lead a socially useful life. For this is what the Quran demands of the faithful, that they remain committed to the *ummah* – the community of the faithful. In this reading of the Holy book, justice is understood to be an ideal that inheres in a disciplined inner life, in practising the tenets of the faith, and in cultivating a life of labour and service.

These points of view are not advanced as abstract arguments, rather they are articulated in the course of specific arguments or campaigns. In the face of routine observations made by male clerics and community leaders that Muslim women enjoy superior rights, the Committee has felt the need to claim these rights. Their attempts to confront and challenge entrenched male clerical authority are often met with disapproval and scorn and have earned them the anger of men who discredit their interpretative exercises as being 'un-Islamic'. It is in trying to answer charges about 'being un-Islamic' that the Committee has felt it important to define its version of Islam and its sense of the Prophet – not only for itself but for all Muslim women.

The Work of Women's Jamaats in the Context of International Efforts at Re-reading Islamic Jurisprudence

In the words of Sayeda Hameed, a fifty five-year old member of the women's jamaat:

> Between Allah and you, there need be no intermediary. You can directly speak to, appeal to Allah – you don't need another person to reach Allah. Allah is close to you, as close as your cheekbone, he is part of what you are and you can read his words – and understand them – as much as you can, and you don't need to listen to what other people have to say about the Quran. There are two things I wish to stress: that in the eyes of Allah there is no difference between man and woman; you should approach the Quran on your own, use your mind and read it. You have the right to do so. Secondly, in the matter of women's rights there are many organizations here in India – the Muslim Personal Law Board, the Wakf Board, and many others – which tell us that the Quran says this and the Quran says that. Often they interpret the Quran to advance their own interests. Now that we can read the Quran, we will know the truth. Nowhere in the Quran does it say that women should not have their own mosque – and in the event of women wanting a mosque, there have been instances of them having their own – where they can speak and pray without fear.

It is significant that for many in the women's jamaats, the Quran is both a text that invites women to an equal civic existence along with men, and a scripture that demands of women a spiritually exacting life. And the women of southern India are not alone in wanting to do this. Women across the Islamic world, in different social and political contexts, are today re-reading the Quran and the traditions of Islamic jurisprudence to claim what they believe is due to them, as citizens and as individual seekers. Some amongst them are actively engaged in returning to the Quran its universality – this, in the face of obstinate and narrow assertions of Islamism which seek to ground their claims in a series of petty practices and rituals directed at women's sexual and social subordination. Others are battling with local authority that attempts to rein in democratic re-readings of scripture – including those by women. Yet others are trying to work through the ambiguities of meaning and the demands of faith – as they embark on their own distinctive spiritual journeys. For all of them, as for the women in southern India, there is much at stake, both in an existential and a political sense. They wish to lead dignified, self-respecting lives, and their sense of the good and the just is defined by the Quran, which frames and marks their social horizons.

Between Faith and Politics

The Tamil Nadu women's jamaats, whose members bring with them a voluntary zeal and energy, appear an unusual vanguard of activists. For one, they are deeply embedded and committed to local life and concerns – their sense of what is owed to them as self-respecting women is not dictated by an anguished alienation from the world of the family and community. Rather it proceeds from an indignant and expressive anger at the manner in which familial and communal structures and institutions exclude and marginalize women, even where there is enough scriptural sanction for them to be considered equal. The jamaat women see themselves therefore as transforming in practical and everyday terms the civic lives of the communities they are a part of, in a manner that allows us to see the limits of feminist political practice in India over the last two decades and more.

The 'second wave' of the Indian women's movements (see above) defined its politics in and through an opposition to the hold of family, caste and community, which were deemed patriarchal. Its ideologues searched out the hand of patriarchal power and authority in all aspects of a woman's life – from the cradle to the grave, as a popular feminist song had it – and attempted to challenge it. Intimacy, desire, personal and social relationships – all of these were understood in terms of violence and control deployed by patriarchal agents who were determined to keep women down and submissive. This rhetoric of violence offered women from diverse social backgrounds a political register of complaint and anger (as I have noted above), but it also prevented them from engaging actively with local civic cultures, whether of the village panchayat (the village commonwealth, so to speak) or jamaat or caste tribunal. These latter appeared regressive institutions when measured by the lofty ideals of abstract democracy and appeared captive to a pre-republican civic ethos, where locally dominant interests determined the meanings of rights and justice. It did not appear possible then to re-work these latter to address feminist demands. Besides, the possibility of challenging masculine authority through a robust invocation of female victimhood was taken up eagerly and with passion – this too precluded many of us in the women's movements from seeing how we, as victims, actually negotiated the worlds around us. We became captive to our own discourses and looked to legislative and rhetorical strategies and struggles to address problems of violence and justice.

The jamaat women are discovering and extending the limits of a discourse they have only known as given and mandated faith. Their reclaiming of the Quran has opened up the holy book both literally and symbolically. They have also sought to bring their actual experiences of arguing and fighting – with families and clerics – to bear on their political practice, as is clear from the manner in which the women's jamaat receives and disposes of petitions. There is an openness to their practice, perhaps because it is dictated less by ideology and more by a sort of Gramscian 'good sense', a homespun logic of right and wrong, which, in the last instance, looks to the Quran for endorsement.

However, Sharifa is not entirely comfortable with this looking to the Quran. She often poses provocative questions such as the following: 'Would you not support a measure that is not ratified by the Quran? What if we find a Quranic stricture unreasonable?' She also attempts to embed the jamaat women's moral sense within a more universal feminist logic – through an invocation of sisterhood, of a greater common good. For instance, when calling upon a fellow feminist to speak at a Muslim women's conference, she noted:

> ...you refer to me all the time, but really, when I set out to work amongst women, it was not my faith that propelled me, but the example of women like this, women whose caste, religious or class status was not important but who felt it important for women to step out, claim their rights. It is women like these who have granted me the courage to speak out. I'll never forget what my friend Lucy said a decade ago: 'As soon as a woman realizes what her family, her caste, religion and state have done to her, there is nothing that can stop her from speaking out, from stepping out.'

Likewise, she situates Quranic arguments for divorce and female autonomy within larger democratic contexts. She does this in a number of ways – by translating the jamaat women's demands into the terms of a more catholic political register; or she invites non-Muslim women as observers to hear what the jamaat women have to say and then solicits their opinion on what they have heard. Yet, for her, the political moment of which she is a part, and which she and STEPS have ushered into existence continues to be a tensely delicate moment – demanding from her vastly inventive responses.

Afterword

The politics and practice that I have attempted to define in these pages are of our time – that is, they are part of the moving present and as such mock all attempts to map them onto a coherent theory. However the processes at play are so amazingly original that they challenge what we have held to be valid and true – whether this has to do with the history of feminist protests, or the manner in which these have been transacted. To that extent, the justice that Muslim women demand in God's name stands to be defined on its own terms – not only as an instance of liberation theology, or feminist strategizing, but as an ideal that offers tantalising possibilities – for our understanding of our feminist pasts, as well as prospects for newer, feminist futures.

Notes

1. In Tamil Nadu and in several other parts of India, personal issues within the Muslim community are settled by the local Jamaat – an all-male body attached to a mosque which applies Sharia law to adjudicate on matters related to divorce, dowry, harassment, domestic violence, and custody. As the traditional belief system does not allow women to enter mosques, they are not represented or heard during deliberations by the Jamaat and do not benefit from its verdicts.

2. *Towards Equality: Report of the Committee on the Status of Women.* 1974. Government of India, Ministry of Education and Social Welfare, Department of Social Welfare. A government-appointed committee was constituted in 1971 to assess the impact of constitutional, legal and administrative provisions on the social and economic status of women in India. This committee's report, titled 'Towards Equality', was submitted in 1974. The report highlighted gender disparities in the country and highlighted the invisibility of women in several sectors of the Indian economy and society. This report is a historic benchmark and a watershed in the contemporary struggle for women's rights in India.

3. Mathura, a 16-year old tribal girl, was raped at a police station in Maharashtra in 1972 after she was brought to the police station in pursuance of her brother's complaint that she had been 'kidnapped' by her lover. She was raped within the precincts of the police station even as her family members waited outside. The Supreme Court concluded, in 1978, that she had consented to sexual intercourse with two constables because she did not raise an alarm. Since she was a tribal girl who had eloped with a boy, and a medical report that said she had no external injuries, and was 'habituated to sexual intercourse', she was labelled a 'shocking liar' and a woman of 'easy virtue'. *Tukaram and another vs State of Maharashtra* AIR 1979 SC 185: 1979 SCR (1) 810

4. In 1978, Rameezabee was raped by several policemen in Hyderabad, and her husband – a rickshaw puller – was murdered because he protested.

5. Premananda was an infamous Hindu religious leader who established a sprawling ashram near Tiruchirapalli in Pudukkottai district, Tamil Nadu. He lured young and old women, adolescent girls and children to his ashram and sexually abused them. He was convicted of multiple counts of murder and rape in 1997.

6. Shariat is the body of legal doctrines that regulate the lives of those who practise Islam.

7. For example, in a 1997 conference on '50 Years of Indian Independence: Politics, Public Life and Women', organised by the Tamil Nadu Women's Coordination Committee, Nazneen spoke on what it meant to be a critical insider in the Muslim community and how she and others like her conceived of women's rights – drawing on the Quran for argument and inspiration.

8. This was the local policeman's interpretation of Articles 25 and 26 of the Constitution of India which guarantee minorities' the right to practise their faith, abide by their personal laws – that is, laws to do with matrimony, divorce, maintenance and guardianship of minor children. What the police, in these do not inform (either out of ignorance or biases) to the Muslim women who come to them with petitions, is that if they wish to avail of them they do have the option/right to access to the country's civil laws.

References

Subramanian, L. 2008. 'Feminist Force'. 26 June 2008. http://indiatoday.intoday. in/story/Feminist+force/1/10442.html (accessed on 5 November 2013).

Anand, S. 2004. 'Getting Ready for World's First Women's Only Mosque'. 2 September 2004. http://www.countercurrents.org/gender-anand020904.htm (accessed on 5 November 2013).

Khanam, S. 'Tamil Nadu Muslim Women's Jamaat: Who Are We and What Do We Do?'. http://www.mazefilm.de/dokupdf/khanum.pdf (accessed on 5 November 2013).

Madhok, S. 2008. 'A Space of Their Own'http://infochangeindia.org/women/ changemakers/a-space-of-their-own.html(accessed on 5 November 2013).

Setalvad, T. 2005. 'Unmanning Males: A Women's Jamaat Battles for Muslim Women's Rights in Tamil Nadu'. *Communalism Combat*. Year 12, No. 111, October.

Venkat, V. 'An Act of Faith'. 2008. *The Frontline*. Vol. 25, Issue 8, 12–25 April.

EIGHT

A Beacon of Hope

Engaging with the Communal Violence Bill[1]

Saumya Uma

Prelude

Ten years have passed since the term Communal Violence Bill (CV Bill) entered the public discourse in 2004; ten years in which numerous drafts of the law were written, re-written, read, analysed and critiqued; ten years of dialoguing with, explaining to and persuading the United Progressive Alliance (UPA) government; ten years of strategising through numerous consultations – big and small, press conferences and public meetings, across the length and breadth of the country; ten years of listing down non-negotiables for any law on communal violence; ten years of agreeing and disagreeing with, brainstorming and discussing aspects of the law with like-minded friends and colleagues; ten years of engaging with a Bill that intermittently went onto the back-burner, only to be resurrected some months later in a new avatar![2] Ten years during which the CV Bill seemed to have become the centre of my professional existence.

Many persons and organizations have been closely associated with the CV Bill campaign – including women's rights activists, human rights activists, secular and humanist individuals and groups, peace activists, lawyers, members of the media and students of varied disciplines. I will name some of those that I worked with closely and collectively in the course of this essay but I do not intend to represent any of them. Even as I trace the trajectory of the engagement of women's rights activists with the Bill, I am aware that there are other narratives stemming from personal engagement with the issue by many others, some complementing and others contradicting my narrative. Recalling a personal journey of a campaign is a contentious one as there are multiple versions of what happened and why. This essay focuses on my personal reflections, and how I believe the collective efforts of women's rights activists influenced the discourse around it.

The Foundation

The secular agenda is not new to the Indian women's movement. Feminist engagements in countering communal forces far preceded the birth of the CV Bill. In the 1980s, the Indian women's movement rallied strongly around the Supreme Court judgment that applied a secular provision of maintenance (S. 125 of the Criminal Procedure Code) for Shah Bano – an old, divorced Muslim woman.[3] The Ram Janmabhoomi movement[4] was also vigorously countered by women's rights groups, activists and advocates, while simultaneously critiquing the role of Hindu women who were in the forefront of the movement.[5] The Uniform Civil Code debate, in the 1980s and 1990s, benefitted greatly from active discourses of women's rights activists, who focussed on gender justice and citizenship rights of all women within their families, while countering the discourse of the Hindu Right on national integration.[6]

Gender-based violence in the context of the Partition had been condemned loudly by women's rights activists, who also observed that justice for such crimes was accorded a low priority in the interests of nation-building.[7] Mass crimes committed against women in the context of the anti-Sikh attacks in Delhi, 1984, gained much visibility through interventions of women's rights activists, who rallied behind some women survivors of sexual violence for decades.[8] In the wake of the destruction of Babri Masjid, mass rapes of women in Surat and attacks on women in other places were documented by women's groups.[9]

During the Gujarat carnage in 2002, many women's rights activists were engaged in aspects of relief and rehabilitation, campaigns for justice, accountability and peace. 'Survivors Speak' – a fact-finding report brought out by a women's panel – focussed on brutal forms of sexual and gender-based violence that Muslim women were subjected to.[10] A feminist analysis of the carnage, seen through the lens of international standards, was also articulated through an International Initiative for Justice in Gujarat (IIJG).[11] Varied forms of consistent and unstinted socio-legal support were provided to victim-survivors such as Bilkis Bano,[12] by secular-humanist organizations as well as women's rights activists.[13] This resulted in a landmark judgment delivered by the Mumbai Sessions court in Bilkis Bano's case[14] – the first case in post-independence India of conviction for sexual assault in the context of communal violence.

Engagements with justice and accountability processes in communal contexts enriched feminist learnings in myriad ways. Interactions with and support to victim-survivors of the violence gave an insight into their lived realities, the day-to-day challenges and dilemmas, the subtle and intangible forms of harassment, ostracism and socio-economic boycott they often faced. The difficulty of social integration in a society where fissures based on religious identity ran deep became obvious. Patterns in the planning, preparation, perpetration of violence and attempts to destroy the evidence subsequently became apparent. By supporting individual survivors through the labyrinth of law and justice, the rigours, challenges and limitations of existing law and legal strategies were realized. This included the difficulty in making the masterminds who plan, facilitate and implement acts of communal violence accountable through the domestic legal regime. The dire need for victim and witness protection became obvious.

The nature of the state became more apparent due to its ad hoc and whimsical attitude towards discharging its responsibilities of providing relief, rehabilitation, compensation and helping the victim-survivors rebuild their lives. The absence of reparative justice came to be exposed. The callous attitude of the police, their institutional bias against minority communities, and the systemic nature of the impunity with which they commit grave dereliction of their duties became evident. The complicity of public officials – police, medical, administrative and others – through acts of commission and omission, became distinct. These are important lessons learnt, that positively impacted why and how women's rights activists engaged with the CV Bill.

Incidents of communal violence subsequent to the commencement of the CV Bill campaign, such as those in Kandhamal and Muzaffarnagar, saw the active participation of women's rights activists and groups. For example, the National Alliance for Women, Odisha intervened in 2008 to ensure that the relief kit distributed by the state government to victim-survivors of the Kandhamal violence met the needs of women and adolescent girls. Gender-based violence on Muslim women in Muzaffarnagar in 2013 gained considerable visibility through the efforts of women's groups and activists.[15] This culminated in a writ petition filed on behalf of seven women victim-survivors of sexual violence.[16]

Background and Context of the Bill and the Beginnings of a Campaign 2004-2005

Against the backdrop of the Gujarat carnage 2002, when the United Progressive Alliance (UPA) government was elected to power in 2004, it issued a National Common Minimum Programme in May 2004. One of the promises made in this document was to enact a 'model comprehensive law on communal violence and encourage each state to adopt that law to generate faith and confidence in minority communities'.[17] This assurance formed the backbone of the government effort to formulate and enact a law on communal violence, and civil society responses to it.

In the period between July and September 2004, there were at least three separate bills drafted by civil society groups consisting of non-profit organizations, judges, lawyers, police personnel, writers and social activists, among others. These were submitted to the government, for inclusion and to influence the content and context of the bill that was being formulated by the government.

In July 2014, I attended one such meeting in Mumbai, organized by the Human Rights Law Network (HRLN), to discuss the bill.[18] There was animated discussion that questioned the need for a separate law on communal violence, the provisions of the Bill on various aspects including the rights of victim-survivors and the strategy to be used in negotiating with the government for formulating an effective law. I recall the interventions of a women's rights activist and lawyer, expressing deep concern about some of the clauses of the Bill, emphasizing the need for arriving at a broader consensus before delving into drafting the law. This was my initiation into the CV Bill campaign.

What drew me to the meeting was also the fact that I was actively engaged with and coordinating the ICC-India campaign – a nation-wide campaign on mass crimes, impunity and the relevance of the International Criminal Court and other international standards to India.[19] Participating in advocacy efforts on the Communal Violence (CV) Bill seemed the perfect and logical corollary to my work on justice and accountability.[20] The ICC-India campaign focussed on strengthening domestic laws to address and end impunity for mass crimes. Communal violence is a major component of mass crimes, the CV Bill was one of the first and historic attempts to fill a legal lacuna in India – the absence of a domestic law on mass crimes.

Another civil society draft, titled 'The Prevention of Genocide and Crimes Against Humanity Act 2004', was prepared through a Citizens' Consultation, consisting of renowned lawyers, judges, activists and others.[21] The draft incorporated many provisions from the Rome Statute of the International Criminal Court. This draft reconfirmed my view that the CV Bill campaign had the potential to incorporate international standards and concepts into the domestic legal regime.

In May/June 2005, the Union Home Ministry drafted the Communal Violence (Suppression) Bill 2005. It was introduced in the Parliament in the session commencing 25 July 2005. Based on feedback and criticisms to the Bill, on 5 December 2005, the improved version – the Communal Violence (Prevention, Control & Rehabilitation of Victims) Bill – was introduced in the Rajya Sabha.

The Bill was referred to the Parliamentary Standing Committee on Home Affairs, then headed by Sushma Swaraj, for consideration.

Engaging with the Standing Committee on Home Affairs: 2006

As done by other civil society groups, women's rights activists and groups too studied the document and prepared to engage with the Standing Committee. A consultative meeting was held in Delhi on 13 March 2006, on accountability of mass crimes against women and the relevance of the International Criminal Court.[22] At this meeting, Urvashi Butalia, Uma Chakravarti and Farah Naqvi highlighted mass attacks against women during the Partition, anti-Sikh attacks 1983 and the Gujarat carnage 2002 respectively. Madhu Mehra, Usha Ramanathan and I highlighted relevant international standards, followed by a discussion on the CV Bill among all participants. The participants were deeply concerned that the Bill rendered sexual and gender-based violence invisible despite the Bill being a response to the Gujarat carnage of 2002, where such violence was used as an engine for mobilization of hatred and destruction of a minority community.

Though we had the option of suggesting amendments to the existing Bill in relation to gender-based violence, it was decided by consensus that since the Bill, in its existing form, had a flawed foundation and framework, incorporating gender-related provisions within this framework served little purpose. As an immediate step, it was decided that a letter to the Standing Committee on Home Affairs was warranted, expressing a rejection of this Bill, and pointing out its various flaws. As a next step, there was a need to formulate provisions on gender-based violence that a law of this kind ought to incorporate and garner the support of women's rights and human rights groups for this.

Thereafter, a small group of women's rights activists, lawyers, law researchers and academics, primarily from Delhi and Mumbai, drafted a memorandum to the Standing Committee, incorporating our main concerns and suggestions.[23] It was submitted to the government on 15 July 2006.[24] The memorandum observed that there was a historic neglect that has existed in making persons accountable for mass crimes against women in India, contributing to a growing climate of impunity for the perpetrators. It further pointed out that the CV Bill 2005 did not acknowledge, address or remedy the major hurdles that have contributed to women's poor access to justice in the context of communal violence in a serious manner. Some of the recommendations made in the memorandum were as follows:

- Include new crimes of sexual violence into the Bill rather than working within the framework of the penal provision on rape, as there were limitations in the definition of rape in the Indian Penal Code.
- Include sexual violence, genocide and crimes against humanity, as spelt out and defined in the memorandum. Attention was drawn to recent international jurisprudential developments, such as the judgment in *Akayesu vs Prosecutor* by the International Criminal Tribunal for Rwanda (ICTR) and India's obligations under the Genocide Convention. [25]
- Include crimes against women documented in other parts of the world, such as sexual slavery, enforced prostitution, forced pregnancy and enforced sterilization, prior to the commission of such crimes in India. This was in conformity with the established principle in criminal law prohibiting ex-post facto law.[26]
- Amend the existing procedural and evidentiary law to address difficulties faced by women in the unsafe and hostile environment in contexts of communal violence – these include challenges in accessing police stations (for lodging FIR), government hospitals (for medical examinations) and in pursuing legal processes.
- Incorporate provisions on victim and witness protection prior to, during and subsequent to the trial, addressing the safety, physical and psychological well-being, dignity and privacy of victims and witnesses, particularly in cases of sexual or gender violence.

- Incorporate the principle of command and superior responsibility.[27]
- Introduce the concept of victims' right to reparations.[28]

The memorandum helped in considerably broadening the discourse on the CV Bill, and bringing into focus aspects of gender-based violence. The concepts of command and superior responsibility, as well as reparations were prominent in the Rome Statute of the International Criminal Court, and were being popularised by some of us in the ICC-India campaign in public discourse within the country. It is significant that Usha Ramanathan and Vahida Nainar, who actively contributed to the content of the memorandum, were also advisors of the ICC-India campaign, and well-versed with international standards. The memorandum also benefited from Vrinda Grover's unpublished paper written for New York University, entitled 'Communal Violence Bill – Invisibilising Sexual Violence' which critiqued the CV Bill from the perspective of sexual violence and international jurisprudence.

The memorandum was thereafter circulated to many civil society organisations and activist groups, including women's organizations in various parts of the country, and received a broad-based endorsement from them. It was followed by an oral deposition before the Parliamentary Standing Committee by some Delhi-based activists.[29]

In December 2006, the Standing Committee gave its recommendations to the government, tabled in the Parliament on 13 December 2006. We were deeply disappointed that it did not suggest any structural changes in the framework of the Bill and that our concerns and suggestions had found no place in its report and recommendations.

Intensive Campaigning and Mass Mobilization: 2006–2007

In addition to engaging with the Standing Committee, a need was felt for a wider consultation, discussion and consensus among women's rights groups and activists on the CV Bill. Several consultations were held across the country, which led to broad-based alignments and support for the campaign. They also facilitated collective strategising.

A consultation was held in August 2006 in Mumbai, with the participation of over 25 representatives of women's organizations and human rights activists.[30] The decision taken at the March 2006 meeting in Delhi to reject the Bill in its entirety due to its flawed framework was reiterated at the Mumbai meeting. The specific strategies decided upon included:

- Dialogue with the Parliamentarians on the shortcomings of this Bill prior to its introduction in the Parliament in the winter session;
- Produce an alternative draft;
- Identify certain non-negotiables for any Bill of this kind and communicate the same to the government;
- Write an open letter to the government questioning its silence on sexual violence, and on the abdication of state responsibility;
- Align the suggested provisions on sexual/gender-based violence in the CV Bill with provisions of the Sexual Assault Bill; and
- Conduct a self-organized workshop in the National Women's Conference (NCC) in Kolkata in September 2006 in order to have a wider consultation on this issue.

Not all that was planned could be implemented. However, the strategies are important to highlight in this paper as they indicate the pulse and course of the initiative of women's rights groups and activists within the CV Bill campaign. Similar consultative meetings were held in Delhi and Bangalore in the weeks that followed.

In September 2006, under the aegis of the 7th National Conference of Autonomous Women's Movements in India, held in Kolkata, a workshop was organised on the CV Bill.[31] Participants included more than 50 representatives of women's rights organizations, lawyers and human right activists from all over the country. At this consultation, it was agreed that substantive provisions on sexual and gender-based violence must be included. The participants expressed concern on various issues. The total absence of any specially trained cadre of police to interact with survivors of sexual violence and other enabling structures would render even the insertion of positive substantive provisions, meaningless in practice. The Bill did not acknowledge state participation and complicity, without which crimes of the scale and nature dealt with in the Bill cannot be committed. The special powers assigned to the Central government were a bone of contention among political parties, as it was threatening to dilute the federal structure of the Indian polity.[32] Inclusion of 'enforced prostitution' as gender-based violence within the CV Bill may encourage courts to make moral statements about prostitution – an issue on which women's groups nationally and internationally have no consensus. The future plan of action decided upon included the following:

- Pass a resolution rejecting the CV Bill in its present form, send the same to the Prime Minister's Office, Parliamentary Standing Committee and others.
- Ask the government to hold a consultation with women's rights groups on the Bill.
- Meet key persons in relevant ministries, and communicate to them our concerns and resolution as an outcome of the present consultation.
- Finalise draft non-negotiables.
- Have wider consultation at the state level.
- Have consultation with victims/survivors, Dalit and adivasi groups, and with groups from North Eastern states and Kashmir.

The meeting was useful in many ways. For one, it created an awareness of the issue among many groups and individuals, especially those situated in smaller towns, semi-urban and rural areas. This was possible only through a discussion at a national platform such as the national conference. The meeting contributed to a more broad-based support for the campaign from the women's movement.

In the first half of 2007, the Union government studied the recommendations of the Standing Committee, and sent the Bill to the cabinet for clearance. The Bill was scheduled to be presented in the Parliament in the monsoon session, commencing on 10 August 2007, with minor modifications. The UPA government expressed a keenness to get the Bill passed. Intensive campaigning was required to stall the flawed Bill and compel the government to return to the drafting table.

With this objective in mind, public meetings were held in Delhi as well as other cities across the country, where the dangers of the government draft were highlighted and public opinion mobilized against the draft. I was actively engaged in the activities in Mumbai and Pune. In Mumbai, public meetings were held in Govandi, Dadar and Bandra.[33] At each, a statement rejecting the Bill in its present form was read out, which was endorsed by the participants of the meetings unanimously. Public meetings and press conferences were also held in Pune, and covered by the local media. A press conference was held in Mumbai on 4 July 2007 on the issue 'Communal Violence Bill: A Remedy Worse than the Malady?'[34] The press conference received massive media coverage.[35] Copies of press coverage of the public meetings, press conferences as well as the statement rejecting the Bill – endorsed by hundreds of victim-survivors at each meeting – were sent to key government officials.[36]

While some efforts in Maharashtra are outlined above as a representative example, many such intensive efforts took place all over the country. As a delegation of civil society activists including women's rights groups, interactions were held with Members of Parliament in several cities, briefing them about the dangers of the Bill, and encouraging them to raise questions in Parliament.[37]

The women's rights activists and advocates based in Delhi performed the arduous task of engaging in a dialogue with key government personnel, as well as leaders of political parties, and presented to them the concerns discussed above. The intense advocacy efforts at Delhi, coupled with the visibility created of the growing dissatisfaction with and vehement opposition to provisions of the Bill among members of civil society, perhaps had its desired effect. The government did not present the Bill in the August 2007 session of Parliament.

Drafting an Alternative Bill: 2008

In January 2008, the Prime Minister's Office (PMO) requested some of us who were working together on the issue to submit a fresh draft, within two weeks. Despite the impossible deadline, the opportunity could not be missed. We held intensive deliberations across Delhi and Mumbai through face to face meetings, telephonic conversations and email exchanges. In this draft, we revised, re-defined and developed further from our previous suggestions.

DELIBERATIONS AND DILEMMAS

In our efforts at drafting the law, we were confronted with many issues and dilemmas. Some of these are highlighted below:

- Should the law be limited to violence between religious groups, or should it also include ethnic, caste, political and class violence? We decided that it should apply to all violence which is targeted and systematic, because this law aims at ensuring state accountability, irrespective of the identity of the group that was targeted for attacks.
- Should communal crimes be related to overt violence and its aftermath, or also to structural everyday discrimination, social/economic/cultural, as well as ostracism/boycott? After much thought and discussion, we decided that it was desirable to separate the two and include only the former within the framework of the criminal law. The latter could be better addressed within the framework of an Equal Opportunities Commission.
- What was the threshold/scale of violence required for the law to become applicable? There was an agreement that any threshold in terms of scale or numbers would be unjust and

may run the risk of excluding many incidents of violence. Hence the Bill we drafted stated that the law would apply to violence that was 'targeted, systematic or widespread': targeted in terms of the identity of the group/community that was attacked; systematic in terms of the manner and patterns of attack, as well as planning and preparation involved in the same; and widespread in terms of scale and geographic spread of the attack.

- How would state accountability be enforced in light of immunity clauses that protect public servants?[38] How do we circumvent the provisions that grant immunity from prosecution to all public servants, which may nullify the principle of superior or command responsibility? These were critical areas, as the entire focus of the Bill, was to make state officials accountable for acts of commission and omission.

- How do we prevent abdication of state responsibility with regard to relief, rehabilitation and compensation to victim-survivors, and promote their right to reparative justice? After deliberations, it was concluded that the right to reparations needed to apply in every case of targeted and systematic violence, according to standards laid down in the law itself, and that the only state discretion should be to give more, not less. We believed that relief camps should be established according to international standards, and run as long as the survivors do not feel safe to return to their homes.

- How do we ensure an independent investigation, as scuttling of justice occurred mainly through shoddy and biased investigations? Should the responsibility of investigation in contexts of communal violence be vested with the police, the CBI, a new independent body or through an oversight mechanism such as the National Human Rights Commission (NHRC)? The legally tenable, desirable and practical aspects of all options were discussed.

In the Bill that we drafted, a solution could not be provided for each of these issues/dilemmas. However, it was significant that from 2006 to 2008, we had broadened our focus beyond sexual and gender-based violence, and deliberated on seeking accountability of public officials.

HIGHLIGHTS OF THE ALTERNATIVE BILL

The alternative Bill titled The Communal Crimes Bill 2008, drafted by us, was submitted to the government on 24 January 2008.[39] While the Bill, in a preliminary note attached with it, acknowledged that many persons and organizations had participated in the consultations over various points in time over the past three years, due to a paucity of time, only the names of persons involved in the final versions of the draft were indicated.[40]

In its list of communal crimes, the Bill:

- Included the following categories of gender-based violence: rape, sexual slavery, forced pregnancy, enforced sterilization, other sexual violence and persecution (including gender-based persecution);
- Excluded the crime of enforced prostitution, in consonance with the concern raised at the National Conference,/discussed above;
- Introduced and defined the crimes of torture, extermination, enforced disappearances and persecution, drawn from international standards;
- Introduced the concept of aggravated communal crime – when communal crimes are committed by public servants and in custodial situations;
- Explicitly included a statutory duty of the court to prevent intimidation of victims and witnesses, and to ensure their safety and dignity prior to, during and after trial;
- Spelt out, for the first time, special procedural and evidentiary rules in prosecutions for sexual violence. These include *inter alia* a presumption of non-consent, exclusion of evidence concerning the past or subsequent sexual history of the victim; provision of victim's counsel, in-camera trials; and onus on the accused to prove innocence.

- Created a special apparatus at the Sessions Court as an interface between the victim-survivor and the court. It was envisaged that this apparatus would provide information to victim-survivors on the status of the cases, referral to appropriate agencies for relief, rehabilitation, legal medical and psycho-social assistance, protect the victims and witnesses, and provide translation/interpretation services of court proceedings to victim-survivors and witnesses as and when required;
- Spelt out reparations as an inviolable and legally enforceable right of all victims, and included principles of restitution.[41] These provisions were non-existent in the previous government drafts, and were intended at making reparative justice a reality for victim-survivors.

While the government exhibited a keen interest in enacting a law on communal violence, they also had serious differences with our draft. The principle of command and superior responsibility was a bone of contention for the government, as its officials felt threatened that they may be vicariously held accountable for communal crimes caused by their subordinates. There was a clear reluctance within the bureaucracy to exclude application of S. 197 CrPC under this law.[42] In short, the government stiffly resisted the state accountability we wanted to extract through this law.

State Level Consultations on the Alternative Bill: 2008–2009

After submission of the alternative draft, we decided to maintain visibility of the issue, by holding meetings in various states. In June 2008, a discussion meeting on the Communal Violence Bill took place in Hyderabad.[43] In July 2008, a consultative meeting was held in Jaipur.[44] In August 2008, a meeting was organized in Bangalore.[45] The same month, a consultation was organized with women lawyers of the High Court at Chennai.[46] These meetings were held with a cross-section of civil society, including women's and human rights groups, groups working on Dalit and minority rights as well as women lawyers. The meetings, illustrative in nature, were platforms where information was disseminated about the content and critique of the government draft of the Bill as well as the salient features of the alternative draft advanced by us. Discussion ensued around feedback and suggestions to improve the provisions of the alternative Bill as well as strategies for the future.

In early 2009, the government announced that it had made 59 amendments to its previous draft of the Bill. However, it did not change the framework of the Bill, which many civil society groups had criticised as deeply flawed and entirely unacceptable. This was followed by another round of advocacy initiatives including an intensive dialogue with key government officials. The Bill was not introduced in the Budget session, and soon thereafter, India went in for Lok Sabha elections. The UPA government was voted back in power. In its election manifesto of 2009, it not only reiterated its commitment to the CV Bill but also elaborated on the same, by expressing its 'unflinching resolve to combat communalism of all kinds', and further promised to ensure 'the right to compensation and rehabilitation for all victims of communal, ethnic and caste violence on standards and levels that are binding on every government.'

The National Advisory Council Conundrum: 2010–2011

In June 2010, the National Advisory Council (NAC) constituted a Working Group on the Communal Violence Bill. Although the National Advisory Council (NAC) was constituted under the Prime Minister's Office as an interface with civil society, it was a largely autonomous body.[47] The Working Group was entrusted with the responsibility of developing a new draft Bill on the issue on a priority basis, and presenting the same to the government by the end of 2010 for its consideration.[48] The Working Group, consisting of a Drafting

Committee and an Advisory Committee, included government representatives as well as members from civil society.[49]

The stated mandate of the Working Group brought the accountability of public officials in the spotlight – as desired. The mandate also gave recognition to a rights-based approach to victims and survivors. Soon after the Working Group commenced its work in July 2010, it laid down and adopted the key guiding principles for the Bill, which are as follows:

- Broaden title and applicability of the law to include 'communal and sectarian violence';
- Shift from empowering the State, to seeking action and accountability of state/public officials;
- Basic framework of law must not rest on declaration of 'disturbed areas';
- Need for an independent national authority to ensure effective compliance with the law, without disturbing the federal structure;
- Ensure accountability and criminal liability of public officials for acts of omission and commission, for preventing or controlling communal and sectarian violence, or extending timely and adequate rescue, relief and rehabilitation;
- Incorporate the doctrines of command and superior responsibility;
- Definition of communal and sectarian violence to cover both isolated incidents as well as mass crimes, against people based on religious, caste, linguistic, regional and other identities;
- Need to specifically define and include new crimes/offences including sexual assault, enforced disappearances, torture, long-lasting social and economic boycott, and genocide, among others;
- Need to remove prior sanction requirement for hate speech (Sec. 153A and 153B – IPC);
- Statutory obligation on government to lay down national standards for the entire spectrum of provisions for victims – including rescue, relief, compensation, rehabilitation,

resettlement, restitution, reparation and recognizing the rights of internally displaced persons;

- Implementation according to the norms in point ten to be a statutory obligation under this law;
- Compensation amounts to be specified in terms of national norms under the law, and revised every three years;
- Need for amendments in the Criminal Procedure Code and Indian Evidence Act to meet extraordinary circumstances of communal and sectarian violence to protect victims' rights; and
- Specific provisions for victim-witness rights to be made under this law.

Several meetings of the Drafting and Advisory Committees of the Working Group were held in 2010–2011. The members of the Working Group had varied interests, expertise, perspectives and worked with varied constituencies – such as Dalits, women and religious minorities. Ideally, the rich knowledge and expertise of the members of the Working Group ought to have facilitated a constructive dialogue, resulting in an effective Bill. However, sharp differences of opinion arose among the members on the content of the Bill. These centred around issues of a) the role and responsibilities of the National Authority; b) accountability of public officials; and c) reparative justice to victims and survivors.

In February 2011, four prominent members of the Working Group withdrew from the NAC process – Shabnam Hashmi and John Dayal from the Advisory Committee, and Vrinda Grover and Usha Ramanathan from the Drafting Committee. In a joint press statement issued by them on 23 February 2011, they stated that the draft in progress was 'severely insufficient to address the lacunae and gaps of the government Bill of 2005.'[50] Despite this setback, the drafting process was finalized internally among the existing members of the Working Group. The Working Group presented the draft Bill – Prevention of Communal and Targeted Violence (Access to Justice and Reparations) Bill (PCTV Bill) – to the government on 28 April 2011, which was, soon thereafter, placed in public domain for suggestions and feedback. Simultaneously it was sent to the Union Ministries for Home Affairs and Justice for their responses.

THE MOVE FORWARD

The NAC draft went beyond existing legal standards in at least five significant ways:

- It recognized identity-based mass violence and targeted/hate crimes as special and heinous crimes, and spelt out a definition of communal and targeted violence for the first time in Indian legislative history;
- It defined new offences such as torture, sexual assault and hate propaganda;
- It provided for accountability of public officials for various dereliction of official duties, as listed out in the Bill – this was the heart of the law and an important agenda for the women's rights groups and activists;
- It incorporated the concept of command and superior responsibility for the first time in Indian law, by which commanders and superiors could be held accountable for the offences committed by their subordinates under certain circumstances; and
- It spelt out various aspects of reparations that had not been hitherto detailed in any law.

CONCERNS RAISED ON THE DRAFT BILL

Despite these positive aspects, the NAC draft of May 2011 was severely criticised by most political parties – not only the BJP but also UPA's allies – as well as a large section of civil society.[51] One contentious issue in the Bill was the definition of 'group' that required the protection of law. The NAC draft, by consensus, defined 'group' as a religious or linguistic minority or Scheduled Caste or Scheduled Tribe, in order to counter institutional bias and prejudicial functioning of the state/district administration.

There was a rationale behind the definition of the group in this manner – institutional bias against religious minorities, SC and ST communities prevented an equal protection of the law to them when incidents of communal violence took place. While the Indian Penal Code and Criminal Procedure Code would deal with all offenders, in the normal course, the definition of 'group' was meant to rectify the disadvantage that marginalised communities faced. The feminist consciousness of intersecting and multiple forms of discrimination contributed to the need for and contents of this definition. However due to the definition of 'group', the Bill itself was severely criticised by the Hindu Right as anti-Hindu and pro-minority.[52]

Another contentious issue related to the creation of the national authority and state authorities with over-arching and far-reaching powers of monitoring, supervision and intervention in contexts of communal violence and its aftermath. These provisions threatened to violate the sacrosanct principle of federalism.[53]

The Bill's provisions on sexual violence were also not satisfactory.[54] The prosecution in cases of sexual assault hinges on the question of consent to sexual intercourse by the concerned woman. The Bill required the victim-survivor woman to prove that she did not consent to sexual assault and that the assault took place in coercive circumstances. This was unrealistic and unjust. Further, women's groups had, for several years, been saying that there was a need to put in place special procedures and evidentiary standards for sexual assault perpetrated in contexts of communal and targeted violence. Yet the Bill made no mention of it. Further, provisions relating to reparative justice were paternalistic, and did not promote the rights of victim-survivors.

Salvaging the Law Reform Initiative: 2012

Seven months after government inaction over the NAC Bill, secular and civil liberty activists, women's rights activists, legal experts, academics, and representatives of over 50 organizations, including women's groups, met in Delhi in April 2012.[55] They urged the government to return to the drafting table for a fresh draft, and offered an alternative framework for the CV Bill, on which political consensus was possible.[56] They proposed an outline that clearly emphasized that the 'inordinate impact of communal and targeted violence on women and children must be recognised in the making of the law'.[57] The essential features focussed squarely on a) securing accountability of public servants and holding them responsible for communal and targeted violence; and b) making provisions for providing reparative justice to the victims and survivors of such violence.

At the same time, another group of secular humanists and women's rights activists, tried to persuade the government to introduce the Bill in its present form, have it sent to the Standing Committee on Home Affairs, and hope to make rectifications to the Bill subsequently. The rationale was that a law, however imperfect it may be, is better than having none, and we can always correct it along the way.

Both approaches had their merits. At the end of the day, all involved in the campaign wanted a workable law (not a perfect law) that can increase the chances of providing reparative justice for victim-survivors and making perpetrators accountable.

Renewed Attempt at Introducing the Bill: 2013–2014

In October 2013, in the wake of communal violence in Muzaffarnagar and Shamli districts of Uttar Pradesh, there was a renewed attempt from civil society to resurrect the CV Bill, and urge the government to enact the same.[58] Although the UPA government did speak of the CV Bill in 2013 and early 2014 from time to time, there was no serious debate. The Union cabinet cleared the Prevention of Communal Violence (Access to Justice and Reparations) Bill in December 2013. In February 2014, the UPA government made a half-hearted effort to introduce a version of the Bill in the Rajya Sabha before the national elections of May 2014. However, it was forced to defer the same due to stiff opposition from a range of political parties.[59] The legislative competence of the central government to introduce such a law, and the overarching powers of the National Human Rights Commission (which replaced the National Authority originally envisaged in the Bill) were questioned.[60] In the national elections that followed in April – May 2014, the UPA government was voted out of power.

Conclusion: Small Successes, Large Challenges

Between 2004 and 2013, there were innumerable Bills, frameworks and sets of non-negotiables related to a CV Bill proposed by many, including women's rights activists and groups. However, for women's rights activists, whose efforts were endorsed and supported by the larger women's movement in India, the CV Bill is an unfinished agenda. Engagement with the issue over a decade led to our creative strategies and advocacy skills being honed; while it sharpened our focus on what we really want from the law – accountability of all perpetrators including state actors – the efforts made us realize that the state and its agents were not going to concede to a standard or system that exacted its accountability all that easily.

Efforts of women's rights groups and activists have been valuable in broadening and strengthening the discourse on sexual and gender-based violence, state accountability for acts of commission as well as omission, reparations and command/superior responsibility. Many of the women's rights activists who were engaged with the CV Bill believed in a multi-pronged approach and engaged simultaneously with other advocacy initiatives, such as law reform processes on rape, torture and child sexual offences. Some of the viewpoints advanced by feminists in the CV Bill campaign were also extended to and replicated in other law reform campaigns, where they have met with modest success. For example, the Justice Verma Committee, which was established to review the penal provisions on rape in 2013, became the first official body in India to recognize the doctrine of command/superior responsibility as a concept and recommended that it be incorporated in Indian law.[61] This is an achievement for those working on bringing home international legal standards and strengthening domestic law.

At the same time, the contents of the CV Bill were also informed by other campaigns for justice and accountability where women's rights activists participated. For example, the demand for inclusion of 'command and superior responsibility' arose partially due to the difficulty in making commanders of armed forces accountable for the commission of heinous offences in the North Eastern states and Kashmir.

The shield of state immunity, resulting in impunity for mass crimes, has been penetrated in other ways. The Prevention of Torture Bill 2010, revised after the recommendations of a Select Committee of the Rajya Sabha, restricts the scope of immunity available to a public servant in prosecutions for torture, by providing for a time limit (three months) within which a decision to deny the sanction needs to be taken, failing which sanction is deemed to have been granted; further, the provision requires reasons in writing justifying the decision to deny sanction.[62] For the first time, the Criminal Law Amendment Act 2013 included commission of rape during communal or sectarian violence, as an aggravated circumstance, entailing more stringent punishment.[63] The same law also dispensed with the need for sanction for prosecution of public officials, where it pertains to certain sexual and related offences.[64] Further, a public servant's act of disobeying direction under law has been specifically made an offence.[65] These are significant amendments, brought about through the concerted efforts of women's rights activists and others for several decades.

Among members of civil society, including women's rights activists, there remains a difference of opinion on the potential contents of the CV Bill. The major areas of difference are as follows:

- *Should the 'group' be defined as a religious/linguistic minority?* Within the NAC, there was a consensus that this should be so as a religious or linguistic minority or SC or ST, due to the huge institutional bias against minorities. However, could the definition lead to a possible exoneration of communally targeted violence by minority groups, which had the potential of causing discrimination? Is it politically viable to retain the definition, or should the definition of 'group' be excluded altogether?

- *Should the National Authority and state authorities have over-arching and wide-sweeping powers that occupy the centre stage of a CV Bill?*
  The NAC draft reflects a need to establish these new bodies to address issues of and to oversee various aspects in the aftermath of communal violence. The government draft subsequently replaced the National Authority with the National Human Rights Commission (NHRC), in response to a caution in creating new bodies that replicate the work of existing ones. However, is the NHRC the appropriate institution?
- *Should the Bill have a limited focus?*
  The NAC draft dealt elaborately with provisions related to definitional, preventive, prosecutorial, monitoring, sentencing and reparative aspects, among others. However, since the Bill is intended to break the culture of impunity, should it focus primarily on definition of crimes, accountability of public officials and reparations for victims and survivors?

These differences are not cast in stone and positions are not hardened to a point of non-compromise. No clear-cut solutions are in sight, and hence further deliberations are imperative.

There have been personal learnings from the journey. I learnt a great deal by observation – of feminist ways of sharing information, discussing, agreeing, disagreeing, analysing and strategizing. I benefitted greatly from the company of women's rights lawyers and law researchers, who had nuanced discussions on various legal provisions, the language used in law and their possible import within the courtroom. The opportunity to make presentations and speak in public fora, including public meetings and press conferences, alongside friends and colleagues from the feminist and human rights fields was valuable too. The CV Bill campaign has helped me understand the politics of law making on a highly contentious issue. Although well-versed in the law and legal processes, senior women's rights lawyers and activists did not assume the self-importance of an expert; instead they took me into their fold as a co-traveller, and helped me learn the ropes; it was a gratifying and humbling experience.

The CV Bill was vehemently opposed by the Bharatiya Janata Party (BJP) – which was voted into power in May 2014. From the manner in which the communal environment is presently gaining ground in India, the pendency of the Bill is, on the one hand, making a mockery of the state's commitment to preventing mass and targeted violence. On the other hand, it is an indication of the abject failure of the state to provide reparative justice to victims and survivors subsequent to the violence. The contribution of women's rights advocates and activists to the discourse on CV Bill remains in the public domain and has the potential to positively influence advocacy efforts in future. Till then, the challenge before us is to persistently make inroads on state impunity for communal and targeted violence – through social, legal and political processes – however negative the present political context may be towards such efforts.

Notes

1. I deeply appreciate the time and effort taken by Farah Naqvi and Vahida Nainar to provide detailed inputs to this essay, which have helped enrich it. A special thanks to Poonam Kathuria who convinced me to write this piece and to Abha Bhaiya and Usha Ramanathan for their encouragement.
2. Avatar, a Hindi word, means version/form/figure/incarnation.
3. The debates around the issue of Shah Bano were dominated by Muslim religious leaders and politicians on the one hand, and autonomous women's groups on the other. For more details, see Flavia Agnes.2012.'From Shahbano to Kausar Bano – Contextualising the "Muslim Woman" within a Communalised Polity'.Loomba, A & Lukose, RA (eds.), *South Asian Feminisms*, Durham: Duke University Press and New Delhi:Zubaan, pp. 33–53; see also Kirmani, N. 2009.'Claiming Their Space: Muslim-led Networks and the Women's Movement in India'.*Journal of International Women's Studies*, 11(1), pp. 72–85 at p. 72.
4. The Ram Janmabhoomi movement was started in 1984 by Hindu right wing activists, advocating for the building of a Ram temple in the place where

the Babri Masjid – a historic mosque in Ayodhya in Uttar Pradesh. The mosque was constructed in 1527 and destroyed by a mob of over 1,50,000 on 6 December 1992. The Hindu Right claimed that a Hindu temple had been destroyed or modified to construct the Babri Masjid.

5. For more details see Kumar, R. 1994.'Identity Politics and the Contemporary Indian Feminist Movement', in Moghadham, V. (ed.), *Identity Politics and Women, Cultural Reassertions and Feminisms in International Perspective*, Boulder: Westview Press, pp. 243–273. See also Agnes, F.1996. 'Redefining the Agenda of the Women's Movement within a Secular Framework' in McGuire, J, Reeves, P and Brast, H. (eds.), *Politics of Violence: from Ayodhya to Behrampada*, New Delhi: Sage, pp. 95–110.
Sarkar, T. 1991.'The Woman as Communal Subject: Rashtrasevika Samiti and Ram Janmabhoomi Movement', *Economic and Political Weekly*, 31 August.

6. Menon, N. 1996. 'Uniform Civil Code: Debates in Feminism Today', in N. Rao, L Rurap and R Sudarshan (eds.), *Sites of Change: The Structural Context for Empowering Women in India*, Delhi: UNDP/FES, pp. 445–459.

7. For example, see Butalia, U. 2000.'Community, State and Gender: Some Reflections on the Partition of India', in Hasan, M. (ed.), *Inventing Boundaries: Gender, Politics and the Partition of India*, New Delhi: Oxford University Press, pp. 178–207; Menon, R and Bhasin, K. 1998 *Borders and Boundaries: Women in India's Partition*, New Jersey: Rutgers University Press; and Butalia, U. 1998. *The Other Side of Silence: Voices from the Partition of India*. New Delhi: Viking Penguin.

8. For example, see Chakravarti, U. and Haksar, N.1987.*The Delhi Riots: Three Days in the Life of a Nation*. New Delhi: South Asian Books; see also Kishwar, M.'We Share Their Agony – Sikh Women Victims of 1984', *Manushi*.

9. See report by Sahiyar, a Baroda-based women's organization, mimeographed copy, report of women delegates to Bhopal, Ahmedabad and Surat, by AIDWA, CWDS, MDS, NFIW in Sarkar, T. and Butalia, U. (eds.) 1995. *Women and the Hindu Right,* New Delhi: Kali for Women, pp. 299–328.

10. The team comprised eminent social activists Syeda Hamid, Ruth Manorama of National Alliance of Women, Bangalore, Malini Ghosh of Nirantar, Delhi, Sheba George from Sahrwaru, Ahmedabad, Farah Naqvi, a journalist from Delhi and Mari Thekaekara of Accord, Tamil Nadu. They visited Ahmedabad, Kheda, Vadodara, Sabarkantha and Panchmahal districts and spoke to a large number of women survivors of the communal carnage. The report, titled *The Survivors Speak: How Has the Gujarat Massacre Affected Minority Women – Fact Finding by a Women's Panel*, May 2002, is available at http://www. outlookindia.com/article.aspx?215433, accessed on 12 May 2014.

11. The report *Threatened Existence: A Feminist Analysis of the Genocide in Gujarat,* International Initiative for Justice in Gujarat, 2003, speaks of the Gujarat carnage as comprising of genocide and crimes against humanity under international law, pp. 104–135; it also articulated the specific location of 'woman' in the political/communal projects as a matter of grave concern.

The organizers of the IIJG included Citizen's Initiative (Ahmedabad), People's Union for Civil Liberties (PUCL) – Shanti Abhiyan (Vadodara), Communalism Combat, Aawaaz-e-Niswaan, Forum Against Oppression of Women (FAOW) and Stree Sangam (Mumbai), Saheli, Jagori, Sama, and Nirantar (Delhi), Organised Lesbian Alliance for Visibility and Action (OLAVA, Pune), and other women's organizations in India.

12. Bilkis Yakub Rasool is a victim-survivor of gang rape committed in the context of the Gujarat carnage 2002. She was pregnant at the time of the brutal rape, and witnessed the brutal killing of 14 members of her family, including her 3 year old daughter. Besides Bilkis, a number of other female family members of hers were raped and killed in the same incident in Dahod district of Gujarat on 3 March 2002. She was the sole survivor of the massacre.

13. Bilkis' case was brought to the attention of the National Human Rights Commission and taken to the Supreme Court due to efforts of fivew omen's rights activists: Farah Naqvi, Huma Khan, Madhavi Kuckreja, Malini Ghose and Gagan Sethi. During the three-year trial in Mumbai, the same activists provided Bilkis and her family with legal support, handholding and protection, and post-trial, with full relocation/rehabilitation.

14. Mumbai Sessions Court convicted 13 out of 20 accused persons, in January 2008.

15. See for example Joint Citizens Initiative (2013), *30 Days and Counting – report of a fact-finding team* comprising women's rights activists, health and medical professionals, and lawyers from Uttar Pradesh, Delhi, and Mumbai, available at www.sacw.net/article5920.html, accessed on 16 June 2014; Anhad.2013. *Evil Stalks the Land.* www.anhadin.net/article192.html, accessed on 16 June 2014.

16. The writ petition was drafted, filed and is handled by Vrinda Grover – a feminist lawyer. The petition has sought, inter alia, compensation and the establishment of an independent investigating team, expressing the survivors' loss of confidence in the UP police for arrest, investigation and prosecution of accused persons.

17. See UPA's Common Minimum Programme 2004, para 2 under the sub-topic 'Social Harmony and Welfare of Minorities', available at www.hindu.com/2004/05/28/stories/2004052807371200.htm, accessed on 16 June 2014.

18. The draft Bill, titled The Communal Crimes Act 2004, was drafted by Human Rights Law Network (HRLN), Act Now for Harmony and Democracy (ANHAD – based in Delhi) and Jan Sangharsh Manch (based in Ahmedabad). These are non-profit organizations working on issues of human rights, justice, peace and secularism.

19. Mass crimes include multiple incidents of heinous crimes in a given context, crimes committed in a widespread manner, crimes committed in a prolonged manner over a given area or those with a systematic/common/consistent pattern. While the essence of such crimes is captured by the term 'crimes against humanity' in international law, the term 'mass crimes' is more popularly used

in India. Distinguishing features of mass crimes as against crimes against individuals are discussed in more detail in Saumya Uma (2011a) at pp. 215–216.

20. I worked as the National Coordinator of ICC-India campaign from 2000 to 2010.

21. The Citizens' Consultation had the participation of Justice PB Sawant, Justice Hosbet Suresh, Justice Ahmadi; KG Kannabiran, KS Subramanian, Brinda Karat, Iqbal Ansari; Teesta Setalvad, Javed Anand, Dr. Siraj Hussain, Indira Jaising; Nitya Ramakrishnan, Chaman Lal, Padma Rosha (IPS) retd, Yusuf Muchhala, Manzoor Ahmed, Suhel Tirmizi, HS Phoolka, Faizan Mustafa, Munawwar Rahi, ND Pancholi and John Dayal, among others.

22. This meeting was held in Delhi on 13 March 2006, organized by ICC-India campaign and Partners for Law in Development, in association with People's Watch.

23. The group included Farah Naqvi, Madhu Mehra, Uma Chakravarti, Usha Ramanathan, Vahida Nainar, Vrinda Grover and me.

24. The memorandum is on file with the author.

25. The judgment of the International Criminal Tribunal for Rwanda (ICTR) in the case of *Jean Paul Akayesu*, advances the treatment of rape and sexual violence in mass crimes contexts. The Tribunal stated: 'Like torture, rape is used for such purposes as intimidation, degradation, humiliation, discrimination, punishment, control or destruction of a person. Like torture, rape is a violation of personal dignity...'*Akayesu vs Prosecutor* Case No. ICTR 96–4–T, judgment dated 2 September 1998 at para 687.

26. Prohibition in subjecting a person to a criminal law created after the commission of a crime.

27. Command or superior responsibility is an established principle in international law to pin criminal liability to the person – military or civilian – under whose command the crimes occurred. This is a principle that is absent in Indian law.

28. 'Reparations' is a broader and more progressive concept than the frequently used 'compensation' or 'relief' in India – the government practice of doling out inadequate amounts to some victim-survivors in an *ad hoc* and arbitrary manner, supposedly in discharge of its responsibilities. Reparations include rehabilitation, compensation, restitution as well as measures that have reparative effects such as reintegration, satisfaction and guarantees of non-repetition. For more details, see Nainar, V.2013. Submission to Justice Verma Committee on the Issue of Reparations, 20 January 2013, available at www. wragindia.org, accessed on 1 March 2014.

29. Farah Naqvi, Uma Chakravarti and Madhu Mehra were among those who made an oral deposition to the Standing Committee, explaining and elaborating upon the recommendations stated in the memorandum.

30. The consultation, held on 16 August 2006, was organised by Women's Research and Action Group and Forum Against Oppression of Women. Organizations represented in the consultation included Aawaz-e-Niswan, Centre for Enquiry

into Health & Allied Themes (CEHAT), Child Relief & You (CRY), Dilaasa (Project of CEHAT), Forum Against Oppression of Women, India Centre for Human Rights & Law, Lesbians & Bisexuals in Action (LABIA), Movement for Peace & Justice, Women's Centre and Women's Research and Action Group (WRAG).

31. The workshop, held on 10 September 2006, was organized by Women's Research and Action Group and Forum Against Oppression of Women. In addition to activists, the workshop had representatives of several women's groups across the country including Anandi, Sahr-Waru and Sahiyar from Gujarat; STEPS from Tamil Nadu; Sama from Delhi; Vanangana and AALI from Uttar Pradesh; Women's Research and Action Group and Forum Against Oppression of Women from Maharashtra.

32. The Bill empowered the Central government to act in circumstances where the state government fails to take appropriate measures with regard to a situation of communal violence, and to deploy armed forces to the state on the request of the state government.

33. The Mumbai meetings were organized through the initiative of Women's Research and Action Group (WRAG) in collaboration with other civil society groups and activists. The Dadar meeting, held on 5 July 2007, was organized by Akshara, Bombay Catholic Sabha, BUILD, Centre for Study of Society and Secularism (CSSS), CORO for Literacy, Committee for Right to Housing (CRH), Dayasadan, Documentation, Research and Training Centre (DRTC), Hukook-e-Niswa, Movement for Peace and Justice (MPJ), Mumbai Initiative for Human Rights Education (MIHRE), Nirbay Bano Andolan, Salvation Seva Kendra, Wisdom Foundation, Women's Research and Action Group (WRAG), YUVA and other organizations and networks. For the Govandi meeting held on 26 July 2007, WRAG collaborated with CORO for Literacy and CORO Federation of Mahila Mandals – community-based organizations; the Bandra meeting was organized by WRAG and Hukook-e-Niswa on 15 August 2007.

34. This press conference was organized by Women's Research & Action Group (WRAG) in collaboration with Documentation Research and Training Centre (DRTC). The panelists were Justice H. Suresh (retired judge of Bombay High Court and an ardent campaigner of human rights), Shakil Ahmed (advocate and human rights activist), Shabana Sheikh (survivor of Bombay communal violence) and me.

35. See, for example 'Communal Violence Bill Dangerous: Activists', *The Times of India*, 5 July 2007; 'Communal Violence Bill 2005 is Rejected in its Entirety', *Free Press Journal*, 6 July 2007; an article in Marathi in *Maharashtra Times*, 5 July 2007; an article in Urdu in *Inquilaab*, 5 July 2007; and 'Bill on Violence Stalled', *The Afternoon*, 9 July 2007.

36. These included the Prime Minister, the Leader of the Opposition and the Union Home Minister.

37. In Mumbai, Priya Dutt (an MP from the Indian National Congress party) and Supriya Sule (an MP from the National Congress Party) were contacted in this regard.
38. For example, S. 197 of the Criminal Procedure Code requires prior government sanction for prosecution of any public servant accused of any offence, creating conditions for immunity, leading to an absence of accountability. A 2013 amendment, which inserted an explanation to S. 197(1) brought about an exception to this procedural requirement, in the case of sexual and related offences.
39. The text of The Communal Crimes Bill 2008 is on file with the author.
40. These included Farah Naqvi – activist and freelance journalist; Harsh Mander – Director, Centre for Equity Studies, New Delhi; Maya Nair – 'Justice and Accountability Matters' programme of Women's Research and Action Group, Mumbai; Saumya Uma – National Coordinator, ICC-India campaign; Uma Chakravarti – feminist historian, New Delhi; Vahida Nainar – founder trustee, Women's Research and Action Group, Mumbai; and Vrinda Grover – advocate, Delhi.
41. The principle of restitution sought to restore dwellings, habitats and livelihoods to levels that match or improve on what victim-survivors had enjoyed earlier.
42. Section 197 of the Criminal Procedure Code makes it mandatory to obtain sanction of the government for prosecution of public servants and judges, where such a person is accused of any offence alleged to have been committed in discharge of his official duty. The sanction is to be issued by the authority that has powers to remove the public servant from office – the central government in the case of armed forces and officers of the central government, and the state government in all other instances. While courts have repeatedly stated that this provision is intended to prevent vexatious litigation against public servants for acts done during their official discharge of duties, in reality, this provision provides almost complete immunity to such public servants from prosecution, resulting in impunity.
43. It was organized and hosted by Asmita Resource Centre for Women based in Secunderabad.
44. This meeting was organized and hosted by Vishakha – a voluntary organization working on issues of women's empowerment in Rajasthan.
45. This meeting was organized by Alternative Law Forum, South India Cell for Human Rights Education and Monitoring (SICHREM), PUCL–Karnataka and the ICC-India campaign.
46. The consultation, titled 'Mass Crimes Against Women: the Communal Violence Bill' was organized by The Women Lawyers' Association of High Court, Chennai in collaboration with Women's Research and Action Group, Mumbai.
47. The NAC was established on 31 May 2004 soon after the UPA came into power at the central government, to provide inputs in the formulation of policy by the government, with a special focus on social policy and the rights

of disadvantaged groups of people. It comprised professionals with diverse backgrounds in the field of development who served in their individual capacity. Notably, the NAC had, as its members, Aruna Roy of Mazdoor Kisan Shakti Sangathana, Harsh Mander, a former senior official of the Indian Administrative Services (IAS) and Farah Naqvi, writer and feminist activist.

48. Details of the mandate of the Working Group and members of the Advisory and Drafting Committees as well as the key guiding principles are available at http://nac.nic.in/communal/com_bill.htm, accessed on 10 November 2010.

49. Members of the Drafting Committee were Gopal Subramanium, Maja Daruwala, Najmi Waziri, P.I.Jose, Prasad Sirivella, Teesta Setalvad, Usha Ramanathan and Vrinda Grover. Members of the Advisory Committee were Abusaleh Shariff, Asgar Ali Engineer, Gagan Sethi, H.S Phoolka, John Dayal, Justice Hosbet Suresh, Kamal Faruqui, Manzoor Alam, Maulana Niaz Farooqui, Ram Puniyani, Rooprekha Verma, Samar Singh, Saumya Uma, Shabnam Hashmi, Sister Mary Scaria, Sukhdeo Thorat, Syed Shahabuddin, Uma Chakravarti and Upendra Baxi. Farah Naqvi and Harsh Mander were the joint convenors of the Working Group.

50. The press statement is available at www.xa.yimg.com/kq/groups/.../name/CV+BILL+PRESS+STATEMENT.doc, accessed on 15 June 2014.

51. See for example, V.Venkatesan, 'A Flawed Bill', *Frontline*, Volume 28 Issue 13, 18 June-1 July 2011.

52. See for example, 'Communal Violence Bill Anti-Hindu Says VHP', *New Indian Express,* 1 November 2013.

53. Federalism under the Indian Constitution is a system that allows states, united under a central government, to maintain a measure of independence. The Seventh Schedule of the Indian Constitution contains three lists of subjects – central, state and concurrent lists – on which the centre, state or both are empowered to legislate.

54. See for example, Rehan Ansari, 'Serious Concerns Persist in New Draft Communal Violence Bill: Saumya Uma', 4 June 2011, available at http://twocircles.net/2011jun04/serious_concerns_persist_new_draft_communal_violence_bill_saumya_uma.html#.U51kDZSSyZc, accessed on 15 June 2014.

55. For more details see Mohammad Ali, 'Civil Society Activists Reject Draft Communal Violence Bill', *The Hindu*, 22 April 2012.

56. See 'Draft Fresh Anti-Communal Violence Bill: Activists', *Daily News and Analysis*, 21 April 2012.

57. Statement Issued at the National Consultation on Communal Violence Bill, dated 21 April 2012, on file with the author.

58. 'PM Urged to Enact Law on Communal Violence', *The Hindu*, 10 October 2013.

59. Political parties who voiced their opposition to the Bill include the Bharatiya Janata Party (BJP), Samajwadi Party, Communist Party of India – Marxist, All India Anna Dravida Munnetra Kazhagam (AIDMK), Dravida Munnetra Kazhagam (DMK) and the Trinamool Congress.

60. The legislative competence of the law was questioned as law and order, maintenance of public order, police power and power to regulate the services of the State are state subjects under the Indian Constitution, so the central government cannot interfere with state jurisdiction. The opposition on the ground of legislative competence is a bogus one, as this was not raised in 2005 when the Bill was introduced in the Parliament; the Parliamentary Standing Committee headed by Sushma Swaraj (a senior leader of the BJP) had clearly said that Parliament had the competence to legislate on the subject. Besides, administration of justice, criminal law and Criminal Procedure Code are issues in the Concurrent List – on which the Parliament has the competence to legislate. For more details see 'Govt Forced to Defer Communal Violence Bill', *The Hindu*, 5 February 2014; see also T.Rajalakshmi and V.Venkatesan, 'A Bill on Hold', *Frontline*, 7 March 2014.

61. In the words of the Committee, public servants 'in command, control or supervision of the police or armed forces' fail to exercise control and allow for criminal offences such as murder, rape, destruction of property etc. to be committed shall be guilty of the offence of 'breach of command responsibility.' – Report of Justice Verma Committee on Amendments to Criminal Law (2013), available at http://www.prsindia.org/uploads/media/Justice%20verma%20committee/js%20verma%20committe%20report.pdf, accessed on 11 February 2014, p. 445. Please note, however, that this recommendation was not accepted by the government when it carried out amendments to criminal law in 2013.

62. Provisions 1 and 2 to S. 7 of the revised Prevention of Torture Bill 2010, available at http://www.prsindia.org/billtrack/the-prevention-of-torture-bill-2010–1129/, accessed on 16 June 2014.

63. S. 376 (2)(g) of the Indian Penal Code, inserted by the Criminal Law Amendment Act 2013.

64. Explanation to S. 197(1) of the Criminal Procedure Code, inserted by the Criminal Law Amendment Act 2013.

65. S. 166A of the Indian Penal Code, inserted by the Criminal Law Amendment Act 2013.

References

BOOKS

Chakravarti, U. and Haksar, N. 1987. *The Delhi Riots: Three Days in the Life of a Nation.* New Delhi: South Asian Books.

Menon, R. and Bhasin, K. 1998. *Borders and Boundaries: Women in India's Partition.* New Delhi: Kali for Women.

ARTICLES

Agnes, F. 2012. 'From Shahbano to Kausar Bano – Contextualising the 'Muslim Woman' within a Communalised Polity' in Loomba, A & Lukose, Ritty A. (eds.), *South Asian Feminisms*, Durham: Duke University Press, pp. 33–53.

Agnes, F. 1996. 'Redefining the Agenda of the Women's Movement within a Secular Framework' in McGuire, J, Reeves, P. and Brast, H. (eds), *Politics of Violence: from Ayodhya to Behrampada*, New Delhi: Sage, pp. 95–110.

Ansari, R. 'Serious Concerns Persist in New Draft Communal Violence Bill: Saumya Uma', 4 June 2011, available at http://twocircles.net/2011jun04/serious_concerns_persist_new_draft_communal_violence_bill_saumya_uma.html#.U51kDZSSyZc, accessed on 15 June 2014.

Butalia, U. 2000. 'Community, State and Gender: Some Reflections on the Partition of India', in Hasan, M. (ed.), *Inventing Boundaries: Gender, Politics and the Partition of India*, New Delhi: Oxford University Press, pp. 178–207.

Kirmani, N. 2009. 'Claiming Their Space: Muslim-led Networks and the Women's Movement in India'. *Journal of International Women's Studies*, 11(1), pp. 72–85.

Kishwar, M. 'We Share Their Agony – Sikh Women Victims of 1984', *Manushi*.

Kumar, R. 1994. 'Identity Politics and the Contemporary Indian Feminist Movement' in Moghadham, V (ed.), *Identity Politics and Women, Cultural Reassertions and Feminisms in International Perspective*, Boulder: Westview Press, pp. 243–273.

Menon, N. 1996. 'Uniform Civil Code: Debates in Feminism Today', in. Rao, N., Rurap. L. and Sudarshan, R (eds.), *Sites of Change: The Structural Context for Empowering Women in India*, Delhi: UNDP/FES, pp. 445–59.

Rajalakshmi, T and Venkatesan, V. 'A Bill on Hold', *Frontline*, 7 March 2014.

Sarkar, T. 1991. 'The Woman as Communal Subject: Rashtrasevika Samiti and Ram Janmabhoomi Movement', in *Economic and Political Weekly*, 31 August.

Uma, S. 2011a. 'Square Peg in a Round Hole: The Use of Ordinary Law for Mass Sexual Violence by Security Forces', in Dhalival, S. (ed.) 2011. *Human rights advocacy: Global approaches, local experiences*. Rajiv Gandhi National University of Law: Patiala, pp. 215–234.

———. 2011b. 'The Communal Violence Bill: Countering Impunity, Seeking Accountability'.*People's Verdict: Civil Society Review of UPA II's Performance*, published by Wada Na Todo Abhiyan, June 2011, pp. 68–71.

———. 2014. 'Aftermath of Muzaffarnagar Riots: Women Bear the Brunt', *Kashmir Times*, 17 March, available at http://www.kashmirtimes.in/newsdet.aspx?q=30083.

———. 2014. 'Muzaffarnagar Aftermath: Mass Marriages to Prevent Abuse: 550 and Counting!', *India Together*, 28 February, available at http://indiatogether.org/mass-marriage-in-aftermath-of-muzaffarnagar-riots-women.

Venkatesan, V. 'A Flawed Bill', *Frontline*, Volume 28 Issue 13, 18 June–1 July 2011.

REPORTS/PAPERS/PRESENTATIONS

Anhad. 2013. *Evil Stalks the Land,* available at www.anhadin.net/article192.html, accessed on 16 June 2014.

International Initiative for Justice in Gujarat. 2003. *Threatened Existence: A Feminist Analysis of the Genocide in Gujarat.*

Joint Citizens Initiative. 2013. *30 Days and Counting – report of a fact-finding team* comprising women's rights activists, health and medical professionals, and lawyers from Uttar Pradesh, Delhi, and Mumbai, available at www.sacw.net/article5920.html, accessed on 16 June 2014.

Nainar, V. 2013. Submission to Justice Verma Committee on the issue of reparations, 20 January 2013, available at www.wragindia.org, accessed on 1 March 2014.

Report by Sahiyar, a Baroda-based women's organization, mimeographed copy, report of women delegates to Bhopal, Ahmedabad and Surat, by AIDWA, CWDS, MDS, NFIW in Sarkar,T and Butalia, U.(eds.)1995.*Women and the Hindu Right.* New Delhi: Kali for Women. pp. 299–328.

Report of Justice Verma Committee on Amendments to Criminal Law. 2013. http://www.prsindia.org/uploads/media/Justice%20verma%20committee/js%20verma%20committe%20report.pdf, accessed on 11 February 2014.

The Survivors Speak: How Has the Gujarat Massacre Affected Minority Women – Fact Finding by a Women's Panel. 2002. http://www.outlookindia.com/article.aspx?215433, accessed on 12 May 2014.

Uma S. and Khan H. *Battered and Betrayed: A Report of Visit to Muzaffarnagar Camps.*http://twocircles.net/2014feb05/battered_and_betrayed_report_visit_muzaffarnagar_camps.htmland also at http://www.sacw.net/article7472.html.

NINE

Voices Against 377

Jaya Sharma

July 2, 2009. Sitting in the courtroom as the judgment was being delivered, I was crying too much to hear clearly as Justice AP Shah read out the conclusion written by him and Justice Muralidhar. Members from Voices Against 377, Naz, Lawyer's Collective and our lawyers witnessed an amazing moment in the history of justice in India. My ex-partner of ten years, who sat next to me on that day, was not only the 34 year old empowered Delhi journalist. Shah spoke to the frightened child who grew up in Bombay thinking that there was no one else like her who did not feel much like a girl and was attracted to girls. The words we heard were like magic, just like Nehru's words which Justice Shah was quoting when he said, 'The notion of equality in the Indian Constitution flows from the 'Objective Resolution' moved by Pandit Jawaharlal Nehru on December 13, 1946'. Nehru, in his speech, wished that the House should consider the Resolution not in a spirit of narrow legal wording, but rather look at the spirit behind that Resolution. He said, 'Words are magic things often enough, but even the magic of words sometimes cannot convey the magic of the human spirit and of a Nation's passion. (The Resolution) seeks very feebly to tell the world of what we have thought or dreamt of so long, and what we now hope to achieve in the near future.'[1]

We had won. After years of organizing, fighting, strategizing, hoping, despairing, we had won. The countless people forced into marriages they didn't want had won. The children growing up afraid and alone had won. The transgender people and men facing extortion for money and forced sex by police had won. The women whose desires were too unthinkable to even reach the khap panchayat had won. The HIV positive people against whom only the virus had not discriminated had won. Every feminist who struggled for the rights of women to have control over their own bodies had won. Every supporter of rights and justice in the country had won.

As we walked out delirious from the courtroom, we were greeted by hordes of cameras. A young journalist said he wanted to interview me; he had seen me crying. He was a print journalist and there seemed no danger of being outed to my family. I had to refuse since he needed a photograph. I was used to refusing. I have done it for ten years now, for the sake of my mother.

I walked past him into the madness, the hugging, euphoria, statements to the press, phone calls across the country and celebration plans. Shalini[2] called to say how thrilling it is that the 'positive version' of the press release was needed. We had worked on two versions of the press release at an emergency meeting of the coalition at Nirantar the previous night, one for victory, one for loss.

What a day it was – the judgment, celebration, press conference, more celebrations, watching the coverage on TV, even more celebration. What a historic day!

As I write now, about Voices Against 377,[3] the Delhi based coalition of women's groups, child rights groups, human rights organizations, queer groups, NGOs and individuals that came together because Section 377 of the Indian Penal Code criminalized all 'carnal intercourse against the order of nature', i.e. all sex which falls outside of procreative sex, whether consensual or not. I remember a day in April 2005 when Voices organized a meeting on Sexuality and Fundamentalism at the Jagori office.[4] Discussions linking sexuality and fundamentalism were part of our ongoing efforts to dialogue with different groups and movements about linkages of queer politics with their core concerns. We had worked hard spending long evenings at the Saheli[5] office figuring out how to focus the discussions and identify resources to draw upon. As we came out of the meeting that went off so well, I remember telling Ponni, a fellow queer activist, 'Oh, we forgot to talk about 377'.

'Forgetting' to talk about the very law which brought the coalition into existence seemed striking to me. It symbolized how much of what Voices did went beyond the law. In fact, Voices pursued a much broader agenda of generating dialogue on queer politics. This is part of what I would like to write about[6] – the relationship between engagement with the law and processes outside the courtroom, the separate spaces they occupy as well as the linkages and tensions.

I write this story up to Voices' contribution to the Naz Foundation (India) Trust's petition to read down Section 377 IPC in the Delhi High Court, and till the subsequent judgment. This part of the continuing case is a story worth telling in itself. Some of my personal experience will illustrate the processes and reflections. This, therefore, is not the entire story about Voices, which moved on to engage much more actively with the media and the discourse on culture, as part of the Supreme Court appeal.[7]

The introduction to Section 377 moves on to a description of the work done by Voices – the social and political – as well as work related to the legal process. I then reflect upon two themes. The first relates to intersectionality between issues and related movements, which captures what inspired member organizations to join and why the coalition pursues the agendas it does. Instead of being an identity-based coalition, Voices brings together organizations with a shared commitment to explore linkages between queer politics and their own core mandates. I seek to share what this intersectionality meant in practice, and some of the ensuing strengths and challenges. The second theme shows the impact of the work Voices did within and outside the courtroom and how the legal and non-legal discourses around Section 377 related to each other.

Section 377

The Indian Penal Code (IPC), introduced in India in 1860 during British rule, drew heavily from laws in the United Kingdom in Victorian times. Section 377, IPC sought to punish 'carnal intercourse against the order of nature', the non bailable arrest which could lead to a sentence ranging from 10 years to life imprisonment.[8]

Contrary to popular belief, Section 377 did not criminalize homosexuality. In fact, the term homosexuality did not exist at that time. The association of sodomy with a particular kind of sexuality that could be named, a particular kind of person and identity, is a phenomenon that began only later in the nineteenth century. [9] The law therefore applies as much to acts such as anal or oral sex between even a man and woman, as it does to these acts between two men or two women or a woman and a transgender person, or any such combination. This Victorian-era law criminalized any sexual act that was not in keeping with the reproductive logic of peno-vaginal sex. The societal sanctity and privacy accorded to married heterosexual couples resulted in the law being effectively used against same-sex desiring and transgender people.[10]

It is not merely a historically interesting detail that Section 377 is not articulated around sexual identities. In the Indian context, most people who experience desire for others of the same sex do not identify as gay, lesbian or bisexual. These identities circulate largely in urban areas, especially among those from middle or higher income groups, since adoption of these identities requires exposure to their existence which, in turn, is related to class and location (urban/rural). There are also those who consciously choose to remain outside these identities, rejecting categories and labels. For this reason, I will be using the term same-sex desiring rather than terms like lesbian, gay or bisexual except when the identity is relevant as in the case of individuals and groups that identify as LGBT+.

A word with a relatively recent history, the term 'queer' has been defined and interpreted in many different ways across the world. The term queer is not the same as LGBT+, even if LGBT+ is extended to include (H)ijra, (K)othi, (I)ntersexed and other identities. As Voices, we understood 'queer' more broadly as an all-encompassing range of expressions of gender and sexuality transgressing social norms. I now use the term queer to explicitly refer to a way of understanding transgression from sexuality and gender norms that in a political sense also includes the underlying ideologies and material realities and linkages with other social, economic and political structures such as class, caste, religion etc. Therefore, an individual or group cannot be queer only by identifying as L, G, B or T and similarly someone queer does not have to identify as L, G, B or T. This is similar to all women not being feminist and that to be feminist you do not have to be a woman. I also use the term transgender as an umbrella term for all those who do not identify with the sex assigned to them at birth, including Hijras.

Returning to the law, while it is true that Section 377 did not criminalize homosexuality, it was a tool for stigmatising and violating the rights of same-sex desiring and transgender people in India. The legal discourse has been almost entirely focused on same-sex desiring men. It is debatable whether Section 377 could technically be applied to those who are biological women because of an explanatory clause that requires penetration; on the other hand, the law does not define penetration, which could be interpreted to include non-penile penetration as well. There have not been any convictions of women under Section 377. However, the same law has been used against same-sex desiring women by family members and police to denigrate their desire as illicit and potentially illegal. The law has also been used to violate the rights of transgender people who are male bodied, including members of the Hijra community.

The significance of Section 377 cannot be captured by the number of persons charged or convicted under it.[11] Other than aiding and abetting blackmail, sexual harassment and violence by the police, the law strengthened the hands of family members who invoked the illegality of same-sex desire to reinforce their own censure. Above all, the law had the power to reinforce that homosexuality was the deviant, illicit, disreputable phenomenon public morality believed it to be. In effect, the law ensured that same-sex desiring people could not gain status and rights as citizens of this country.

As Section 377 refers to sex 'against the order of nature', it had been used in the context of child sexual abuse (CSA), which is not explicitly covered in IPC rape laws. This was a highly imperfect legal remedy and is no substitute for a law designed to address CSA. Section 377 is also used by women in cases such as a wife wanting a divorce on the grounds that her husband wants to have anal sex.[12]

Section 377 did not distinguish between consensual and non-consensual sexual acts between adults. The Delhi High Court petition filed in 2001 sought to ensure that this critical flaw in the law was corrected to exclude consensual sexual acts between adults. Submitted by Naz Foundation India,[13] the PIL argued that Section 377 was a hindrance to carrying out HIV and AIDS interventions – amidst MSM.[14] A partner in this legal struggle was another NGO, the Lawyers Collective.[15] The petition challenging the constitutional validity of Section 377 was mounted on the grounds that the law is arbitrary in its classification of natural and unnatural sex and that it causes a serious setback to HIV and AIDS outreach work amidst MSM, thus violating their right to life.[16] Essentially, the PIL called for the section to be 'read down' and not repealed. This was for several reasons, including the fact that, however imperfect, Section 377 remained the only legal recourse for cases of CSA and marital rape; and that non-consensual sexual acts must remain criminalized.

As I trace the history of the petition, memories almost forgotten are returning. I remember how angst-ridden I used to be about legal reform related to 377. The 'forgetting' once again is significant. To me it indicates the power of the law and legal change, and the significance this grows to acquire within us. I want to locate the angst in an earlier time in the women's movement. In the mid-1980s, I recall processes in which feminist activists and lawyers – even feminist lawyers – worked together. Although they had expertise with the law, these lawyers were neither considered nor saw themselves to be 'the experts'. When working together, it was the women's rights activists who took the lead. Over the years, I felt a shift in the dynamics. Gradually, lawyers were becoming 'the experts' and feminist activists were the ones 'supporting' them, criticising them when they were not consultative enough and praising them when they were. Interestingly, this is a more recent phenomenon in which lawyers are at the centre and activists are meant to engage in ways that can be appreciated as participatory. The term participatory is truly vexed – implying a power centre with mechanisms designed to 'allow' others into the process. This is so entirely different, of course, from a paradigm of equality, camaraderie or a collective way of working.

I also now recall the angst of how engaging with the law pushed us to take positions as queer activists. In Prism, we were completely caught up in the gender neutrality debate.[17] Some of us held gender neutrality as an ideal even as we remained committed to fighting gender subordination. The law made us choose the latter in a way that had no space for the rest of our politics as it related to gender and sexuality.

Engaging with Section 377 brought the same ambivalence to the fore. The law did not seem a priority particularly when so much LGBT+ activist energy was focused on crisis intervention and generating dialogue on queer politics along with battling our own families. There were of course stunning incidents of the law being used to persecute people which we protested against. In fact, the arrest of four health care workers of Bharosa Trust in Lucknow in June 2001[18] under section 377 had brought Prism together, even if most of Prism's work had little to do with the law. Interestingly, it was the law again that brought Voices together.

Although law was not the focus of Prism's work, we had to respond when in September 2003, the then NDA government[19] in its reply to the Delhi High Court argued that Section 377 was needed in 'the interest of public safety and the protection of health and morals'. The government claimed that deleting the section could 'open the floodgates of delinquent behaviour'. In addition to asserting that Section 377 was needed to deal with cases of child sexual abuse, the government claimed that the vast majority of Indians were not concerned about homosexuality. [20]

The anger and outrage against this led us in Prism to call a larger meeting to respond to the petition. This was the meeting that led to the creation of Voices.

Voices: The Beginning

Soon after the September 2003 hearing when the government filed its response, I recall leaving an evening meeting at the India Coffee House, a Delhi institution that has supported activists from a wide range of movements across the political spectrum, who sit around tables and engage in long discussions while arguing over endless cups of wonderful, terrible coffee. I spotted a meeting of the AIDS Bhedbhav Virodhi Andolan (ABVA) underway at another table. ABVA had filed the first ever challenge to Section 377 in 1994 following the debates triggered by the then Superintendent of Tihar Jail Kiran Bedi's refusal to allow condoms to be distributed to prisoners, so as not to 'abet' violations of Section 377. The contents and arguments in the ABVA petition were far ahead of the times even if it did not survive the legal system.[21] I joined the ABVA activists and we talked animatedly about the need to counter the government's response. An ABVA member said, 'Call a meeting, but make sure it's a large meeting, invite all those who call themselves progressive'.

And indeed, it turned out to be a momentous meeting. Members of women's groups, queer activists, lawyers and human rights activists were packed into the outer room of the Saheli office. We discussed how to counter the government's assertion that 'homosexuality' was not a concern for the vast majority of people in the county. A human rights activist proposed putting together a report showing how different sections of Indian society, as represented by women's groups, groups working on child rights, LGBT+ groups and others were all opposed to Section 377 and stating why they were concerned about the rights of same-sex desiring people. This would be a powerful way for a cross section of Indian society to assert that this law is not acceptable. All present threw their energy and hard work into creating the report entitled 'Rights For All: Ending Discrimination Against Queer Desire Under Section 377'.[22]

The report provided, perhaps for the first time, understandings and perspectives from different movements about the significance of issues around same-sex desire. The chapter titled 'A perspective from the women's movement' contributed by Saheli, begins thus:

'The personal is political' has long been a rallying point for the women's movement and never has it been as applicable as in the realm of sexuality. From abortion rights to the use of contraception, women's groups have campaigned for the right to control sexuality and bodily integrity. For women, the only legitimate expression of sexuality has been within heterosexual marriage, rigidly circumscribed by caste and community. Sex for pleasure has traditionally been taboo for women who are merely expected to submit to the sexual act to satisfy their husbands and produce children, preferably sons. Of course, whores/prostitutes/sex workers are at the other end of the scale, their entire existence constructed around sex. Patriarchal control over women's sexuality is reinforced by laws as well as biases of the judiciary to bolster attempts to maintain the unit of the family – however oppressive or violent it may be. Section 377 and the government's unwillingness to repeal it sums up the historical attitude of the Anglo-Saxon legal system toward non-procreative eroticism.

The chapter locates and analyses the construction of same-sex desire, particularly between women, and the responses to it in the larger context of women's sexuality, patriarchy, the women's movement and colonial history. Responding to the categorization of same-sex desire as being 'unnatural', it asks what truly could be called 'natural' in a context in which reproductive technologies are making even human reproduction possible without heterosexual intercourse. The chapter raises questions about whether there really is a silence on sexuality, on the limiting heterosexual-homosexual binary, and whether people are as 'straight' as they appear to be. It also foregrounds the centrality of the issue of consent in the women's movement in light of Section 377 failing to distinguish between consent and non-consent.

This is an illustration of why groups who were part of Voices engaged with it — not merely as allies supporting another's cause, but by squarely locating queer issues as part of their mandate and ideology, thereby claiming the issues as their own.[23]

There are several references in the report to transgender as an identity, which is part of LGBT+. Testimonies of human rights violations faced by transgender people were also included. However, we did not address the reasons why transgender people face violations and the linked issue of the particular challenge to gender norms and patriarchy that they pose. This needs to be located in time, as well as in terms of the class composition of Voices. At the time Voices was formed, members of the Hijra community had already been raising their issues for several years but the larger LGBT+ community/movement had not yet joined in. A few groups working on HIV and AIDS issues were working with transgender people who were male bodied. It is only in recent years that transgender issues have come to be centrally addressed by the LGBT+ community/movement.

Most members of Voices were largely middle or upper middle class. Although their organizations worked with economically and socially marginalized communities, such as Dalit, rural poor, or women, there was no experience of work with transgender people. And even members who identified as queer did not identify as transgender, though several were far from being strictly 'masculine men' or 'feminine women'. One more reason why Voices did not engage with transgender issues might lie in part in the rejection of identity-based politics as expressed, for instance, in preference for the term 'same-sex desiring' rather than LGBT+. Perhaps also the articulation in terms of 'queer' made us less cognisant of the differing extent to which specific issues and identities were being addressed.[24] We often did not add 'gender transgressing' to 'same- sex desiring'.

The publishing of the Voices report energized and motivated us to continue the work of raising awareness about queer issues. That's when we decided to form a coalition and name it Voices Against 377.

How Voices Worked

Any outside observer would have seen little in terms of a rhythm or predictability in how Voices functioned. A coalition of typically overworked NGOs and activist groups, it's a miracle that Voices survived this long without a structure. Numerous unsuccessful attempts were made to form committees and have rotating co-ordinators. What is significant is that there have been phases when someone has taken the lead, brought in energy and pulled the group together. Voices has seen a fluid leadership even if leadership is not a term that has been consciously used within it.

Even though the membership was organizational, the engagement of individual representatives was intense; this was the strength and limitation of Voices. Perhaps if such members acted only as representatives of organizations, their engagement might not have been as intense. Or, if the engagement and accountability had been more organizational, perhaps Voices could have worked more systematically. Although examples abound of networks and coalitions where participation by member organizations tends to be mechanical, they often do not tend to last long because of the lack of sustained interest on the part of member organizations.

The queer approach of Voices meant that the perspective building on issues of same-sex desire called for a broader understanding of sexuality. This happened in organic ways in meetings and intense joint work for events. From time to time, Voices conducted workshops for member organizations that sought to deepen their understanding of sexuality, including the politics of sexuality that recognized positive affirmation going beyond violations.

SOCIAL AND POLITICAL ACTIVISM

The key initiatives undertaken by Voices as part of its social and political activism are as follows:

Actions and Events: In July 2004, Voices organised a *dharna* at Jantar Mantar as a mark of the continued struggle of diverse groups and individuals against Section 377. For the first time, a united coalition of different groups — not just LGBT+ — came together to make 377 everyone's issue. Voices also organized a panel discussion on Section 377 that included Robert Wintemute's talk on 'Lesbian and Gay Human Rights in India: International and Comparative Perspectives' in February 2006.[25] Voices also participated in the national consultations on the 377 petition organized by Lawyer's Collective.

Dialogue with Other Movements: In August 2004, Voices organized a public meeting to address the violations faced by those who are marginalized on the basis of their sexuality, and how different struggles waged by other oppressed groups like Dalits, women, workers, and children are related to the struggle for sexual rights.

The engagement of women's groups needs to be located in queer activism even before Voices was formed, after the release of the film

Fire in late 1998. The film enraged Hindu fundamentalist groups, especially with the female leads in the films having names of Hindu goddesses. They vandalized cinema halls, intimidated cinema-goers and called for a ban on the film, saying that there were no lesbians in Hindu families. The left-linked women's groups and other progressive groups protested against the vandalism and censorship. However, it was only certain autonomous women's groups and queer groups who raised the issue of lesbian women and women's sexuality as part of the Campaign for Lesbian Rights (CALERI). Other women's groups refrained with the stance that including lesbian women's and women's sexuality issues would dilute the fight against censorship and freedom of speech. Thereafter, some of the left-linked women's groups refused to let the autonomous women's groups and queer groups raise lesbian women's issues during International Women's Day celebrations. Queer groups made several unsuccessful attempts to dialogue with these women's groups about the significance of lesbian women's issues. After a gap of several years, Voices made an attempt in February 2005 to dialogue once again with groups like the National Federation of Indian Women (NFIW) and the All India Democratic Women's Association (AIDWA) that are associated with left parties.[26]

There was dialogue with the Jan Swasthya Abhiyan (JSA), an integral part of the Right to Health movement, on the linkages between sexuality and health. Voices and Sama[27] felt the need to incorporate issues of sexuality within the health discourse. A series of dialogues was initiated between the JSA and Voices to explore the relationship between sexuality and health and include queer issues within the Right to Health framework. A residential national-level workshop included an in-depth understanding of issues of sexuality more broadly from a queer, feminist perspective.[28] Some of the participants – especially clinical psychologists and activists working on disability issues – later shared that they had been able to weave in the interlinkages between health and sexuality within their organizational/institutional work including workshops, campaigns and interactions with the community/groups they work with.

Outreach: Voices engaged with mental health professionals to educate them about the trauma and humiliation same-sex desiring and other queer people undergo when subjected to aversion therapy to 'cure' them. In November 2005, Voices conducted a meeting with members of the Psychological Foundation, where we presented a brief on the research conducted by Arvind Narrain and Vinay Chandran.

Voices also made efforts to network with organizations like Anhad and Sahmat to link issues of sexuality and fundamentalism. In April 2005, Voices held a public meeting on fundamentalism and sexuality.

Voices also participated in protests organized by other movements. For instance, Voices members participated in the protest against the Sardar Sarovar Dam in April 2006, in solidarity with the Narmada Bachao Andolan. Although we were told that 'humare yahan aise log nahin hain' (we don't have people like this here), we sat with our placards and even mustered up the courage to read out a statement of solidarity. Voices was also part of the queer contingent that joined a big rally in March 2006 protesting former President George W. Bush's visit to India. In response to a request from Sangat, a representative of Voices spoke at a Human Rights Day event in December 2007 in Delhi.

Voices did many rounds of leafleting in different public places in Delhi. Voices also launched the 'Million Voices Campaign', meant to be a nationwide campaign to gather voices against Section 377 as well as various expressions on sexual rights and sexual diversity. The year-long campaign was launched on December 9, 2004 – the eve of Human Rights Day – as a means of generating dialogue and making visible the opposition to Section 377. The idea was simple. People everywhere – on the streets, at meetings, conferences – wrote or drew whatever they wanted to about Section 377, same-sex desire, sexual diversity, and sexual rights, on pieces of cloth. The campaign went through periods of lull as well as bursts of energy. The work done by Partners for Law and Development (PLD) helped take the Million Voices Campaign beyond Delhi.[29]

In February 2007, Voices launched its website as a ready reference for people on Voices Against 377, to get greater visibility and engage in online advocacy such as online petitions and signature campaigns.

Crisis Intervention: Reflecting back, it is interesting that a coalition like Voices also got involved in crisis intervention, which proved quite challenging. Voices also joined other fact-finding efforts.

In January 2006, when the UP Police arrested four men in Lucknow under Section 377, Voices joined a fact-finding team that was sent to Lucknow to investigate the matter and expose the role of media and police in stigmatising and discriminating against same-sex desiring people. We also became part of a fact-finding team to Shillong in March 2006, in response to the murder of a queer individual, which was feared to be a homophobic attack.

Voices called a meeting in July 2007 regarding Shahzina and Shamail, a couple in Pakistan imprisoned under charges of perjury and Section 377. Shamail, who identifies as a man, was accused of lying to the court about his gender.[30] In December 2004, Voices wrote to the Kerala government, Kerala Police and NHRC expressing shock at the police abetment of the attempts by families of two adult women, Rashiath A. (aged 20) and Neethu Saji (aged 18) from Parathode, under Kanjirappally Police jurisdiction, to prevent them from staying together.

In mid-April 2006, two Delhi-based women, Neha and Victoria, contacted Sangini[31] for assistance. A warrant of arrest had been issued against Victoria under Section 166 of IPC, which is a gender-specific law against abduction of a woman with intent to marry her. Voices organized financial support and became involved in planning the legal strategy to counter the charge of Section 166.[32]

In June 2007 a media report announced that Manpreet Kaur, 21, and Ranno Kaur, 20, (names changed) from neighbouring villages of Batala, Gurdaspur district, Punjab had got 'married' against the wishes of their parents at the Vaishno Devi shrine in Jammu and Kashmir.

Voices went as a team comprising members from Naz Foundation and two autonomous women's groups that were its member organizations. The team arranged bail and returned to Delhi with Manpreet where she took up shelter with some Voices members.

Over a period of two years, Voices handled the case in the district court and made several trips to Batala, often with support from the LGBT+ community.[33] The process of handling the case long distance, working with local lawyers, fearing what Ranno's family might do, concerns about the masculine appearance of Manpreet in the court and how to sustain this engagement were the key challenges. A silver lining was when Manpreet's mother told her daughter that she didn't care what she was and what she did as long as she was happy.[34]

In February 2005, a memorandum was sent to the National Council of Education Research and Training (NCERT) regarding inclusion of sexuality education with special emphasis on sexual choice and diversity for its national curriculum. It outlined the role of sexuality education in creating an aware and confident individual who knows about her/his choices and makes informed decisions without being bound by the narrow parameters set up by society. In 2007, Voices presented a paper on education and sexuality towards incorporating issues of sexuality within the education chapter of the CEDAW shadow report.

In March 2005, Voices participated in the national consultation on Child Sexual Abuse organised by AALI[35] in a context in which the continuing existence of Section 377 has been justified as a preventive measure against child sexual abuse. In March 2006, Voices submitted a memorandum to the Committee to Reform the Police Act entitled, *Sexual Minorities and the Police in India: Towards a regime of accountability.* In June 2006, Voices actively participated in a National Consultation on the proposed Sexual Assault Bill. Also, Voices used the media to strongly condemn two homophobic actions in the country in June 2004 — the release of the film *Girlfriend* by director Karan Razdan and the protests by the right-wing fundamentalist groups at cinema halls screening the movie. The press release condemned the irresponsibility with which the film chose to represent lesbian sexuality as well as the violent and undemocratic ways of the fundamentalist groups in trying to curb the freedom of expression of others. Voices also organised a press conference in August 2004, condemning the media for sensationalising the murders of Pushkin and Kuldeep.[36] Members of Voices were also instrumental in coordinating the process of several open letters which sought to impact the government on Section 377.[37]

Dialogue on LGBT+ issues: In May 2007, Voices organised a National Consultation for LGBT+ and LGBT+-supportive groups to dialogue on issues facing the LGBT+ community.[38] The Consultation witnessed wide ranging discussions and debates including those related to the media. It also focussed on crisis interventions and their legal, medical, psychiatric and personal dimensions. It addressed issues of how work with agencies and actors such as the police, politicians, doctors, media, corporates, lawyers and colleges could be strengthened. Linkages were discussed between LGBT+ groups and groups working with women's rights, child rights, displacement, labour and so forth. Participants shared about their own LGBT+ work, the gains made, the strategies explored and the challenges inherent in the course of such work.[39]

VOICES' WORK AS IT RELATED TO THE LAW

The year 2006 was packed with new developments. In a crucial move, NACO[40] filed an affidavit in the court saying that the existence of Section 377 on the statute books was a serious impediment to HIV and AIDS prevention work in the country. At the same time, a petition by the ex-BJP Member of Parliament B.P. Singhal stated that the law should be retained in order to protect Indian values and culture. In his affidavit, Mr Singhal claimed that homosexuals were more prone to murder, accidents and diseases, and that the human body was not designed for anal sex.[41]

Voices decided to file the intervention in December 2006 in support of the Naz petition. This involved identifying and working with senior lawyers. The role of the Alternative Law Forum[42] was central in this process and their being queer lawyers and highly supportive of the LGBT+ movement was very significant. They briefed the senior lawyers who argued the case, along with Voices. The work involved tremendous research and drafting undertaken by ALF. A key role that Voices played, other than decision-making regarding positioning of arguments, was the identification and documentation of testimonies of individuals who had experienced violations because they were same sex-desiring or transgendered.

The testimonies were one of the most important contributions made by Voices, especially in a context in which the Delhi High Court had earlier dismissed the petition on grounds that the petitioner had no locus standi and that the PIL had not been filed by those directly affected by section 377. It was decided not to include testimonies of same-sex desiring women, particularly because of the fear of gender neutrality being added to the existing section 377 thereby making lesbian and bisexual women even more vulnerable as had happened in Sri Lanka. However, some members of Voices maintained that the inclusion would have been important. According to them, whether section 377 technically applied to women or not, it was part of the persecution they faced. The Voices lawyer Mr. Divan ensured a reference to this when he narrated the incident in April 2006 of two adult lesbian women in Delhi who were in a relationship, shared above as the case of Neha and Victoria.

The testimonies submitted came to form a critical part of the overall case. The Voices lawyer was particularly brave and strategic to begin with the testimony of Gautam Bhan, someone who is privileged in many ways. Quoting from the affidavit filed by Gautam Bhan, Mr. Divan showed that the legal repercussions of Section 377 hindered the lives of homosexuals even though society and family could be supportive. In his affidavit, Bhan states that he felt like a second-class citizen in his own country because of 377. Mr. Divan argued that, 'Section 377 operated to criminalise and stigmatise people for being themselves. There is no justification for such a law.' He elaborated on the importance of the notion of identity. 'We were discussing the issue of caste. In parts of India, men identify themselves by their caste. Women often identify by gender. For some, religious identity is paramount. When you are enumerating identity, a heterosexual person may not consider sexual orientation as important, but for a homosexual, sexual identity may be paramount. Sexual orientation is often the first thing that governs a person's life. As we saw in Gautam Bhan's affidavit, he asks why, though he is equal to persons in all other aspects, he still suffers from the stigma of section 377.'

Another contribution that the Voices intervention made was to define the notion of privacy in a manner that took it well beyond the spatial realm. This is highly significant in a context in which the Naz petition had run into considerable controversy within the LGBT+ community because of the use of the argument of privacy which many felt was an elitist positioning, given that so many same-sex-desiring men have no choice but to have sexual and erotic encounters in public spaces.[43]

Not all of us were in court, but we checked our mails every night to read the updates with nervous excitement. This happened only because Voices members and those from the community took prolific notes of what transpired in the courtroom. These narratives for me capture more than what any judgment possibly can.[44]

The limitations in the Voices discourse around transgender identity and concerns got addressed when Voices moved beyond its own member composition and began to draw upon the work done by Sangama and ALF in Karnataka. Thus, the testimonies submitted included those from members of the transgender and Hijra community. Engagement with the law in this instance gave Voices an opportunity to move beyond its class composition and related limitations.

It needs to be mentioned here, that members of the LGBT+ community in other parts of the country contributed financial support for the Voices intervention, which was crucial and an important reflection of how the larger community was invested in the legal struggle.

INTERSECTIONALITY AT WORK

The approach of intersectionality taken by Voices was its very inception; Voices countered the myth that Indian society was not concerned about the rights of homosexual people. The coalition represented a wide range of civil society organizations who worked with different sections of society as well as on a range of issues such as legal rights, health and education. This was also important in the context of the legal strategy with representatives of a wide range of organizations directly intervening in the legal case. Intersectionality was reflected not only in the composition and nature of Voices, but also in much of its work. This also had direct impact on the work of constituent organisations, in particular those who had not gone beyond sexual violence.

But before this, I would like to locate Voices as part of a tradition in Delhi of queer, non identity-based activism.

AIDS Bhed Bhav Virodhi Andolan (ABVA) was a Delhi-based activist, non-funded group that worked on a range of issues related to HIV and AIDS in a manner that was highly political, passionate, committed and rigorous. ABVA effectively used a mix of methods including protests, the media, law and publications. Members of ABVA consisted of a nun, a professional blood donor, doctors and laywers. They took up a range of issues including those related to same-sex desiring people, professional blood donors, intravenous drug users, sex workers and HIV positive people. It was a truly pioneering activist group as it demonstrated in an unstated, low profile way the politics of intersectionality and how such work need not be defined by identities. ABVA members could address in a highly informed manner the range of issues that the group took up, irrespective of their identity. There was, of course, a lot of ground work and heated discussions that took place for this to be possible.

My friend Sidhartha Gautam,[45] who was one of the founding members of ABVA, used to share his experiences and would also sometimes ask me to join its meetings. Sidhartha used to share the passionate and animated discussions of ABVA on issues of same-sex desire and how energizing it was to see others engage head on with these issues, which were new for some. And from this kind of ground work, and tremendous research, emerged ABVA's amazing pink book, *Less than Gay*, which was way ahead of its times in terms of the understanding that it held about same-sex issues. The tradition of non identity-based politics based on recognition of intersectionality,

even before these terms came into circulation, was continued by
CALERI referred to above.

The Significance of Intersectionality: Voices, not being an identity-
based coalition, acquires particular significance in a context in which
identity-based politics is becoming increasingly important as a
paradigm in politics, activism, the development sector etc. [46]

There is a need to recognise some of the challenges inherent in
narrowly defined identity politics. Most often the diversity that is
recognized is that which exists around us with respect to identities
such as caste, religion and increasingly also gender and sexual
identities. However, there is often a failure to recognize the diversity
that might exist within us. To use the example of sexuality, while
there is a growing recognition of sexual diversity, the identity-based
paradigm means that if we need to, we identify as heterosexual,
lesbian, gay or bisexual. This does not allow us to recognize that there
might be a diversity of desires within us, not just around us. Rather
than seeing sexual desires as being fixed, unchanging and unitary,
a queer understanding of sexuality recognizes that a multiplicity of
desires could co-exist within each one of us, and also that desires can
change, and that our sexual desires are not, and need not, be limited
to what we have experienced so far in our lives.

That we truly do not know what the future holds can be both
exciting and frightening. It is much safer to believe that we are what
we are, forever and ever. The system of punishments and privileges
does not help matters. If we identify as heterosexual, the privileges
we gain from the identity are not likely to make us want to be open
to the possibility of it being a tenuous or fragile reality. In the case
of a stigmatized identity, we might feel that the stigmatized identity
that we have been able to claim with such difficulty is one that we
need to keep identifying with, in solidarity with that identity as it
were. It is like what many of us feel as feminists when we are now
challenged by the trans discourse to place ourselves on a slippery
gender continuum because we have struggled to assert our identity
as women and formed communities and a movement around this
identity. Interrogating identities is tough.

Being open to diversity within is also logical if we reject an essentialist world view and adopt a lens which recognizes that nothing is 'natural' and 'normal', and that social construction cannot be wished away. No matter how 'natural' and 'normal' even being gay or lesbian or transgender seems, there is a need to recognize and accept that nothing is, in fact, natural or free from the influence of social factors. Hence, identity politics needs to be looked at critically because it is not in sync with the lived realities of diversity and fluidity. Non-identity based politics allows for possibilities of self and collective actualisation, which we might otherwise deny ourselves and each other.

Further, the framework of intersectionality helps deepen our understanding about 'alliances' as part of which one identity lends its support as an ally to another identity or cluster of identities. Even if this alliance is intensive in terms of time, energy and resources, there will still be a distance between the allies, the support will be extended from a distance, and in the case of stigmatized categories, from a safe distance. We can see how this might play out in terms of same-sex desire.

For example, a woman who identifies as heterosexual is likely to be more comfortable lending her support to lesbian women as the 'other' perhaps or even empathetically, thereby affirming her identity as a heterosexual. This is indeed easier than being open to the possibility of the stirrings of desire that she might feel for another woman. This paradigm also does not allow for a deeper recognition of the inherent linkages between different social, economic and political forces. However, a framework of intersectionality opens up the space to recognize and act upon these linkages.

In the case of Voices, the nature of the coalition compelled us to recognize these linkages. For example, when activists focussed on the struggle against communalism were invited to the meeting on sexuality and fundamentalism, the positioning stemmed from a framework of intersectionality. This is indicated in the title of the meeting, Sexuality and Fundamentalism – Exploring Linkages, Confronting Challenges. The framing was not LGBT+ but sexuality, and it sought to explore linkages between sexuality and fundamentalism. The power of such a framework is that it seeks to forge energies based on recognition of real linkages that do exist but are hazy or invisible because of the cloud of identity politics instead of linkages that need to be artificially evoked. It strikes me that progressive forces often work in silos whereas right-wing forces are often better at recognizing linkages. In Nazi Germany, the wing of the police force which targeted homosexuals also targeted sex workers and women who refused to oblige the system by producing Aryan babies.[47]

Far from being a 'fancy' or an 'evolved' concept as is sometimes critiqued, the need for an approach based on intersectionality mirrors the nature of reality, the various dimensions of which are interconnected and co constitute each other.

Let's take, for instance, how intersectionality manifests itself in terms of sexuality and gender. Does it not make perfect sense for women's groups to be a part of a coalition like Voices? For starters, women who desire women are stigmatized and denied rights. Also, for long the women's movement has been challenging ideas about what is 'natural' – for example how natural is it for a woman to feel maternal, how natural is the sexual division of labour. It is therefore 'but natural' that the women's movement should join hands with the queer movement to challenge naturalness accorded to homosexuality.

What Intersectionality Meant in Terms of How We Worked Together: Voices did not have a formal structure. There have been many phases, however, when someone has taken the lead and brought energy and focus into Voices. Many of these individuals were not people who identify as LGBT+. Many who came at different points in time were often in learning mode. There was interest in learning as well as in contributing to the work. Often these members would not be the most vocal ones in meetings, especially the newer and younger members of NGOs. However, being part of Voices was an important, alive and organic learning ground in which they felt challenged to think about issues of sexuality.

Purwa had been actively involved in left politics, in particular in theatre and literature, as a student and activist in Bihar. She had an increasingly intensive engagement with women's issues as part of Nirantar.[48] When she came for Voices meetings, she initially tended to be quiet. I remember our working on the Hindi translation of the Voices report and facing the challenges of capturing the meaning of the English version in Hindi. It was a struggle, but a struggle worth undertaking. There is much less baggage associated with terms, and one has to start almost afresh. There is therefore a compulsion and opportunity to write in a manner that seeks to capture and to describe, without falling back on words in the sexuality realm that are already in circulation in English, words that are contested or words that often mean different things to different individuals.

When Lawyers Collective called national level meetings on legal strategies, representatives from Voices were perhaps the only ones at the meeting who were not necessarily identifying as LGBT+. Sometimes this also meant that the manner in which they were able to participate in the discussions was somewhat circumscribed and perhaps processes of orienting and preparation before meetings might have been desirable. That, however, may have been asking too much from a coalition which had neither full time members nor a formal structure.

A particular challenge facing the coalition was getting many groups who had not engaged with issues of same-sex desire to work together. Working together on planning and organizing events was an organic way to overcome this challenge. A tangible sense of being part of the same entity was created, despite the different backgrounds that people came from. This working together was made easier because most groups had a broader political understanding and a commitment to justice and social change.

What Intersectionality Meant for the Work of Member Organizations
Nirantar's[49] engagement with sexuality was specific to sexual violence and rape as part of the women's movement. Through its involvement with Voices, Nirantar began looking at its ongoing work on education from the lens of sexuality. One significant initiative was the advocacy undertaken by Voices for the inclusion of issues of sexuality in the school curriculum with NCERT.

Here too, the positioning and the issues raised were not limited to the LGBT+ community but a larger framework of sexuality. This has also meant intensive partnerships with organizations working with rural women to work towards more positive and political ways of approaching sexuality, and to see the linkages with ground level work, in particular Gender based Violence (GBV).[50] This entailed building an understanding about sexual norms, including the norm that desire should be experienced only between a man and a woman and why these norms are upheld, the linkages with patriarchy, caste and religion, challenging sexual and gender binaries, etc.

Sexuality and gender diversity are presented in the frameworks of continuums, while the importance of identity is recognized in the struggle against stigma and towards building communities. There is also recognition that understanding issues of same sex desire and gender transgression are central to our work and politics as feminist groups.

Nirantar highlights the exclusions from current GBV interventions. For instance, Violence against Women simplistically implies 'married, heterosexual' women. Sex workers, same-sex desiring women, widows, single women, even younger married women tend to be excluded, as are transgender people. With respect to same-sex desiring and transgender people, Nirantar's work now seeks to enable GBV programmes to recognize the exclusion and create willingness and preparedness to respond to the violence faced by all these women.

Sexuality has over the years become an integral part of the mandate, political understanding and work of Nirantar. Sexuality is a part of gender trainings, including those with teachers. It has become a lens through which Nirantar undertakes its research such as that related to curricula, development policies and interventions.

Nirantar's experiences are only one example. Similar examples can be found among other member organizations.

THE RELATIONSHIP BETWEEN VOICES' LEGAL AND
NON LEGAL WORK

Social and Political Work Made Possible the Legal Work: Many people, including activists, journalists and others in the development sector, assume that the battle against Section 377 was begun and won in the courtroom. While the legal processes as well as the judgment were historic, it is critical to remember all that preceded the judgment. When the PIL was first filed in the Delhi High Court in 2001, there was already a national level movement through groups and individuals spread across the country. The relationship between social and political processes and legal processes is often seen more clearly in the case of the women's movement or the Dalit movement. Perhaps it is easier to recognize that the legal processes were greatly strengthened or sometimes even made possible by these movements. Similarly, the legal victory too was an outcome of the LGBT+ movement's active and growing presence in India.

The Implications of Legal Work on Social and Political Work: The legal work became the entire focus of Voices. This phenomenon is not unique to Voices. Law-related work, including the urgency that timetables set by courts bring, has the ability to draw heavily on the time and energy of activists. For a fluid, non-structured coalition like Voices, the immediate nature of the legal work made members gathering around the work to be done. It seemed as if we emerged from the law, did much outside the law and then were back to focusing only on the law.

However significant the legal struggle was, there continue to be challenges and opportunities in the social and political realms. The LGBT+ movement, like the women's movement, Dalit movement and others is up against long-standing, deep rooted norms about same-sex desire and gender transgression, norms which underpin powerful entrenched systems like patriarchy and ideas about what is natural and normal. We are questioning the family, how we should be, how life should be organized, intimate relations, the relationship between love and sex, inheritance and private property, the continuity of caste and religious identities and so on that need progeny born of the union of a woman and man belonging to the same religion and often the same caste. Why would the threat that same-sex desire and gender transgression pose to all of this, go away with any change in the law, however significant?

Who Speaks for Whom? Any engagement with the law brings up the question of representation, namely who becomes the voice for queer issues. Among those engaged with the processes, many were either LGBT+ identified or lawyers. Perhaps responding to the legal milestones seemed more daunting for those who were not LGBT+ identified to speak about it in the public realm. Speaking on the legal case can be intimidating in a context where the media too expected those who 'belong' to the directly affected identities to speak about the issue. Right after the Delhi High Court judgment, those from Voices who spoke in the public realm were largely from the LGBT+ community. In fact, they addressed the media from their location as members of the LGBT+ community and not as representatives of Voices. This is not a critique; but a reflection on what happened spontaneously and in an unplanned manner after the judgment. In a context where Voices was trying to work within the framework of non identity politics and intersectionality, this needs to be reflected upon, especially by members from outside the LGBT+ community.

THE RELATIONSHIP BETWEEN LEGAL AND NON LEGAL PUBLIC DISCOURSES

How Progressive Legal Discourse Can Counter Mainstream Discourses: The Delhi High Court judgment made a huge difference. However much one might critique the idea of the nation or not look to the state for legitimacy, one's sexual orientation being criminalised means that one does not feel like a citizen. As I was sitting in the courtroom, hearing the Voices lawyer Shyam Divan argue for and assert our rights, I felt my mother's presence in the courtroom, in a tangible, palpable way. I was saying to her, can you hear him, listen to him! Even as I write, I can feel tears stinging, threatening to interrupt my writing.

Here I am, a woman touching fifty, 'empowered' in many ways, highly privileged, sitting in a house I own, someone who has been part of the women's movement for over thirty years and the LGBT+ movement for almost half of that, not vulnerable to my family in any obvious or direct kind of way, and yet it's there. The sense of validation I received from the queer community is what, in essence, the queer community meant to me, a reminder that I'm okay. Besides talking about these issues and marching on the street in protest, these reminders matter in knowing that there are people you can talk to, touch and feel. In similar ways, it matters what the law says. Because the law has power. It wields power over my mother. My mother respects the law. She can choose not to come to my house because I lived with a woman, but she better listen along with the judges to what Shyam Divan is saying.

This house that I 'own' has given shelter to many a runaway, crazy lesbian couple at times when we had to deal with a niggling fear of what if the police find out and dramatically come crashing in, see the books, magazines, films in the house? And the police have come sometimes. Either me or my ex-partner have had to sit over tea with the police in our living room as they asked questions or suggested we were involved in trafficking women. Though the police never moved any further into the house, they could have. And that is the frightening thing. They could have.

I remember how scared I was once when I had to tell the police that my gay friend was my boyfriend when he was picked up cruising in a park one night. They were reluctant to believe our story because our names betrayed our families were of different faiths. I also remember the fear both Akshay and I felt as I waited for him outside the Police Station while they interrogated him, along with many 'gay' men, after the Pushkin murder case. Akshay, inspired by his fear, even as he sweated, gave the police a lecture about how to describe him as 'gay' was limiting and inaccurate, stopping short only of quoting Foucault! One empathised with the cops too that day. The hysterical laughter over all this when he came out also sprang somewhere from fear.

Another memory that comes to me as I write is that of how the team from Voices travelling to Punjab to accompany a young transgender person to the courtroom felt reassured by the presence of the big hunk of a Jat boy who was a staff member of Naz. We discovered how he identified much more with the feminine than the masculine and were left with our worries about the impression the trans person, female-bodied but very masculine, would make on the court and how we coached her to be very polite before the judge. I remember when a trans female bodied friend got into trouble with the police, worrying about his childhood photos framed on my bedroom shelf at home. And these are some memories, as I said, of an empowered, privileged woman. Clearly the law assumes significance in countering such fears.

Beyond this, there is a beauty, a stunning beauty, in the manner in which the legal arguments made by Voices and also the judgment stretched the rights language to its maximum.

The judgment[51] was in no way weakened or diluted by the fact that there had not been any convictions under Section 377. One of the many strengths of the judgment was the significant distinction it made between 'prosecution' and 'persecution'. Even if there is no prosecution, there is clearly persecution. Prosecution was difficult. One of the reasons for this is that it was difficult to get third parties to testify in cases of consenting adults. Justice Muralidhar also seemed to refer to the situation that the lack of convictions under section 377 was at the High Court or Supreme Court levels. He pointed out that the lack of convictions at the trial court level might relate to criminal law invariably being used against the poor in the country.

Chief Justice Shah compared discrimination based on sexual orientation to discrimination based on caste. 'If you belong to the 'untouchable' category, you suffer a disadvantage in every aspect of life. The effect of criminalization (of homosexuality) is like treating you as a member of a scheduled caste', he said.

The judgment was powerful and highly strategic in countering the morality argument. '[P]opular morality or public disapproval of certain acts is not a valid justification for restriction of the fundamental rights under Article 21. Popular morality, as distinct from a constitutional morality derived from constitutional values, is based on shifting and subjecting notions of right and wrong. If there is any type of 'morality' that can pass the test of compelling state interest, it must be 'constitutional' morality and not public morality.' (Naz judgment 2009, para. 79)

It made a new and useful interpretation of Article 15 that specifies prohibition of discrimination: for the first time in India, sexual orientation was considered a ground analogous to sex (Naz judgment 2009, para. 85). Discrimination on the basis of 'sex' was deemed to include 'sexual orientation'.

In its conclusion, the decision invoked the first Prime Minister of independent India, Pandit Jawaharlal Nehru, 'If there is one constitutional tenet that can be said to be an underlying theme of the Indian Constitution, it is that of 'inclusiveness'. This Court believes that the Indian Constitution reflects this value deeply ingrained in Indian society, nurtured over several generations. The inclusiveness that Indian society traditionally displayed, literally in every aspect of life, is manifest in recognizing a role in society for everyone. Those perceived by the majority as 'deviants' or 'different' are not on that score excluded or ostracised.' (Naz judgment 2009, para. 130, p. 104)

As shared by Geeta Mishra in her article,[52] at a public debate in Delhi[53] on the 377 judgment, moderated by ex-Attorney General Soli Sorabji, Shohini Ghosh[54] explained how the judgment had radically transformed the terms of debate. Other than moving debates on sexuality from public morality to one of constitutional morality, the judgment had reconfigured the notion of harm. The question was no longer whether homosexuality 'harmed' abstract notions of family values and the social fabric but about how the provisions of 377 had harmed members of the LGBT+ community by marginalizing, oppressing and exploiting them. Lastly, and most importantly, said Ghosh, the scope of the judgment far transcended the LGBT+ issue with its implication of unprecedented protection for all minorities. By so doing it had introduced, for the first time in South Asia, the idea of sexual citizenship.

The legal victory also opened up spaces. For example, in the work that Nirantar is engaged in with respect to Adolescent Education and Life Skills Education, the negotiations around addressing heteronormativity in the curriculum with NCERT had a different flavour. The resistance was less. We were now at least able to argue against assumptions and assertions of desire being only heterosexual. To illustrate, we were able to argue for a rearticulation of the existing material that referred to 'attraction to the opposite sex' in terms of just 'attraction'. It might be a small move forward, but it was one that entailed much struggle.

The Ways in Which Legal Discourses Might Delimit/Bind: I remember watching the news on TV, even as I felt the euphoria of the day in court. I so wished that the 'progressive' TV anchors would let the dharam gurus talk instead of, for example, aggressively and self-righteously asking the Chairperson of the Maharashtra Minority Commission whether he was living in the 21st century. However much the modern, liberal discourse tries to steer clear, religious leaders were raising issues of the family, marriage, children, morality and culture, which are our issues too. I welcomed Baba Ramdev saying a son needed a mother. The levels of threat perception – related to the patriarchal building blocks of society as we know it – were high and rightly so. Sexual and gender transgression does pose a challenge to how society is currently structured; as we become secure in our newfound status as citizens accorded dignity by the courts, we need to debate these issues more and more in the public realm.

Although there was more space in the Supreme Court,[55] in the High Court we stuck to the safer territory of rights and dignity and chose not to engage with the 'cultural' debates. There was no knowing where the conservative forces on the other side of the legal debate might take the debates about culture, family etc.

Prior to the start of the High Court hearings, I remember the acute disappointment bordering on distress as we sat in a lawyer's office, seeking her advice on matters related to the case. The judges will not understand the language of queer, she said. We were already really pushing the boundaries, and it was not useful or necessary to push the boundaries in terms of language. It would be counterproductive. So we settled for LGBT+. Same-sex desiring people including those who identify as LGBT+ was clearly a tongue twister. But inconvenience was hardly the issue. It was about a paradigm, a language reflecting how we understood sexuality, desire, identities and politics. It was a big compromise to drop the language of queer symbolizing what it meant to seek legitimacy in the eyes of the law.

I recall another moment sitting in court, with the right wing, conservative forces on the left of the courtroom, marvelling and at the same time feeling shock and horror at how Mr. Malhotra, the lawyer representing the Home Ministry, was holding forth on the anus.[56] Explaining what the expression 'order of nature' in Section 377 meant, he said, 'for intercourse, nature has specified a place. That place is scientifically designed by nature. If it is done at that place, probably there is no injury, or if there is an injury, it is of minor nature.' He said that nature had devised scientific methods. 'You breathe through your nose, eat through your mouth. Similarly order of nature would mean that intercourse should be in the place specified by nature in all human relationships even among animals.' Mr. Malhotra noted that, 'In normal sex, man is required by law to have sex with one person. Now if they are having sex with hundreds of persons, two hundred, five hundred even more, it's more likely to transmit disease.'

His views were echoed by Mr. Sharma, the lawyer representing B.P. Singhal, the ex BJP MP whom Mr. Sharma described as a social worker representing the matter so that it is seen as the majority view. Mr. Sharma stated that the 'physiology of every organ has a special purpose and that the anus was only for excretion, and no other purpose. The ejaculatory ducts were meant for the carrying of semen and that there were no such muscles in the anus. In the science of sexual physiology and anatomy, it is completely logical that intercourse is heterosexual and any other way of releasing semen is unnatural.'

I was struck by the ease with which the lawyers representing the opposition were being able to talk about the anus, the body and sex while our arguments were strictly couched in the language of rights and dignity and sexuality with no reference to the body. Truly, we had to be disembodied in order to ask for rights.

In the legal realm, we could not engage more with interpretations of what construes the 'natural'. In popular discourse, including in discussions or arguments with friends and family, or in the media, queer individuals and activists often settle for agreeing or asserting that 'homosexuality' is 'as natural' as 'heterosexuality'. This assertion seeks sameness to make a claim for equality. There was no scope to further articulate that no phenomena are natural and that sexuality, including homosexuality, is no exception. We did not engage with the Voices senior lawyers much on this issue. Justice Shah, who in other respects has such a nuanced understanding, said during one of the hearings that homosexuality was 'by nature, and not by choice.' Shyam Divan was also of the opinion that homosexuality was as natural as someone who might have six fingers instead of five.[57] Clearly, the legal discourse does not easily lend itself to engaging with the bigger challenges.

The limits of the legal discourse were evident in other ways. Neither Voices nor the lawyers or the judges highlighted this as an intervention on behalf of organizations that represent different sections in society. The intersectionality inherent in the composition and work undertaken by Voices mattered less in the legal discourse as it did for large sections of the media too. This intersectional and non identity based nature of Voices assumed much more importance in the social and political realms of activism.

Conclusion

Although Voices was born in response to the Section 377 case, much of what we did was not about the law till we made a legal intervention in the case. Voices did of course contribute significantly to the historic victory, but there were other implications too. Implications for all the other work that we did as Voices, particularly in a context of the limited time and energy available to a non funded coalition without a formal structure.

The legal discourse, even though it is hugely and unarguably important, has its own logic and limitations. During the Delhi High Court petition, we did not have the choice to speak in any other language. Our lips were sealed even as the opposition held forth on what is normal and what is natural, marriage, family and what part of the body is designed for what sex act. We stayed strictly within the language of rights and dignity, although with tremendous imagination. The judges too stretched the limits of the rights discourse to the fullest in an awe-inspiring manner. It remained true however that to win the huge victory in the Delhi High Court, we had to be citizens worthy of respect and make peace with being limited to the identities of LGBT+ and not same-sex desiring or transgender. The language of sex and the body were not part of our interventions. We also had to contend with our ideas as expressed in the introduction to the Voices report not finding their way into the court.

> We live in a society that constantly tells us that there is only one kind of acceptable desire: heterosexual, within marriage, and male. Social structures further define and defend rigid notions of what it means to be a man or a woman, how the two should relate, and the family unit that should result. All those who dare to think outside this perfect ideal are considered threats to 'morality' and to society at large...Section 377...legitimises notions of what is 'natural' and 'normal', with a view to upholding institutions of heterosexuality and patriarchy such as marriage and the family in order to maintain the existing inequalities inherent in these systems.

Even as one wept with happiness, some questions remained. Why could we not address what is love, what is family, why marriage, why not the anus? Why did we 'have to' use the term LGBT+ instead of queer? Why did only those of us identified as LGBT+ speak to the press? Will Voices continue after the legal battles are over? These questions linger even as I wait, with anxiety, for the Supreme Court verdict.

POST THE SUPREME COURT JUDGMENT

I am beginning with reflections on the Supreme Court judgment in December 2013 and what followed. This is a later addition, but, needless to say a crucial one.

On 11 December 2013, the Supreme Court delivered its judgment on Koushal vs Naz, setting aside the Delhi High Court order of July 2 2009, which read down Section 377 to effectively decriminalize same sex acts in India. The Indian and global LGBT+ community, the government of India, and a majority of the Indian media were left in shock. Only the leading opposition party spoke up that day in favour of the Supreme Court verdict. The first thing I did that day was to go on to Facebook to rage at those LGBT+ people who had till then been supporting this opposition party, which openly targets religious minorities. I wanted them to know, ideologies of hatred don't spare any minorities. They too were in a state of shock that day.

Once the hysteria and anger settled into a calmer place in me, I began to feel that we could turn this judgment to our advantage. It had jolted the LGBT+ community, the anger had galvanized us, not least the younger ones for whom the Delhi High Court judgment had placed them in a different India to the one we grew up in, and who could not locate that victory in the history of activism and struggle for change. The other good change the SC judgment brought was the tremendous show of support across the board from different sections of society, like never before.

In later months, as we moved closer to the General Elections of 2014, for the first time, Indian political parties came out in open support for LGBT+ rights in their manifestos, without knowing what possible electoral gain or loss taking such a stand could bring. This solidarity by such powerful voices has been a tremendous shot in the arm for India's LGBT+ people. Whatever the SC judgment, for this community, there is no going back to the days before July, 2009.

One striking sign of this is the growing awareness and willingness within the LGBT+ community to organize on political lines. It is these elements that take me back strongly to the themes in the draft of the chapter on Voices against 377. One is the primary theme of the relationship between social and political activism and the law. The SC judgment illustrated starkly, the need for social and political activism. This was apparent to, as I mentioned above, the youngest and least politically aware members of the LGBT+ community. And the energy poured out and was focused in events like the Global Day of Rage across India and even other parts of the world. It relates to what I have argued that in our engagement with the law, we cannot and must not lose sight of social and political activism, because that is at the heart of all change and justice processes. The SC judgment is cruel evidence of that.

This is not to say that it is an either/or paradigm. I'm not arguing that it is only social and political activism that matters and that the law is irrelevant. In fact, the legacy of the Delhi High Court's judgment was palpable in the support that came pouring forth from many quarters after the Supreme Court judgment. The logic that the Justice Shah and Muralidhar had offered made a critical contribution to the framework and a basis on which people could not but support the LGBT+ community against the SC verdict.

This takes me to the second theme that the aftermath of the SC judgment evokes with respect to what I have written. And that is what all this has meant for intersectionality. As I stood there at the Global Day of Rage, it was surreal. There was Jagmati from AIDWA (All India Democratic Women's Association) talking about how when she left Punjab and the fight against the khap panchayat (in the Right to Choice the cases) to come to Delhi to take on a leadership role of AIDWA at the national level, she was relieved. But on her arrival in Delhi, she was welcomed by the Supreme Court judgment, she felt it was not that different from the khap panchayats she thought she had left behind.

The same AIDWA which had all those years ago, said 'come for the women's day rally but not to spell out the word lesbian in your banner'. The same AIDWA with whom we had engaged and engaged... there were magical moments in the rallies and protest of watching students from left linked political parties...of that particular body language, the way that the arm slices the air, that comrades from the left have, that oh so familiar tone and tenor of slogans which I have heard in rally after rally over the years, different slogans this time though, but the revolutionary passion in the sound of the slogans felt the same.

Never had the LGBT+ movement seen so much support from students groups affiliated with leftist parties in Delhi. And yet support is what it was; support 'for' LGBT+ people; not an alliance built on common cause. 'Reclaim the Republic' was an important event held on the 26th of January that was organised by queer activists in Delhi, to which a wide range of activists and movements were linked. And yet, the feeling I was left with was that here were supporters of the LGBT+ movement, not allies of the common cause for which I yearn. However, I'm not undervaluing their support.

For me, personally the sight of Kavita Krishnan, at protest after protest, event after event, was extremely reassuring; as was the sight of the hyper intellectual Shuddhabrata Sengupta from Sarai taking photographs at each of these gatherings. But the discomfort, the yearning for more remains. I'm not even sure I can articulate it, but when Arundhati Roy got up on stage at Reclaim the Republic event and said that she was proud to be among criminals, it was a strange moment. What she said was profound and smart, and yes I am proud to be a criminal, but there it was again, the othering. We were the criminals and who was she? With all the challenges that she poses to norms and to the law and the idea of the nation, was she not one of us, was she not a criminal too?

One thing about the progressive media that continued, was that the poor priest was lambasted once again on TV shows. Once again, we missed the opportunity to talk about the underlying issues of patriarchy; and the potential for understanding and engaging differently with ideas of the family and love. Perhaps we will never be able to have these dialogues in the mass media, not at least till the legal battle is hovering around us.

It seemed that the law had the power to take us to the heights of euphoria and then to smash us to the ground, or below. This resonated with what one of the lawyers closely involved with the case said to me in a conversation where we tried to make sense of what had happened. He said that while the Delhi High Court judgment was ahead of its time, the Supreme Court judgment was well behind the time. I completely agreed. And I feel the need to think through what that means for us as activists. One is that developments related to the law have the power to buffet us around. It also shows the need for activists to have a kind of *sthirta* (stability), in the middle of a gale.

This, in a sense, is what I heard my queer activist ex-partner say after innumerable, draining rounds of strategizing that she had been involved in, along with other queer activists. Should we go for this legal strategy or that? Analysis of the judges involved: 'What are they really like? Which way will they go?' And she said to me the other day, 'You know what? I'm fed up. I'm fed up with these discussions.' Even while she remains centrally engaged with the legal question, she has directed her energies to other activities that are happening within the LGBT+ movement in this very new phase post the Supreme Court judgment, like a meeting in Delhi with parents and family members of LGBT+ people; and an initiative to archive the numerous identities and terms that same sex desiring and gender transgressive people in the country use for ourselves. I feel this is the way forward. A continued engagement with the law, with a primary focus on social and political activism, and that is what has begun to happen.

Notes

1. (1999) Constituent Assembly Debates, Vol. 1, Lok Sabha Secretariat: New Delhi, pp 57–65.
2. Shalini is my colleague at Nirantar, a women's group that is part of the Voices Against 377 coalition.
3. For more about Voices Against 377, please see the website http://www.voicesagainst377.org/, accessed on 8 March 2014.
4. Jagori is a women's group that was part of the Voices coalition.
5. Saheli is a feminist collective that is part of the Voices coalition.
6. I am among the people and groups who set up Voices Against 377.
7. I have shared these reflections with fellow activists and colleagues in Voices to ensure they bear semblance to those tumultuous events. I would like to thank members of Voices for their inputs here. I would like to thank Sumit Baudh for sharing his article for the sections that relate to the law, Madhu Mehra from Partners for Law and Development (PLD) and Sunita Kujur from CREA. Many many thanks to Ranjana Padhi and also to Lesley Esteves who have both been members of Voices for editorial work on this chapter and to Ranjana a big thank you also for making the wonderful offer, in a context in which our busy lives have made such generosity almost extinct.
8. For the full text of Section 377, please see www.vakilno1.com/bareacts/indianpenalcode/S377.htm, accessed on 15 March 2014.

9. Jeffrey Weeks (2003), 'The Invention of Sexuality' in Robert Heasley and Betsy Crane (eds.), *The Invention of Sexuality in Sexual Lives: A Reader on the Theories and Realities of Human Sexualities*, Boston: McGraw Hill.

10. Versions of Section 377 exist or have done so in the laws of all countries that shared the legacy of British rule under the Commonwealth. In some countries, Section 377 continues to criminalise same-sex acts long after sodomy was decriminalised in Britain in 1967.

11. For details about the manner in which section 377 has been used in courts, please see A. Gupta (2006), 'Section 377 and the dignity of Indian homosexuals', *Economic and Political Weekly*, 4815 18 November.

12. Sexual violence within marriage is overlooked in the law. Despite the women's movement making this demand since years, marital rape is yet to be criminalised in the IPC.

13. Naz Foundation is an NGO working on HIV and AIDS and sexual health in Delhi.

14 . Men who have sex with men.

15. Lawyers Collective is a public interest service provider involved in human rights advocacy, legal aid and litigation.

16. The petition challenged Section 377's violation of four fundamental rights guaranteed by the Indian Constitution: the right to equality before the law (Article 14), since Section 377 discriminates against particular groups; the right to be free from sex discrimination (Article 15), since the law primarily targets homosexual sex; the right to fundamental liberties (Article 19); and the right to life and privacy (Article 21), since Section 377 imperils lives by impeding HIV prevention activities and intrudes upon the private consensual sex of adults. For further details please see Sumit Baudh (2013), 'Decriminalisation of Consensual Same-sex Sexual Acts in the South Asian Commonwealth: Struggles in Contexts' in Corinne Lennox and Matthew Waites (eds.), *Human Rights, Sexual Orientation and Gender Identity in The Commonwealth: Struggles for Decriminalisation and Change*, London: School of Advanced Study, University of London, pp. 287–311.

17. For more on this gender neutrality debate please see the following: Jaya Sharma and Dipika Nath (2005), 'Through the Prism of Intersectionality: Same sex sexualities in India' in Geetanjali Misra and Radhika Chandiramani (eds.), 2005. *Sexuality, Gender and Rights: Exploring Theory and Practice in South and Southeast Asia*, New Delhi: Sage Publications, as well as Naisargi N. Dave. 2012. *Queer Activism in India: A Story in the Anthropology of Ethics*, New Delhi: Zubaan.

18. Since 377 was a non-bailable offence, the health care workers were jailed for 48 days. For more details please see Human Rights Watch (year), *Epidemic of Abuse: Police Harassment of HIV/AIDS social workers in India*, New York: Human Rights Watch.

19. The National Democratic Alliance (NDA), a centre-right coalition of political parties in India, including those with Hindu fundamentalist ideologies, which was in power from 1998 to 2004.

20. For more details please see Bondyopadhyay, A.2004. 'A perspective from India: Homosexuality stands criminalized because of a mid 19th century colonial law', speech delivered at the International Panel Discussion: Breaking the 'Cultural' Straitjacket: Why Sexual Orientation and Gender Identity are Issues on the Global South's Agenda, Palais des Nations, Geneva, April 13. http://ilga.org/ilga/en/article/64, (accessed on 15 March 2014).

21. For more about the history of the 377 petition please see the Voices Against 377 website http://www.voicesagainst377.org/?page_id=140, accessed on 16 March 2014.

22. Voices Against 377 (2004), *Rights for All, Ending discrimination against Queer Desire under Section 377*, the English and Hindi versions of the report are available at https://docs.google.com/file/d/0BwDlipuQ0I6Zc0xXUzAyYkZqM2c/edit?usp=sharing&pli=1 and https://docs.google.com/file/d/0BwDlipuQ0I6ZZlJ0MEFvZVl3R0k/edit?usp=sharing&pli=1, accessed on 16 March 2014.

23. Articles in this report show how the law affects HIV and AIDS-related outreach and prevention efforts as well as how the law limits any effective work against child sexual abuse thus countering the myth that assertion of queer rights works against the rights of children. Another chapter looks at violations against queer people and how section 377 promotes homophobia in mental health spaces. The final section documents intersections with the women's movement and the human rights movements.

24. I would like to clarify that I don't suggest that this is a logical outcome of rejecting identity-based politics or the adoption of queer as language and approach. I'm merely reflecting on whether, when using broader, non identity-based approaches, particular care needs to taken to consider possible omissions, exclusions and marginalisation.

25. It was at first scheduled to take place at the British Council, but due to a last minute, unexplained cancellation by the British Council, it was held at an alternative venue. A protest letter was sent to British Council.

26. A representative of one of the autonomous women's groups in Voices prepared a brief presentation on why the issue of same-sex desire needed to be engaged with by women's groups. The response was fairly positive; however, no further dialogue took place.

27. Sama is an active part of the autonomous women's movement, the health movement and Voices Against 377.

28. The workshop was conducted in August 2004. Participants were from varied backgrounds – working on gender issues, women's health and rights, disability issues, reproductive health, rural technology, environment; working with

prisoners, tribals, adolescents and children. They included health activists, sexuality rights activists, lawyers, counsellors, clinical psychologists from organisations working on health issues from different states and regional and national networks.

29. PLD is a member of the Voices coalition. Each PLD workshop those days included a session dedicated to discussing Section 377 and the problems with it, leading to a discussion on sexuality as a ground of discrimination, after which participants would sign, write verses etc. on banners, which poured in from Ranchi, Bhawanipatna, Patna, Bodh Gaya etc.

30. Nighat Khan from ASR, Lahore, who had been a vital source of support to the couple, shared with Voices the details of the case and outlined the support that was needed.

31. Sangini is a Delhi-based helpline and support space for women who desire women.

32. In mid-April 2006, two Delhi-based women, Neha and Victoria, (names changed) contacted Sangini for assistance. As it turned out, they had confided in a colleague about their relationship. The colleague then told their employer, who sacked the older woman and informed the parents of the younger woman Neha about the relationship. Subsequently, the family kept her under virtual house arrest. Sangini managed to rescue her. Neha's family however continued to hound her and also abducted one of the workers of Sangini who was helping the women and took her to the police. Voices got involved in due course of time. A warrant of arrest had been issued against Victoria under Section 166 of IPC, which is a gender-specific law against abduction of a woman with intent to marry her. Voices organized financial support and became involved in planning the legal strategy to counter the charge of Section 166. An application was made to the magistrate's court under Section 164 that Neha is an adult woman who has left the family home of her own free will so there is no question of being abducted. However, the magistrate refused to entertain the application as she was not present in the court. She was in fact outside the court but was afraid to go in as her family was present in a 20–strong contingent. The lawyers said they were ready to produce her if the magistrate would entertain their sec 164 petition and hence provide her the protection of the court. The magistrate refused. The Magistrate recorded that it 'appeared prima facie that under the guise of the section there were hidden allegations of an offence under section 377 as well.' The investigating officer then said that if the victim left 'of her own free will', then she would no longer be a victim and both she and the other woman could be prosecuted under Section 377 IPC (a charge not present in FIR or charge sheet). The matter was then taken to the Delhi High Court.

Voices assumed responsibility for sheltering Neha in an undisclosed location because Neha's family was trying to find her, and she needed to be moved away from the Sangini space immediately. Voices members went to the Sangini space and spirited Neha out in the midst of their group, and took her to the undisclosed, new safe space, where she stayed till the resolution of the matter. Voices also explored the option of moving Neha to a women's shelter, but decided against it as there was no shelter which could be sympathetic to a same sex relationship case. Lawyer's Collective argued the matter before the Delhi High Court, which set aside the magistrate's order. This time, Neha was at the court, escorted by Voices members. Neha's family, also present, openly threatened and intimidated the Voices members. The FIR was finally quashed.

33. Eventually, an autonomous women's organisation, which is one of the Voices member organisations and routinely handles case intervention, took over the responsibility and costs of producing Manpreet at the court.

34. Manpreet came from a family where violence was an everyday affair. Even the 2-year-old grandchild was not spared. His bone was broken by his own father, who beat his mother every night when he was in the village. Manpreet and her mother were routinely assaulted by Manpreet's father.

35. Association for Advocacy and Legal Initiatives.

36. Pushkin Chandra and Kuldeep, who media reports said were 'homosexual' were killed on the night of August 13–14, 2004, at Chandra's residence at Anand Lok area in South Delhi.

37. The first open letter was signed by 'eminent citizens' such as Vikram Seth, Swami Agnivesh, Soli Sorabjee, Aditi Desai and Captain Lakshmi Sahgal. This letter was supported by an open letter by Amartya Sen, both in 2006. Another open letter was sent in response to a newspaper report 'Gays have no legal rights: ministry', Hindustan Times, 28 Aug 2008, in order to counter the myth that the case would endanger the rights of women and children. The signatories included almost 35 legal and human rights groups, women's groups, child rights groups, groups working on HIV and AIDS as well as health, LGBT+ groups and research organizations. .

38. The Consultation was organised prior to a meeting which focussed on legal issues, initiated by Naz Foundation and Lawyer's Collective.

39. Like all events conducted by Voices Against 377, this Consultation too was supported through finances raised by LGBT+ community groups and individuals, supportive groups and fundraising events.

40. The National AIDS Control Organisation is a statutory organisation under the Union Health Ministry.

41. LGBT+ activists across the country were seized with these developments. Being based in Delhi, the city in whose High Court the case was ongoing and with the possibility of access to some of the other players in the case such as the Ministry of Law or Health, LGBT+ activists from other parts of India urged Voices to intervene in the petition.

42. ALF is a space that integrates alternative lawyering with critical research, alternative dispute resolution, pedagogic interventions and more generally maintaining sustained legal interventions in various social issues. ALF is based in Bangalore.

43. The manner in which the Voices lawyer articulated the privacy issue was as follows. 'Matters involving the most intimate and personal choices that a person may make are central to the personal dignity and autonomy of the individual and are protected from unwarranted intrusion. At the heart of personal liberty is the right to seek and develop personal relationships of an intimate character.' Mr. Divan argued that the notion of autonomy extended beyond the spatial dimension. 'It projects beyond the home or the closet, since individuals to attain growth and fulfilment cannot be confined to such spaces,' he said.

44. The edited summaries of oral proceedings were originally posted by Siddharth Narain and are based on notes put together by lawyers representing Naz Foundation and Voices Against 377 and can be found on the Voices Against 377 website.

45. Siddhartha Gautam was a lawyer and human rights activist and worked on a variety of issues related to discrimination against vulnerable groups of people in India. He was one of the first people in India to talk about HIV and AIDS as a human rights issue.

46. The growing significance of identities and their assertions is not only a phenomenon in the realm of sexuality. We can see this with respect to other social and economic contexts as well, such as those related to caste, gender, age etc. A part of this phenomenon is the demand for recognition and to be visible on the part of those who have thus far been at the margins, such as sex workers, domestic workers and those who live with disabilities. Another factor contributing to the importance being placed on identities are priorities of donors and agencies that are working on particular issues. For example, the focus on the part of substantially funded agencies working on HIV and AIDS has enabled the emergence of HIV positive people's groups. Some activists and researchers (and those who straddle both these identities) have also argued that the manner in which 'kothis' have emerged as an identity and who the kothi refers to has been strongly shaped by the HIV and AIDS industry as it has operated in India. I am not arguing here that the emergence or assertion of identities is problematic. I am merely placing on board the observation that identities have acquired growing significance and that there are larger social, economic and political factors that influence these processes. Much more can be said on this issue, but this is not the place for further reflections on the issue of identity politics. This is in no way to deny agency on the part of the marginalized identities that have asserted themselves, nor the significance of the assertion of identities that have thus far been marginalized.

47. Mosse, George. 1985. 'Introduction: Nationalism and Respectability', 'Fascism and Sexuality' in *Nationalism and Sexuality: Middle-Class Morality and Sexual Norms in Modern Europe*. Madison: University of Wisconsin Press.

48. Nirantar is a feminist NGO which has been working in the area of gender and education since 1993 and is now also working on issues of sexuality.

49. I focus here on my knowledge of how being a member of Voices impacted Nirantar's own work. Being part of the organisation, I directly experienced the changes that it underwent.

50. For more details please see Jaya Sharma.2011. 'Bringing Together Pleasure and Politics: Sexuality workshops in Rural India', Practice Paper, London: Institute of Development Studies, January, available at http://www.ids.ac.uk/files/dmfile/Pp6.pdf, accessed on 18 March 2014.

51. *Naz Foundation v. Government of National Capital Territory of Delhi and Others*, judgment of Justice AP Shah and S Muralidhar JJ, of the Delhi High Court on 2 July 2009, 160 Delhi Law Times 277.

52. Decriminalizing Homosexuality in India, Geeta Mishra, in Reproductive Health Matters, 2009.

53. Panel discussion on Section 377 High Court Ruling, Indian International Center, New Delhi, 23 July 2009.

54. Shohini Ghosh is a Professor of Media, an essayist on popular culture and a documentary filmmaker.

55. For details regarding the case in the Supreme Court, to which High Court judgement was sent after being challenged upon the victory in the Delhi High Court, please see the Voices website, http://www.voicesagainst377.org/, accessed on 20 March 2014.

56. The following quotes were recorded as part of the summary of oral proceedings written by lawyers associated with Voices and can be found here http://www.voicesagainst377.org/?page_id=137, accessed on 20 March 2014.

57. Panel discussion on Section 377 High Court Ruling. Indian International Center, New Delhi, 23 July 2009.

TEN

Special Cells for Women and Children

Redefining the Scope and Strategies for Interventions in Violence Against Women

Anjali Dave, Yashoda Pradhan and *Taranga Sriraman*

Background

The Special Cell for Women and Children needs to be understood in the historical context of the Indian women's movement of the 1970s and 1980s, and of Mumbai as a city. These two decades saw a change in the broad agenda of the women's movement, the emphasis shifting from questions related to the promises of Independence, to a focus on women's oppression due to patriarchy and its manifestations in public policy and law. During these years, increasingly, violence against women became a central question for the movement and activists turned their attention to dismantling state patriarchy, finding the state's responses to questions of gender justice inconsistent (Basu, 1998).

The 1970s and 1980s saw a transformation in the urban landscape of Mumbai. The initial exponential growth of the textile industry led to considerable migration into the city, and as a result a great deal of urban expansion. Later, when manufacturing declined and there was mass unemployment, the city had to cope with a different reality. These two developments also had an impact on the women's movement in the city. Increasing numbers of cases of violence against women began to come to light. Media reporting on issues such as the open letter written by four lawyers to the Chief Justice of India protesting what they saw as a miscarriage of justice in the case of the rape, in police custody, of a minor tribal girl in Maharashtra, or on the publication of the report of the Committee on the Status of Women, kept the issue on the public agenda. Alongside these developments there were others: women in political parties and groupings were beginning to raise their voices against internal patriarchal practices. All of these factors came together and influenced women's mobilization on issues of violence against women. More cases of violence began to be reported and activists had to respond to these. Alongside, women in political groups and parties also began to raise their voices against resilient patriarchies within their institutions. This and many other local and international factors influenced the mobilization around issues of violence against women.

At the international level, the Convention on the Elimination of All Forms of Discrimination against Women (CEDAW) formulated objectives which were adopted in 1975 by the World Conference of the International Women's Year held in Mexico City. Thus, violence against women came to be an issue that attracted global attention during the mid-1970s.

In Mumbai, women mobilized across class and caste: activists came from urban, educated, middle class backgrounds, as well as from grassroots communities and from marginalized groups. A number of middle class women spoke out about the domestic violence they had experienced. As Aruna Burte puts it: 'They stated that unless there was external pressure such as effective laws, interventions by the police and social discrediting and ostracism of offenders, domestic violence would not stop' (Burte, 2008). Gaps in the functioning of the state machinery, such as in the work of the police and the courts, were identified and brought under public scrutiny. In 1974 women's groups came together to demand state action on the issue of custodial rape; this was one of the first large-scale public protests on violence against women. Concerted campaigning by women's groups resulted in the state taking cognizance of the recommendations and the demands for structural change made by the women's movement. Thus started the process of engagement between the women's movement and the criminal justice system (CJS); women felt the system must recognize the stark reality of violence on women in general and domestic violence in particular. It was within this larger socio-political- context that the Special Cell for Women and Children (hereafter Special Cell) was conceived, in 1984, as a collaborative effort of a social work educational institute, the police, state systems and women's groups.[3]

Preparing the Ground

The project for Women in Distress was conceptualised by Prof. Meenakshi Apte, then Head of the Department of Family and Child Welfare at the Tata Institute of Social Sciences (TISS), as a collaborative effort between academic-practitioners of social work, and the police. As the driving force behind the establishment of family courts in Mumbai and a member of several women's networks, Professor Apte brought together her experience as an interventionist working with the system and as a social work academic in TISS,[4] to the fore of public discourse and advocacy.

The rationale behind establishing the special cell was to provide immediate psycho-social and legal services to women and children survivors of violence at the police station. Addressing violence of any kind is a state mandate and hence, locating oneself in the police station proves to be a strategic vantage point for entry into the criminal justice system. Despite the existence of the Social Service Branch (SSB) at the office of the Commissioner of Police, social work academic-practitioners at TISS with expertise in working with women and children, found that the police officials/personnel with their training could not fully address the needs of the violated women. Hence, the need to have trained social workers located within the police station.

Social work is defined by the International Association for Schools of Social Work as '... the profession that promotes social change, problem solving in human relationships and the empowerment and liberation of people to enhance well-being.... Principles of human rights and social justice are fundamental to social work.'5 Thus in the context of working with the police and the criminal justice system, social work intervention is crucial to facilitating an effective response to VAW.

It is critical to note here that the criminal justice system and the police have historically been the subject of governmental control and have not been particularly receptive to the issue of violence faced by women – this is true of India as well as elsewhere. Hence, there continues to this day, within the larger women's movement/s at home and abroad, a debate on the practicality of working with male-dominated, patriarchal systems such as the criminal justice system and police. Can these systems ever respond effectively to the needs of violated women? This is more so as the experiences of women who approach the CJS are a testimony to the fact that the state actors often perpetrate further violence on the violated woman.

Therefore, the response from within the Maharashtra police to the idea of initiating a women-centred special cell within police stations was both rare and remarkable. It displayed the potential within the state administration/CJS to support the integration of women's concerns into existing governmental structures. Since the police system works on the principle of command and control, the approval of Mr. J. F. Rebeiro, the then Commissioner of Police, Mumbai, for initiation of the first special cell in the police commissionerate, was a critical step in the system's acknowledgment of the need for what is termed as multi-agency response to VAW today. The special cell started its work with two trained social workers in July 1984.

The support and enthusiasm from the top level of police administration opened the doors of the subsystems within the police. The special cell workers were granted permission to access records, police stations/officers and the office of the Commissioner of Police began referring relevant cases of VAW to the special cell, thus giving it visibility, legitimacy and credibility. This was followed by eventual expansion of special cells in other police stations across the city. This is detailed below.

Strategic Location within the Police System

The police station was chosen as a location to intervene in cases of violence against women and children, as this is usually the first institution where a violated woman goes to seek help. However, this was not all, harnessing police authority to help her access her legal and normative rights is also important. This can be done by enabling police authority to find those legal and procedural paths that will best suit the circumstances and protect the interests of the violated woman. Further, the fact that there is a special cell enables the police to recognize the issue of violence against women, including violence that occurs in familial (natal and matrimonial) and other intimate and significant relationships, as *crime*, in their daily practice. This orientation takes place at different levels of the police system: by sharing information, practice and experiences of police interventions and by disseminating research findings within the police system. Police help is also harnessed to discuss case specific laws, for the retrieval of *streedhan*, child custody and other relief which a victim-survivor/violated woman may want.

Thus, the special cell functions on the premise that the violated woman does not want to be isolated from the family and community, and hence, it is important for cell workers to facilitate dialogues to negotiate a violence-free future with other stakeholders in her life. The male perpetrators, especially, become a part of the dialogue and process at the special cell. The workers also reiterate, especially with the perpetrators, that violence against women is unacceptable. The special cell also works with the CJS to advocate for the rights of the violated woman for protection from violence.

Building a Feminist Perspective and Practice

The 'special cell ideology' is a term often used by special cell workers; this intervention grew from the feminist understanding that the personal is political. Hence, the entire perspective and practice built by the special cell rests on more than just an 'approach', and the programme and its functionaries practise the principle of self-determination in this respect as well, by using the term 'special cell ideology'. This includes work on the premises of feminist social work practice, which is process oriented and is committed to ensure that all women involved are engaged in constantly (re)shaping it. In other words, its value-base is egalitarian and democratic.[6]

As mentioned above, social work practice is where the special cell draws its values, perspectives and interventions from and this is the reason for engaging trained social workers to help survivors of violence live a violence free-life. Some key characteristics of social work practice as reflected in the special cell's own processes include:

- A human-centric approach and a belief that every individual has the capacity and potential to change.
- Practice/s built on the premise that a planned intervention can bring change—both individual and societal/structural.
- Commitment to the most marginalized in society.
- Adherence to principles of self-determination, acceptance and confidentiality while working with a survivor of violence.

The special cell's moorings in feminist understanding enable the combination of the above-mentioned aspects of social work praxis with a focus on structured/planned intervention.

'Feminist social work is a form of social work practice which takes women as its starting point for intervention and advocates social changes linked to advancing women's welfare.'[7] The amalgamation of social work praxis and feminist perspectives to work with the violated woman was developed here. The practices and principles applied at the special cell set the precedent for feminist social work practice while working to influence government systems or to work from within them.

This is not to say that the tools and techniques of a contextually-relevant feminist social work intervention were ready at the time special cells were thought of. The development of the tools, strategies and techniques of work with the violated woman and other stakeholders in her life was in itself a process that evolved over time as it grew in scale and intensity.

Strategically, the selection and training of qualified/professional social workers has been key to the success of the intervention. The special cells' unique location within the supportive but continually challenging setting of the police system required a team of individuals, not just skilled but also committed to facilitating and empowering both the individual and the system.

The selection of social workers, therefore, is a rigorous combing of candidates involving different levels of recruitment. Following selection, they are then introduced to the concepts of feminist praxis and the strategy of the special cell in an intensive three week long training programme, including a week of observation. This is followed up with regular, need based, refresher trainings.

Methods and Practices of Intervention

As mentioned above, the special cell's practice evolved over a period of time, and its many methods and techniques emerged from the needs of the violated woman who approached the cell. These methods and practices covered the following:

WORK WITH THE INDIVIDUAL VIOLATED WOMAN

Special cell practices are geared, as we have said, towards the empowerment of the woman. For instance, the assurance paper—a document written and signed by the violator in the presence of the cell worker, in the police-based location of the cell, assuring the violated woman a violence-free future, economic support or any other action that the woman wants—came into existence after the women requested the cell workers to get the male violator/s to keep to the assurance/s made during joint meetings. This does not mean that the special cell workers do not concern themselves with roles and responsibilities that are created through various familial relations, but they '…actively seek to go beyond this narrow approach to locate women within their broader social networks and ensure that women have access to the support and resources that ensure holistic well-being across the totality of their lives in a holistic manner.'[8]

A violated woman, on an average, comes to the special cell five to six times over a period of six months, and therefore it is essential to employ a multi-dimensional approach. During this crisis period, the special cell worker engages in developmental counselling. The worker provides the woman with emotional support and strengthens her psychological self, enabling her to build external support systems. The survivor is introduced to various forums and groups to facilitate self-reflection as well as to expand her social world. Emotional support is rendered by facilitating the woman's process of self-determination and by rebuilding her human dignity. The cell worker also builds a support system by facilitating legal services for the woman. Information regarding the criminal justice system and the police system is given to the survivor to develop her capacity to access the systems. Support systems are built by engaging the woman's capacities in other women's groups.

WORK WITH SYSTEMS, INCLUDING THE SOCIETAL CONTEXT AND STAKEHOLDERS

At the special cell, working with systems has emerged as an important area of work, as has working with survivors and perpetrators of violence. Workers in the cell are conscious of the constant interplay of power within the patriarchal structure and therefore they understand the importance of recognizing and consistently and strategically challenging it. They understand that it is because of the way power plays out in a patriarchal society, that women are deprived of access to resources and opportunities, 'The pro-woman perspective within which the Special Cell intervenes recognises that the violated woman is not responsible for the violence inflicted on her, and that within a patriarchal society, the misuse of power by men makes her vulnerable to and a victim of violence.'[9] Hence, VAW is not a 'private' matter and is an issue that needs to be addressed in the public domain. This is why the special cell workers also organize and engage in programmes to increase awareness on issues of VAW, as well as critical consciousness on gender and gender-based discrimination and violence for various stakeholders.[10] Such programmes form a part of the core work of the special cell.

WORK WITH MEN

While the special cell strategically adopts a framework protecting the best interests of women for its intervention/s on VAW, the programme's own work has, from the very beginning, included working with men. This has emerged from the expressed need of several of the women approaching the special cells, who wished to renegotiate existing relationships for a violence-free domestic life. For this the special cell worker may undertake efforts to counsel the men and facilitate behavioural changes, so as to protect the interest of the violated woman. Apart from this, the special cell interacts with, and works to transform attitudes and behaviours of various hegemonic patriarchal, justice giving institutions (such as the courts, as well as the police and administrators of shelter homes).

COORDINATION WITH MULTIPLE AGENCIES

The cell is also a crisis intervention centre and so it has to network with shelter homes, hospitals and other such institutions. It works in close contact with other organizations to enable the process of empowerment for the woman. The special cell workers, coordinators and the coordinating agency, TISS, are all involved in evolving advocacy plans and work with the system in different ways, at different levels. However, it is the trained worker at each special cell unit who is the pillar of the programme. The following listing helps understand the design of the intervention through its linkages and work carried out on various fronts by each special cell worker.

- Work with violated women including provision of professional quality psycho-socio-legal services;
- Work with men in society, including men as members of families of violated/at-risk women, communities and government systems and structures;
- Work with the community as a larger entity, including other stakeholders in intervening/responding to VAW on the ground. These include civil society organizations, community elders/bodies, local self-governance institutions such as

panchayats, and traditional/informal bodies such as the caste panchayats[11] and jamaats;[12]
- Work with families as part of the larger community;
- Work with support systems of legal aid, shelter homes, health, education and livelihood interventions for the violated woman, and more recently with the protection system under the Protection of Women from Domestic Violence Act (PWDVA) 2005; and work with the CJS (including the law and courts) as well as the police.

The Expansion of Socio-Legal Services for Violence against Women

Once it was established that the special cell is an effective strategy for intervention on the issue of VAW, the Maharashtra police were willing to increase the outreach and the cell was expanded to two additional locations in Mumbai: Dadar (1988) and Kandivli (1994) police stations.

With consistent efforts from the Tata Institute of Social Sciences and the support of UNIFEM, the Department of Home and the Department of Women and Child Development of the Government of Maharashtra took over the special cell model in 2005, and made it into a grant-in-aid programme. This was an important development as it established the issue of VAW as a concern to be addressed by the state. In 2011, the collaboration that once started with an academic institution and the police department was also brought under the purview of the State Women's Commission for monitoring and technical support.

Currently, the special cell has expanded to various police stations in Mumbai as well as in districts across the state of Maharashtra. In 2002 cells were set up in seven new districts including Navi Mumbai, Pune, Yavatmal and Aurangabad. In 2003, cells were started in Nasik, Wardha and Nanded. As of 2012, there are 39 special cells within the state and another 100 sanctioned; three in each district to be located at the block level.

The special cell has been replicated as a pilot initiative in other states such as Andhra Pradesh, Madhya Pradesh, Uttar Pradesh and Delhi, and has been accepted as a state programme in Rajasthan, Haryana, and Odisha.

Many innovations have taken place through the flexibility of replication and expansion processes. For instance, in Haryana, special cells have been set up in the police stations, and workers have been appointed to work as Protection Officers under the provisions of PWDVA and The Prohibition of Child Marriage Act (PCMA) 2006.[13] These officers work with the assistance of a multipurpose worker and a data entry person.

The Experience and the Learning

It has been twenty-nine years since the special cell was initiated in Maharashtra and the learnings have been many. These have helped formulate strategies to address VAW and are as follows:

THE IMPORTANCE OF WORKING WITH THE STATE

Engaging with the state is essential and is necessary for social change. Article 37 of the Directive Principles of the State Policy states that the application of the principles '...shall be the duty of the State'[14] and Article 38 (1) holds that 'the State shall strive to promote the welfare of the people by securing and protecting as effectively as it may a social order in which justice, social, economic and political, shall inform all the institutions of the national life.'[15] It is thus evident that it is the state's mandate to promote and ensure a life free of violence for its citizens and by situating itself within the state system, the special cell works for and advocates this goal. Only the state is equipped to scale up an intervention through which an ideology and perspective is also spread, on the issue of VAW. Hence, the special cell's original belief of the criticality of engaging with the state and working with/in the system to forward the feminist agenda of responding effectively to VAW, has only been strengthened by the scale of outreach and impact that has been achieved over the decades.

BEING EMBEDDED IN SOCIAL WORK ACADEMIA

The special cell came into existence as a result of feminist discourse within and around social work and in academia, on social issues and activism. Thus it has always associated itself with the causes and concerns of the women's movement. The Criminal Justice System is historically resistant to this particular type of ideological mooring and does usually pose a challenge for feminist interventionists across all pursuits (not only VAW per se, but also health, livelihoods, etc.) However, because the special cell emerged out of a prestigious academic institution founded on values of dignity, equality and social justice, the special cell model was able to overcome the resistance.[16] The TISS, in itself, has chosen *not* to limit itself to a traditionally benign notion of social work education, but to take on the broader onus to leverage its expertise to advocate and consistently work to influence state systems/the police and the bureaucracy. New strategies and intervention techniques were also applied in accordance with the evolution of social work practices, although the learning, unlearning and reworking of these have been possible solely due to the direct work with survivors of violence.

SUPPORT FROM MULTIPLE STAKEHOLDERS

The special cell has experienced the advantages of having allies within the system as well as being able to leverage power from outside it. The combination of belonging to the women's movement as well an academic institution helped the programme to remain true to its ideological premises. The special cell demonstrates on a day-to-day basis how action and reflection can be combined within a feminist framework

The experience of the special cell also shows that when the state is open and willing to work with its citizens, and if there is support from a team of dedicated personnel this can result in successful tackling of an issue such as violence against women in a transformative manner, something that is beneficial both for the individual and society.

The collaborative process between an academic institution, the criminal justice system and the state has helped survivors of violence to lead violence-free lives. It has also led to the integration of social services within the police system for the violated woman, as a joint programme of the Department of Home, which provided infrastructure/location, crisis support etc., and the Department of Women and Child Development (DoWCD) which provided administration and funding support. Thus, even within the state, a unique alliance was formed and inter-development/convergence of a new kind has taken place, wherein various departments and their specific sub-systems (police and State Women's Commission, respectively) are actively part of monitoring and support for integration and sustainability of feminist social work praxis. This convergence has led to a collective system, thinking and actions, making it a strategic alliance that the special cell has built through continuous and simultaneous engagement with all governmental stakeholders. The acceptance and integration within the state system is not only at the official level, but exists in the practical, 'everyday' aspects as well.

According to an evaluation report of the special cell conducted in 2004, 94.7 per cent of the police personnel who worked in the same police station as the special cell affirmed the need for its services.[17] This indicates that the police has accepted, appreciated and acknowledged the need for such a strategy. This is also confirmed by the 84.2 per cent police personnel who referred cases to the cell.[18]

The cell therefore shows the importance of a formal systemic response to violence against women. The creation of the role of the Protection Officers under the Protection of Women from Domestic Violence Act, 2005 is an outcome of the work of the special cell in recognition of the intensive process work that is required to support a survivor of violence through facilitating both formal and informal systems of justice.

Work within male-dominated and patriarchal structures such as the criminal justice system requires persistent reiteration of the pro-woman approach and the feminist perspective. The fact that the special cell has been replicated, expanded and institutionalised in other states is proof of its relevance and success.

Challenges and Limits

Some challenges and limitations in the replication, expansion and institutionalisation process are also listed and discussed here:

1. With expansion and institutionalization, some state governments have seen fit to make changes that affect the principles of the special cell model. Maintaining the core ideology, processes and structure is far easier in the initial stages/pilot phase, but as the programme expands and a larger number of government departments are involved, the technical support role of TISS as the ideational source institution for the entire state/country recedes and gets somewhat restricted. For example, in Haryana, ten out of twenty PPOs (cell workers) appointed at the beginning were trained lawyers as per the state DoWCD's perception of the legal mandate under the PWDVA 2005; the other half were trained social workers. Similarly, in recent years, the Maharashtra state DoWCD has funded the special cell programme as a 'franchised', grant-in-aid scheme where local NGOs are involved in the implementation of the cells in various districts. In both these cases, it has been difficult for the coordinating and technical support agency to ensure the requisite standardisation of quality of services provided to women in the cells. However, advocacy (on the basis of existing work and impact related documentation, evaluation and research) by TISS and the special cell programme ensured maintenance of the core work of the cell. The DoWCD, Government of Haryana, has now sanctioned the appointment of trained social workers as additional Protection Officers in each district-level cell. In Maharashtra, the judiciary and the state departments are considering standardising the programme through establishment of a uniform system of coordinated, (at state and regional levels) comprehensive programme management that also allows greater autonomy, as against the existing

piecemeal system of direct grants to small NGOs – a system that does not allow uniformity of training and monitoring of programmes.

2. Pilot demonstration of special cell units on a small to medium scale (one to three units at police stations/district SPs' offices) requires the specific support of the police department itself, as well as funding support. However, the process of expansion and institutionalisation (the latter in particular) as a scheme jointly supported by both Home and DoWCD of the state government takes much longer and requires a multi-pronged strategy. The time and place of this phase of work is also largely dependent on the socio-political-economic milieu of the particular state/region, and how the state government/ administration has historically viewed/related with civil society actors (especially organizations and women's groups). Thus, awareness of this limitation is a key factor to be kept in mind while planning the programme design and building partnerships with pilot supporting donor agencies.

3. Following from the above, the dynamics between state departments and their willingness to work together on VAW need to be assessed and worked upon/with during the process of institutionalisation of the special cell in the state. Considering the state's historical slowness of pace to accept the existence of VAW, especially DV (domestic violence), there is increasing withdrawal of the state from actual implementation (not funding, necessarily in policing/CJS) and the public sphere, even though the state is mandated to respond to the issue on the grounds of women's citizenship and the country's own global membership. Also, different governmental departments have different levels of willingness to adopt or even consider feminist social work praxis within their implementation structures.

4. Departmental structures and personnel (including officials) at sub-state (i.e. regional, district, block and sub-block levels), as well as other community-level stakeholders/civil society actors need to be constantly networked with in terms

of awareness and sensitisation for effective coordinated functioning. The quantum of this work also increases with the expansion of the programme into newer centres/areas, and dealing with newer kinds of violence against women and children. Key challenges faced on the ground by cell workers also include the general lack of awareness among many influential stakeholders about the PWDVA 2005 and the PCMA 2006, women's and child rights, VAW, DV, the special cell programme, and so on. In this context, it is essential to constantly keep creating platforms for dialogues in conference-cum-workshop mode, perhaps on scale for officials of various levels of police, the Health Department, the Department of Legal Affairs, the Department of Social Welfare and the Education Department, judicial magistrates, as well as other stakeholders (other civil society organizations, community bodies, and so on) to encourage appropriate referrals of cases to the special cells as well as to increase actual reporting of ongoing VAW and child marriage in particular.

5. In newer states where the model has been replicated and expanded, there has been some difficulty in moving beyond addressing only cases of DV. In the context of feudal history and social/gender discrimination and the violence-filled milieu of most states in the country, it is all the more pertinent for the special cell programme to address the larger ambit of VAW perpetrated consistently by/upon women by local communities (especially their own natal communities of caste/clan and village). Hence, cell workers also need refresher training in both perspectives and skills to re-strategize and begin to respond to the more widespread VAW within local and natal communities in particular.

6. Due to the power differentials that exist within government departments and government and civil society organizations, inter-departmental work becomes a challenge.

7. It has been the Institute's (TISS) objective, to build perspective and capacities of academic/research institutions in other states where the cells are being set up and institutionalized.

However, there has been extremely limited progress towards the larger goal of informing social work education on feminist praxis models, approaches and methods, as well as creating more contextually rooted knowledge partners for the DoWCD and the programme in the long term.

Conclusion

In conclusion, it is important to reiterate that while the special cell for women and children remains the only feminist praxis of its kind in India, it also remains caught at the heart of the continuing debate within the women's movement and in general, on the efficacy and practicality of working with the CJS on an issue that requires specialized skills, nuanced understanding and strong sensitivity and belief in women's right to a violence-free life that goes beyond theory and into practice.

Not undermining the challenges that have been faced and continue to be faced in working with the duality of the hegemonic and patriarchal state which does not truly practise liberal, egalitarian principles enshrined in the Constitution, the special cell has demonstrated the need to persist in working with the duality-as well as the potential for building successful strategic alliances. This in turn, it is hoped, will feed back into the need to come together to discuss strategies for advocating establishment of a 'social infrastructure' for delivery of socio-legal services to (in)justice survivors.

Notes

1. The *Towards Equality* report (1974), was prepared by the government-appointed Committee on the Status of Women in India. The report was a historic landmark when it was first published in 1974.
2. Mathura, a minor tribal girl, was raped in police custody in Maharashtra. The Supreme Court rejected her contention that she had not consented, and had in fact resisted the rape, naming her as a 'shocking liar'. Four law professors – Upendra Baxi, Lotika Sarkar, Raghunath Kelkar of Delhi university and Vasudha Dhagamwar of Pune University – wrote an open letter to the Chief

Justice of India, pointing out the flaws and patriarchal/class bias in the judgment. This is discussed in greater detail in the article by Madhu Mehra in this volume.

3. 'Arising from activist perspectives and commitments, and catalyzed by an academic institution and School of Social Work, it has developed systematically over the years, steered by feminist and women's activists, some of whom lay claim to the term "feminist", and some who do not' (Dave, in press; Special Cell, 2004; see also Jung Park [with Peters & De Sa], 2000). The special cell developed, then, out of activism in India although—vitally—it was facilitated, resourced, and encouraged throughout by the TISS, without whom it would not have existed. TISS gave institutional academic support, which facilitated the project in gaining further resources that would not have been as easily accessible to a women's NGO on its own.' Gill Hague, 2013. 'Learning From Each Other: The Special Cell and Domestic Violence Activist Responses in Different Contexts Across the World,' *Violence Against Women* (Sage Publications Journal) published online 20 October (viewed on 30.10.2013, at http://vaw.sagepub.com/content/early/2013/10/18/1077801213506286.full.pdf+html).

4. The Tata Institute of Social Sciences (TISS) was originally established as the Sir Dorabji Tata Graduate School of Social Work in 1936, hence social work education has remained the Institute's first and core priority. In 1988, the Institute had already held the status of Deemed University under the UGC for 24 years. As a pioneering academic institution for social work education (eventually expanded to the social sciences) its work was never limited and hence also included 'social intervention through training and field action projects, and contribution to social and welfare policy and programme formulation at state, national and international levels'. Widening its academic ambit to the social sciences also strengthened the advocacy ambit of the Institute correspondingly, and its acceptability as a negotiator for policy and/or strategy design/change with the state also only grew.

5. http://www.iassw-aiets.org/index.php?option=com_content&task=blogcategory&id=26&Itemid=51.

6. Dominelli.L.1998. p. 919.

7. Ibid, p. 918.

8. Ibid, p. 918.

9. Special Cell for Women and Children, Mission Statement and the Monitoring Indicators for Special Cell for Women and Children (2004), p. 10.

10. Women, police, CBOs, other interventionists and Government officials.

11. Personal issues related to family and community norms are settled by the caste panchayats, all male bodies who adjudicate on matters related to divorce, dowry, harassment etc.Women are not represented in these highly patriarchal bodies and do not benefit from its verdicts.

12. In several parts of India, personal issues within the Muslim community are settled by the local Jamaat – an all-male body attached to a mosque which

applies Sharia law to adjudicate on matters related to divorce, dowry, harassment, domestic violence, and custody. As the traditional belief system does not allow women to enter mosques, they are not represented or heard during deliberations by the Jamaat.

13. The PWDVA 2005 requires Protection Officers to be appointed as part of its implementation machinery. Similarly the PCMA 2006 warrants the appointment of Prohibition Officers to implement the provisions of law. These posts are crucial for an effective implementation of the laws.
14. http://www.constitution.org/cons/india/p04037.html, referred on 17 September 2012.
15. Ibid.
16. http://www.tiss.edu/TopMenuBar/about-tiss/vision-mission.
17. V. Apte (2004), p. 58.
18. Ibid.

References

Apte, V. 2004. Report of the evaluation study of Special Cell for Women and Children within the Maharashtra Police System, for the period of January to December 2003, Mumbai: Tata Institution for Social Sciences.

Basu, A. 1998. 'Appropriating Gender' in P. Jeffery. and A. Basu (eds.). *Appropriating Gender: Women's Activism and Politicized Religion in South Asia*, New York: Routledge, pp. 3–14.

Burte, A., 2008. *Breaking the Culture of Silence: Uniting to Fight Domestic Violence*, Mumbai: CEHAT.

Dave, A. and Dharmadhikari, A. 1987. Working with the Establishment: A New Challenge, *The Indian Journal of Social Work*, Vol. XLVIII, No. 3, 315–323.

Dave, A. and Solanki, G., 2001. *Journey from Violence to Crime: A Study on Domestic Violence in the City of Mumbai*, Mumbai: Tata Institute of Social Sciences.

Dominelli, L. 1998. 'Feminist Social Work: An Expression of Universal Human Rights', *Indian Journal of Social Work*, Vol.59 (4), 917–929.

Definition of Social Work, IASSW. 2014. available online at http://www.iassw-iets.org/index.php?option=com_content&task=blogcategory&id=26&Itemid=51, accessed on 25 November.

Ganesh, I.M. 2008. *Next Steps: Taking the Special Cell Process Ahead*, Mumbai: Tata Institute of Social Sciences.

Hague, G. 2013. Learning From Each Other: The Special Cell and Domestic Violence Activist Responses in Different Contexts Across the World, *Violence Against Women* XX (X), 1–22 (Sage Publications Journal, published online 20 October 2013 DOI: 10.1177/1077801213506286, available online at http://vaw.sagepub.com/content/early/2013/10/18/1077801213506286.full.pdf+html, accessed on 30 October 2013.

Madhu, P. 2005. Towards a Praxis of Social Work: A Reflexive Account of 'Praxis Intervention' with the Adivasis of Attappady, (Unpublished Thesis), Kottayam: School of Social Sciences, Mahatma Gandhi University, available online at http://www.google.com/url?q=http://habituspraxis.sprinterweb. net/praxisintervention.pdf&sa=U&ei=hYlzUuj3EIGRrQeZ2YHwBw&ved= 0CCwQFjAE&usg=AFQjCNHxXhvY3mVX2Sfgx5mvzGqoOCKW6g, accessed on 1 November 2013.

Special Cell for Women and Children. 2004. *Mission Statement and the Monitoring Indicators for Special Cell for Women and Children* Mumbai: Tata Institute of Social Sciences.

The Twentieth Century. 1995. *Mumbai Pages* available online at http://theory.tifr. res.in/bombay/history/c20.html, accessed on 6 August 2012.

Vision and Mission of the Tata Institute of Social Sciences. available online at http://www.tiss.edu/TopMenuBar/about-tiss/vision-mission, accessed on 21 September 2012.

ELEVEN

Domestic Violence

Women-Centred Approaches and the Need for Feminist Counsellling

Sangeeta Rege and *Padma Deosthali*

Introduction

The psychological perspective on domestic violence in the Western world has largely viewed women who have faced violence through a bio-medical approach. (DSM–IV (2000) 4th rev. ed.) The premise was that violence was triggered because of some kind of lack in the woman. This could range from problems in adjusting to the marital home, an inability to perform gender-ascribed roles laid out for women, their so-called impulsive behaviour, their irrational expectations, their sexual coldness and more. Such an approach continued to view violence against women as a result of the intra-psychic make-up of women.

Feminists across the world have been strongly critical of this approach as it blames women for the violence they face, and expects them to adjust to the home environment and even conform to traditional norms in order to maintain the institution of family and/or marriage. Victim blaming was common in the traditional counselling approach. As against this approach, a feminist perspective in counselling is premised on the belief that it is essential to explore external and contextual factors that contribute to problems, thus making the connection between the personal and the political.

In feminist counselling the counsellor is aware of the socio-economic-political and cultural context, as well as the patriarchal norms within which women live and the myriad ways in which these influence and impact women's physical, mental and emotional health. This understanding of the environment is critical in helping women rebuild their lives.

Our essay discusses the need for a feminist perspective in developing domestic violence response interventions. It highlights the contribution of the women's movement vis-à-vis feminist values and beliefs and describes emerging feminist practices prevalent in the country over three decades. It speaks of the contribution made by the women's movement in India with respect to the beliefs and principles underlying feminist perspectives in responding to women facing domestic violence and the ways in which organizations over the past two decades have built on those principles. We also make a case for the need to follow standards in counselling women who face domestic violence and we provide basic steps in regulating the counselling practices of organizations.

A Brief History of Feminist Counselling

Countries of the West have contributed in major ways to feminist counselling. Some of the early insights on ways in which women cope with domestic violence came from Lenore Walker (1974–1980). Though the theory 'battered women syndrome' was later critiqued for being too exclusive in defining the 'victim' of domestic violence, it brought to light the circumstances of abuse and how women deal with it. The theory attempted to reject gender stereotypes and questioned power imbalances. (Walker, 1979) Feminist psychitarists and mental health professionals in Western countries heavily critiqued the bio-medical approach used by mental health professionals and simulatenously contributed to the formulation of different feminist intervention models to effectively respond to women facing abuse (Worell and Pamela, 2003; Chaplin, 1998).

The trajectory of the formulation of feminist interventions was very different in the Indian context. It was the second wave of the

Indian women's movement that brought forth the issues of oppression faced by women within their homes. Different forms of protests by activists in the movement enabled women to come out in the open and question inequality, discrimination as well as the violence faced by them. While more and more women started speaking out against abuse at the hands of their families, the movement realized the need to create spaces for responding to individual women. In India, the women's movement was critical of psychiatric and psychological counselling for survivors of violence (Vindhya U, 2013). Activists critiqued how psychiatry medicalised women who faced abuse and made efforts by reaching out to survivors at an individual level. Providing alternatives such as shelter in their own houses, legal and emotional support was consistently done by those from within the movement. The principle 'personal is political' was discussed with them to help them recognize that if so many women faced abuse, it could not be an individual and isolated problem. Such consciousness raising efforts were made by activists for over a decade in order to change the power relations between men and women. These strategies aimed at taking away the aspect of shame from survivors of abuse and drove home the point that women face violence as a result of power structures, especially patriarchy, that allow those in power to inflict abuse. However much of the movement's energy from the eighties to the nineties was focused around awareness and mobilization on the issue of violence and abuse and not on creating models for psychological counselling.

The early nineties saw the growth of non-governmental organizations, organized funding sources and concerted efforts to respond to violence faced by women in their private lives. Most of these new and evolving organizations were dissatisfied with institutionalized hierarchies and rejected the traditional and formal structures. They created alternate structures based on principles of decentralization and collective participation. Just as women's groups had started formalising their initiatives, they had to struggle against getting co-opted by the government and fundamentalist lobbies which had appropriated the language of the movement. Fundamentalist groups and organizations providing counselling to women facing domestic violence did not place the issue of violence in the context of power and control, but rather applied the notion that the family as a unit had to be preserved at any cost. This implied that women would be asked to change their behaviour and adjust, something they believed would stop violence. Further women who were tolerant of abuse were also glorified and premium value was placed on gendered characteristics such as being tolerant, adjusting and so on. These practices were challenged by the women's movement. Despite these challenges, feminist principles such as the validation of women's experiences, belief in women's agency and the capacity to make independent decisions, also encouraging women to take steps to stop abuse, continued to be central to services being provided by feminist organizations to respond to domestic violence. (Kumar, 1993)

Most organizations/groups of the seventies and eighties were involved in political activity related to creating awareness on the issue of violence against women. Methods such as protest marches, pamphlet distribution, picketing, street plays were implemented to bring the issue of violence against women out of the closet. Slowly this awareness led women to approach groups/organizations and individuals from the campaign. Around this time, a need for setting up counselling services and shelter spaces was felt and many of these groups worked out of the homes of volunteers or makeshift offices. As the number of women approaching groups/organizations grew, volunteers and activists struggled to ensure that women were supported and that the campaign to end violence against women continued. An additional constraint was that most groups were volunteer based and sought no funding whatsoever. Despite a rich body of experience within women's groups, not much has been documented of the actual counselling or support services provided by them.

At CEHAT (Centre for Enquiry Into Health and Allied Themes), we documented different feminist intervention strategies in domestic violence responses from the inception of the women's movement to record the varied efforts made by activists in reaching out to women facing domestic violence. (Bhate-Deosthali, Rege and Prakash, 2013) This essay draws upon these documented practices.

Early Feminist Interventions

The early eighties were marked by intense protests and action, as well as raising awareness by women activists on the issue of violence, more specifically domestic violence. Awareness building in the community often involved drawing attention to popular myths about women in street plays and performances and then using law, fact, and evidence to refute them. At some point women activists began to feel the need to go beyond protesting against the state or making demands of it and pushing for changes in the law. It was also important to focus on the individual situation of women. Protests were often reactive, and took place only when a certain incident had taken place. By then, the harm had been done. It was thus that activists began to think of setting up direct services for women victims and survivors of domestic violence. Organizations and groups such as Vimochana, Saheli, Stree Sangharsh, Jagori, Karmika, Awag and Sahiyar were some of the first ones to set up services at the level of the community.

Reaching out to women and intervening in individual cases of women facing domestic violence stemmed from the belief that activists too are from the same social milieu and thus even they are not protected from the experience of being abused. Hence there was always a very thin line between those who sought services to deal with the abusive situation and those who provided support. Most of these groups did not call their interventions 'counselling' at that point because counselling was a term derived from the discipline of psychology, and most mental health professionals invariably ended up pathologizing women instead of seeing women's response to the situation of abuse as a way of coping with abuse.

The nature of interventions in the eighties included listening to women's narrations and validating their experiences. Interventions did not always have a single counsellor and a single client but sometimes the discussions would take place in groups. The idea was to enable women to not feel that they were to blame and to remove the shame at being abused and place the onus of abuse on the person who abused them. The objective of these interventions was not just to enable the woman to question the abuse in her life, but to ensure that she also became an advocate and could provide similar support to others facing abuse. The personal disclosure of abuse was used as a method to enable other women to deal with similar situations in their lives. 'Sisterhood' was a powerful and constantly used slogan to unite women against abuse.

Though women's groups made several demands of the state, asking for shelter services, improved laws to deal with violence against women, creche facilities for children of working women and so on, they knew too that it would take time for these to be put in place. Given this, the groups developed several innovative methods of dealing with abuse. Saheli, for example, set up a people's committee comprising of well known and respected members of the community who could hold the abuser accountable for his actions. Vimochana and Jagori engaged in dialogue with natal families who were reluctant to support their daughters facing violence in marital homes and Sahiyar created a structure of support at the level of the community to protect women against abuse. This meant that specific people from the community would be located and they would then help women at the receiving end of abuse. (Rege and Chandrasekhar, 2013)

Responding to Domestic Violence in Rural Settings

Efforts to respond to domestic violence were not restricted to urban areas. In fact in the eighties, organizations such as Vanangana in Uttar Pradesh and Masum in Maharashtra to name only two, initiated efforts to respond to domestic violence. Vanagana recognized caste and the feudal system as additional axes of discrimination. Women from marginalized castes often had to travel for hours to fetch water because they were not allowed access to water from the village tank or well. While challenging the feudal power structure in rural settings, Vanangana also equipped women with technical skills of building and using hand pumps. Vanangana's active presence in the rural areas also worked as an enabling factor and gradually women started to talk about their personal lives with activists from the organization. This prompted Vanagana to respond to domestic violence. While doing so, there was also a realization that women from the marginalized castes, especially Dalit women, needed to build leadership skills to unite against abuse from upper castes as well as provide support to each other in situations of domestic violence. Vanagana's consistent work in Uttar Pradesh led to the formation of Dalit Mahila Samiti, an organization of rural Dalit women.

Masum is another organization where the founder members moved from a city base to a rural drought prone area. One of the biggest problems for communities in this area was access to health care. Masum engaged in extensive discussions with women and men from the community to identify health care issues. *Dais* (midwives) and rural women were trained to look into health aspects connected to women's lives, whether these were gynaecological issues or reproductive health issues. Through a process of engagement, women started sharing histories of abuse faced by them and Masum helped women to make connections between violence and its impact on their health. Masum firmly believes that women from the community can be trained to provide support to each other. Several of the organization's programmes, such as the right to health care, and support services to deal with domestic violence are led by rural women who are trained to respond to these issues.

Specialized Feminist Counselling Services

By the late eighties, the women's movement had succeeded in putting in place some reforms in the legal system. An important development was the establishment of family courts. Setting up of family courts gave women the assurance that they could access a more 'approachable' formal structure to seek redress in situations of domestic violence. The mandate of such courts was that they have a gender sensitized judiciary with an understanding of the issue of violence against women. It was during this period that Section 498A Indian Penal Code (IPC), a provision in the criminal law that enabled women to file a criminal complaint in cases of domestic violence, was brought in. This law established and named domestic violence as cruelty at the hands of the husband and/or his family members. Cruelty was defined as both physical and psychological cruelty which can lead to a woman ending her life or attempting to end her life.

By the nineties the efforts of women's groups to get the government to set up shelters and day care facilities for children of working women had met with some success. There was also a steady increase in feminist counselling services across the country. Susamvad in Pune, Olakh in Gujrat, Swayam in Calcutta were some of the many organizations that set up such services. By this time, groups had also managed to have counsellors who were formally trained, unlike in the previous decade where things were much more informal. Several of the principles of the women's movement were operationalized in these set ups and efforts were made to document the process of counselling and maintain such information in a systematic manner.

Activists had also begun to unpack the category 'woman' and look at women as differentiated by caste and class and religion and education, and so on. This recognition translated into the setting up of organizations such as Tarshi, Seher and Rahi. Tarshi (1996) was one of the first organizations to set up a telephone helpline to respond to the questions that women and young people have about sexuality. The aim was to enable women to seek support, no matter what the issue. Rahi was set up in 1996 to respond to adult women survivors of incest (non-consensual child sexual abuse by member of the family) and enable them to cope with life challenges when they found that experiences of incest were interfering with their lives. The issue of sexual abuse was brought to fore by Rahi and besides providing counselling services, the organization also creates awareness about incest in schools and colleges. Rahi believes that individual healing is an important step and healing could also lead to survivors becoming advocates to fight against abuse.

Seher, a psycho therapeutic programme, set up in 2004 under the Bapu Trust, challenged the bio-medical model of dealing with mental distress and illness and introduced a community model of responding to people with mental illness. The programme catered to both men and women and was based on the firm belief that living with abuse leads to mental health consequences and thus it also attempted to demystify the issue of mental illness. One of its unique features was that it addressed the issue of healing by moving away from intra psychic focus to locating the reasons for emotional/ psychological distress in a social context in which women live. (Davar, 2004)

Engaging Public Systems

The Resource Centre for Interventions on Violence against Women (Special Cell) in 1984 and Dilaasa in 2000 have been two important efforts at working with public systems, namely the home department, the women and child department and also with health systems to make them accountable to survivors of violence. The special cell was set up in 1984 by social workers who found that the police response to women reporting domestic violence was abysmal and that there was a need to engage and make the police machinery responsive to women. Those involved with the formulation of the special cell were also backed with experience of having been a part of the women's movement. (TISS, 2014)

The Special Cell for Women and Children started as a field project of the Tata Institute of Social Sciences (TISS) and was established to respond to women facing domestic violence and seeking redress from the police machinery. Thus, the programme had a direct link with the criminal justice system and, under it, trained social workers are based in police stations. Evidence from their work shows that women reach police stations only when abuse escalates. Therefore, providing effective crisis intervention services and preventing further abuse has been an important objective of the cell. In many instances, the abuser was brought to the police station to get him to stop abuse. The backdrop of the police system helped the special cell members to summon perpetrators and negotiate for non-violence. Such negotations have been invaluable because, all too often, despite heightened abuse, women want to continue in the relationship. This has been a challenging situation not just for the special cell but also for organizations working on preventing domestic violence. The special cell was brought under the ambit of the Home Affairs and Women and Child Department of the Government of Maharashtra in 2011 and 39 such cells were set up in Maharashtra alone. The Research Centre for Interventions, (RCI) of TISS has been instrumental in setting up, expanding and upscaling these cells in states such as Orrisa, Haryana, Gujarat, Delhi, Rajashthan and Andhra Pradesh.

Dilaasa, a hospital-based crisis intervention department, was backed with research and evidence related to the impact of violence on women's health from CEHAT, a health research organization set up in 1994 under the Anusandhan Trust. CEHAT drew from both the women's movement and the health movement. Backed with field evidence from Mumbai as well as internationally, it aimed to set up a model in collaboration with the health department to respond sensitively to women. (Bhate-Deosthali, T K and Vindhya, 2012)

Dilaasa was established on the premise that women facing any form of violence reach the health system for health care, they may not approach a police station as complaining against a family member is still difficult, but they will almost always have some kind of contact with the health system. Dilaasa's primary efforts were to sensitize the health professionals to the issue of domestic violence and enable them to play a role in responding to the needs of women. At the same time, counselling was recognized as a health care need and so the Dilaasa hospital based department set up crisis intervention services to respond to women. Dilaasa's efforts had a significant impact on bringing an understanding of domestic violence as a public health issue to the system. Set up in 2000, the centre was replicated in another public hospital in Mumbai. The department was externally evaluated and found to be an upscalabale initiative. Efforts have been under way in four other states to replicate the model. Anweshi, a Women's Counselling centre in Kerala, (Anweshi, 2014), North East Network (NEN, 2014), a North East based network, Soukhya (Soukhya, 2014) and SWATI (Society for Women's Action and Training Initiatives) a non-profit organization that works for the socio-economic empowerment of women in the state of Gujarat (Swati, 2014) are undertaking the setting up of similar models in their respective states.

Beliefs Underlying a Feminist Perspective

The last three decades have been marked by several different kinds of services and support systems created for women facing domestic violence. The nature of support services has also evolved over the years. The early groups that were linked to the movement reached out to survivors and encouraged them to break their silence vis-à-vis domestic violence. Protest rallies, posters, street plays as well as speaking to survivors and opening their own houses as shelters, were the highlights of the movement in the eighties. The focus was on encouraging women to break their silence vis-à-vis domestic violence. However the groups never looked on the support they provided as counselling. More recently, groups have consciously been developing counselling practices as shown in the examples cited above.

The Personal is Political: The second wave of feminism in the West coined the term 'The personal is political'. (Gupte, 2013). In the Indian context too, groups and organizations set up to respond to women facing domestic violence, clearly held the belief that violence faced by a woman is not a personal problem, but is connected to the social and political environment in which she lives. Several methods have been used by different organizations to translate this belief into practice. Engaging women vis-à-vis gender ascribed roles and how these get operationalized in their daily lives, connecting the socio-political understanding related to abuse of power, are some of the ways to encourage women to arrive at the fact that abuse is not because of inadequacies in them, but rather that it occurs because it is used as a tool to maintain the status quo in favour of men. However, these discussions are aimed at enabling women and prompting them to share their views of abuse and why it occurs. The aim of doing so was to explain how those in positions of power use violence as a means to establish control as well as assert/establish their position by being violent so that the power equations within the family are not challenged.

Dealing with Psychological Distress: It is well known that mainstream counselling treats anxiety and negative emotions experienced by women in a vacuum without addressing the underlying abuse faced by them. In contrast, the feminist approach stems from an understanding that being subjected to violence has not just a physical but also a psychological impact. Such an approach enables women to recognize that living in abuse can expose them to tremendous psychological distress. At the same time it is also possible that coping mechanisms to deal with violence may fail. Such a breakdown is interpreted in feminist interventions as a temporary phase and it is felt that counselling will help those at the receiving end of violence to reflect upon ways in which they have dealt with the ongoing abuse in their lives. This kind of acknowledgement is essential to prevent women from perceiving themselves and their emotions negatively. Feminist interventionists are also aware of the fact that women suffering from mental illnesses are often abandoned by their families and do not receive any care. In such circumstances, interventionists engage with the families and discuss the need for care.

Accepting Ambiguity: An important belief in feminist interventions is to recognize women's vacillations. When a woman enters a counselling centre, she may express anger about the ongoing abuse and say that she wants to end the relationship. However, her decision may change after a few days when she comes back to the centre; this time round she may say that she wants to give the relationship another chance, as she believes that the abuser will change or that she can change him. Feminist counsellors recognize and give scope for a woman to examine her personal vacillation. Such a recognition is based on issues such as women being economically dependent on the abuser, the fear of living alone, the apprehension of being stigmatized as someone with a 'poor' character, the fear of losing children and also the hope that the abuser may change.

Consciousness-raising: Feminist interventions do not occur in a vacuum. The goal of feminist consciousness is to create awareness about institutions such as the family and marriage as products of a patriarchal system, and that these have inherent contradictions, mostly to the disadvantage of the woman. Consciousness raising is done with the purpose of understanding different social disadvantages that women face. To cite an example, women who are in a heterosexual relationship, married and have children gain far more respect than women who are married and don't have children. Women who are in a same sex relationship are often dismissed as 'not normal' and may not be allowed to marry or raise a family. Parental families disown women who may have a relationship outside the marriage. Consciousness raising enables women to see their social locations, advantages and disadvantages based on these and also reach out to other women living in abuse.

Principles of Feminist Counselling

Feminist principles for responding to domestic violence have emerged from the work carried out by the women's movement in India. A similar line of thought was seen in the interventions carried out by women's organizations consistently in the eighties, nineties and into the new century. The principles described in this section have emerged from an acute consciousness among women's movement activists about women's subversive status within the family and the community, and a belief in women's own agency. These principles are described below.

Self-awareness: The nature of feminist counselling constantly calls upon the counsellors to re-examine their own values, both personal and professional, vis-à-vis each woman who comes to them for help. This value implies that a counsellor needs to be aware of his or her own beliefs. It also implies that the counsellor has to be introspective and responsible. When counsellors are aware or do not accept women's beliefs, they risk becoming prescriptive in their approach. What sets apart a feminist interventionist is analysis of the intersections to which a woman belongs and the disadvantages she may face due to her social locations such as caste, class, religion etc. Hence, unlike mainstream mental health counsellors, feminist counsellors have the responsibility of understanding women's social location and to be aware of their own sense of these.

Self-determination: Mainstream psychological counselling follows a method of assessment of the woman that is both intellectual and emotional. But, feminist counselling seeks to follow the path of recognition and acceptance and the development of alternatives. Feminist intervention does not perceive the woman as a helpless victim of uncontrollable circumstances, but as an active participant in determining ways and means of dealing with the abusive situation at hand. In a situation where women are often reprimanded about their decision-making capacities, feminist principles aim to increase the woman's confidence and control over the situation.

Awareness of Diversity or Multiple Identities: Feminist intervention recognizes that women are not a homogeneous category and belong to different social, political, cultural, religious, economic and sexual identities and backgrounds. Such a perspective in counselling helps women to identify the ways in which these identities impact their situations. For example, a woman belonging to a Dalit community and facing violence would be at a social disadvantage, not only because she is being abused but also because she comes from a community which has faced oppression for several decades. Therefore, it would be crucial to develop interventions that recognize such multiple axes of oppression.

Commitment to Question Sexist Beliefs: Living in a patriarchal society, women and counsellors both absorb the same milieu and form opinions about others within that social context. For example, a client says that her husband is having an extra-marital affair with a widow and that widows are promiscuous. In such a situation, a feminist approach would enable a counsellor to clarify her beliefs about widows in general, but also empathize with the woman and seek to place the responsibility of the extra-marital affair on her husband. This principle also seeks to challenge the beliefs and prejudices that are common among women, for example that women are women's worst enemies, and explain these as patriarchal constructs developed to divide women.

Recognizing Power Relations: The issue of power between a counsellor and a woman facing abuse has been discussed extensively in western feminist literature (Enns, 2004). The very nature of help-seeking behaviour by a woman facing abuse makes it a challenge to work towards an egalitarian relationship between the counsellor and the woman. Therefore, awareness on the part of feminist counsellors about the power they hold is necessary and important. This awareness will also enable counsellors to ensure that they value women's perspectives in counselling. One way of dealing with power between the counsellor and the counselled is by the former demystifying the process of counselling itself. This in turn can empower the woman and give her a sense of being an educated consumer. (Worell and Pamela, 2003)

SETTING STANDARDS IN INTERVENTIONS/COUNSELLING FOR DOMESTIC VIOLENCE PREVENTION

Opportunities for providing services and reaching out to survivors of domestic violence have grown exponentially after the passage of PWDVA. The new law provides for infrastructure, human resources, new appointments such as protection officers and service providers. But there is also a danger that groups/individuals/organizations will not be adequately equipped to carry out these interventions. It is important to understand that counselling centres do not work in isolation; they negotiate spaces within the institutions of the family, the police, the health system and the judiciary that are riddled with insensitivity and biases against women. Moreover, it is well known that all groups/organizations working with survivors are not necssarily feminist in their perspective and approach to survivors of domestic violence. Such groups may well be invested in preserving the family as an institution rather than helping the survivor to heal.

Despite several services for domestic violence reduction, no systematic effort has been made to set standards to regulate counselling services. In order to respond to the gap in regulating counselling practice in domestic violence prevention, Dilaasa, a joint initaive of the MCGM and CEHAT, instituted a case conference and supervision for those carrying out counselling. This enabled the counsellors to reach out when support was required as well as voice their concerns, dilemmas vis-à-vis interventions carried out by them. As Dilaasa team members, we felt we needed to underdstand the discourse on counselling ethics and whether such standards can be set for self regulation by institutions and organizations. In 2011, CEHAT set up an expert group at the national level comprising women's rights advocates, lawyers, ethicists, psychologists, psychiatrists and practitioners to develop ethical guidelines for domestic violence counselling. The committee examined ethical standards for counselling practices in different parts of the world and evolved a set of principles and guidelines for determining such standards in counselling for responding to domestic violence in India. A set of standards was thus developed in consultation with the expert body and a set of ethical guidelines evolved to develop a comprehensive and ethical response to women seeking counselling services. These guidelines have been evolved keeping in mind different settings, both rural and urban, as well as both sectors such as working with the public system and for setting up counselling services. A set of guidelines has been listed in brief in this section (CEHAT, 2012).

Informed Consent for Counselling – Counselling is not a passive process and consent is essential. Though consent is implicit in a counselling relationship, this is the first step in counselling as it helps women facing violence to get a fair idea of the counselling relationship. Similarly, it is important for women to know (at the outset) what the counselling centre can and cannot offer. If a woman demands a job, she should be informed that the centre may not be in a position to provide it. Once she consents to receiving services, it is important to explain the procedures followed, such as the timings, the assurance of confidentiality and that the counsellors (looking into her case) may change, among other things.

Safety Assessment and Safety Plan – Counsellors play a significant role in each of these situations. They focus on understanding the woman's narration of the history of violence and determine whether there is a threat to her life. Counselling centres need to have a series of questions to assess the severity and frequency of violence, its changing nature over time as well as the woman's perceptions of her safety. These questions are useful in assessing whether it is safe for the woman to return to the violent home. These issues are discussed with the woman to determine and explore alternative shelters, if necessary. The presence of informal support systems, such as the natal family, friends, neighbours, colleagues and employers, is also explored during this time. If a woman lacks such support, then information about temporary shelters is provided to her. Simple strategies such as pre-empting an incident of violence, leaving the room if the abuser is present, getting out of the house, holding his hand, calling the neighbours and shouting, are some practical ways of resisting violence and reducing further harm. Thus, understanding the history of violence and assessing the immediate safety of the woman forms an important step.

Suicide Assessment – Just as the physical safety of the woman is determined so also her emotional safety is an important aspect of the safety assessment and plan. It is important for the counsellor to know whether a client has considered suicide. Not every woman acts upon these thoughts, but many do. It is therefore necessary that counsellors be trained to provide suicide prevention counselling. It may also help the counsellor to ask a woman about her emotional state and her feelings – her mood, does she feel low or sad; does she feel like crying and so on. The counsellor can enable the woman to see for herself how the abuse that she faces has pushed her into attempting suicide and develop a plan for overcoming such feelings.

Legal Counselling – Training of counsellors with regard to the laws related to custody, divorce, maintenance, and the provisions of section 498A of the Indian Penal Code and the ramifications of such actions are imperative as they have to provide updated information to the woman seeking counselling. A lawyer should be available for those women who wish to pursue legal action. The most frequent legal assistance needed by women involves processing an injunction order, petitioning for maintenance and, occasionally, filing for divorce. It is however also important to understand that even if women seek legal counselling, many do not pursue litigation

Negotiation for Non-violence – Often women express a desire to call the abusive person/persons for a meeting, and demand that the counsellor resolve the issue immediately. A counsellor should validate the woman's feelings; at the same time, it is important to counsel the woman that there is a need to understand her life situation and those aspects which she wishes to negotiate. If the woman is not adequately prepared, the meeting may not achieve the purpose. The premise of a joint meeting is to build confidence in the woman so that she can negotiate and put an end to the violence she faces. Therefore, the counselling must be geared to providing her the required training to table the issues that she wishes to discuss with the perpetrator. It is also pertinent to seek details about whether such an effort was made in the past, its outcomes, the aspects that need to be covered in the joint meeting and so on. These details can help the counsellor to set the objective for the meeting. It also helps the woman to concretise the base for a joint meeting. It must be kept in mind that such a meeting is not called to bring about an 'adjustment' or a 'compromise' between the abuser and the woman. If this is done, the woman will be at the receiving end; being blamed for not doing or not acting in ways demanded by the family. As a consequence of this, the purpose of negotiating for preventing violence will be defeated. Women also need to be given a realistic idea about the outcomes of these meetings. Sometimes joint meetings do not work. The counsellor can prepare the woman beforehand and enable her to convey alternative demands.

Preparing the Woman to Seek Police Assistance – While dealing with the issue of domestic violence, it becomes important to register a police complaint if the woman wishes it. The counsellor therefore has to state the importance of ensuring that the complaint is recorded as evidence for the violence a woman faces. Much of the time, women's experiences with the police are anything but positive. These so called 'settlements' that the police broker amount to a kind of arbitration. A woman seeking help needs to know what the fallout of such arbitration can be as these rarely end up being in favour of women. Counsellors should explain the nature and extent of the complaint that can be made depending on the nature of the violence. Differences in cognizable and non-cognizable offences also need to be explained. Further, the woman must also be informed about the importance of gathering evidence of abuse, including getting herself examined at a government hospital, preserving the medical report, taking photographs of the bruises and injuries, preserving her letters to her parents/relatives/friends.

Importance of Referrals – Domestic violence is a complex issue. Therefore, the outcomes of counselling are difficult to ascertain. Also even though they may have filed complaints women have to move on with their lives. But counselling centres can do little in this regard so it becomes important for them to have a good network of organizations that can provide the required support. Counsellors can keep lists of trusts and organizations that provide material resources and financial aid for different needs such as schooling for children, shelter homes and employment opportunities for women. Counsellors also need to be certain of organizations to which they make referrals as this too is an ethical responsibility. (Bhate-Deosthali, 2013).

Emerging Issues and Challenges

A number of different services have been created for women in the past three decades.The nature of the support systems has also evolved. In the early days of the movement activists reached out to survivors and encouraged them to break their silence about domestic violence but they did not term their support counselling. The belief that 'the personal is political' enabled women to speak out against abuse in their private lives. This slogan later became very important in feminist counselling. But activist groups also realized that women seeking abuse did not necessarily participate in the struggle for social change.

Consistent pressure by women activists on the state to develop services for women has yielded some results and shelter homes, family courts and counselling services have been set up. The understanding that domestic violence should not be tolerated and is unlawful, has also gained ground. And there is a growing understanding of the need to develop gender sensitive individual solutions in counselling. But the process has been slow as organizations are unsure of the wisdom of engaging with the state. Some, like Stree Mukti Sanghtana and Swadhar in Maharashtra did take this step and set up family counselling centres with the women and child department of the state to create services for women facing domestic violence. Vimochana, in Bangalore, also decided to engage with the state and set out to build capacity building workshops with public servants on issues concerning women and violence. This engagement was done with the purpose of educating government officials on the need for good quality services.

The passage of the domestic violence prevention law (PWDVA) by the Government of India and its implementation through the Ministry of Women and Child Development helped to create institutional mechanisms to deal with domestic violence. The appointment of protection officers, schemes for setting up of family counselling centres, hostel facilities, the extension of shelter homes such as 'swadhar' for survivors of domestic violence were some of the steps taken by the government. Though these schemes may have greater outreach than civil society organizations, these have not been evaluated and therefore it remains a challenge whether they really reach women living with abuse.

The Planning Commission in its Twelfth Five Year Plan consti-tuted a working group under the chairpersonship of the Secretary,

Women and Child Development, for the creation of hundred One Stop Crisis Centres (OSCCs) across the country to mitigate abuse against women both in their personal lives as well as in workplaces. However, the roll out of the actual OSCC scheme and its operational aspects have not been presented to civil society yet. Thus, while it is true that at one level the state seems to be responding to the needs expressed by women's groups, at another the perspective with which the schemes and services are offered needs to be assessed as these schemes do not necessarily follow a pro-woman approach. This poses a challenge to the efforts to do away with domestic violence

The Way Forward

It is clear that counselling has gained momentum over the past three decades. Psychologists, social workers, lawyers, protection officers, barefoot counsellors, outreach workers across the country both in urban and rural communities, are involved in counselling work. The Protection of Women from Domestic Violence Act (PWDVA) 2005 brought in a new cadre of professionals, termed 'Protection Officers' Their role has been to assist women to seek services beyond the law. There is a need for such professionals to understand the conditions that lead to violence against women, and it is important that they be equipped with a feminist perspective while counselling women. We are cognizant of the fact that a feminist perspective in counselling has still not been integrated into the disciplines of psychiatry and psychology, disciplines from which counselling actually emerged. There is an urgent need for organizations working in the field to produce evidence related to the utility of feminist counselling and its effectiveness in responding to domestic violence because only such evidence will prompt the academia to integrate feminist analysis in the academic counselling discourse.

Closely associated with feminist counselling is the importance of the regulation of counselling services. For counselling to be effective, organizations should ensure supportive supervision to enhance and maintain the quality of counselling. One of the ways in which this can be done is for organizations to adopt ethical principles and guidelines in their counselling services. Counselling ethics discourse can sensitize counsellors, protect and promote the rights of women as well as enable counsellors to seek guidance and support when needed.

As professionals enter the arena of domestic violence counselling, it is important to bear in mind that organizations raise the consciousness of professionals by participating in campaigns on ending all forms of violence such as the one based on caste, class and religion as domestic violence cannot be dealt with in isolation.

References

American Psychiatric Association. 2000. *Diagnostic and Statistical Manual of Mental Disorders* (4th ed., text rev.). Washington, DC: American Psychiatric Association.

Anweshi 2014. *Anweshi a women's counselling centre.* Kerala. Retrieved from http://anweshi.org/.

Bhate-Deosthali, Padma. 2013. 'Evolving Guidelines For Running A Crisis Counseling Centre', in Bhate-Deosthali, Padma, Sangeeta Rege and Padma Prakash (eds.) *Feminist Counselling And Domestic Violence In India.* (Pp. 302 -17). New Delhi: Routledge.

Bhate-Deosthali, Padma; T K Sundari Ravindran and U. Vindhya. 2012. 'Addressing domestic violence within healthcare settings: The Dilaasa model', *Economic and Political Weekly,* 47(17), April, 66–75.

Centre For Enquiry Into Health And Allied Themes (CEHAT). 2012. 'Ethical Guidelines For Counseling Women Facing Domestic Violence', Mumbai: CEHAT, p. 32.

Chaplin, Jocelyn. 1998. 'Rhythm Model', In Seu, Bruna and Colleen M. Heenan (eds.) *Feminism and Psychotherapy: Reflections On Contemporary Theories And Practices,* London: Sage Publications, pp. 135–56.

Davar, Bhargavi. 2004. 'Treating mental disorders: Bijli', 39 p. Pune: Center For Advocacy In Mental Health: A Bapu Trust, p. 39.

Dobash, Emerson R. and Russel P. Dobash. 1992. *Women, Violence And Social Change.* NewYork: Routledge.

Enns, Carolyn Z. 2004. *Feminist Theories And Feminist Psychotherapies: Origins, Themes and Diversity.* (2nd ed.). New York: The Haworth Press.

Gupte, Manisha. 2013. 'Why Feminism Should Inform Our Routine Interventions In Domestic Violence', in Bhate-Deosthali, Padma, Sangeeta Rege and Padma

Prakash (eds.) *Feminist Counselling And Domestic Violence In India*. New Delhi: Routledge, pp. 48–89.

Kumar, Radha. 1993. *The History of Doing: An Illustrated Account* of *Movements for Women's Rights and Feminism in India, 1800–1990*. New Delhi: Zubaan, p. 203.

Masum. 2014. 'Mahila sarvangeen Utkarsh Mandal', Pune. Retrieved from http://www.masum-india.org.in/.

North East Network. 2014. *North East Network (NEN) is a women's rights organization*. Assam. Retrieved from, http://www.northeastnetwork.org/.

Bhate-Deosthali, Padma, Sangeeta Rege, Padma Prakash (eds.) 2013, *Feminist Counselling And Domestic Violence In India*. New Delhi: Routledge.

Rege, Sangeeta and Aarthi Chandrasekhar. 2013. 'Feminist Domestic Violence Interventions In India' in Bhate-Deosthali, Padma, Sharmila Rege and Padma Prakash (eds.) *Feminist Counselling And Domestic Violence In India*. New Delhi: Routledge, pp 126–75.

Soukhya. 2014. *Soukhya Dr Mathai's International Holistic Health Centre*. Bangalore, India. Retrieved from, www.soukya.com.

Swati. 2014. *Society for Women's Action and Training Initiatives*. Gujarat. Retrieved from, http://www.swati.org.in/.

Vanangana facebook page. 2014. *Vanangana*. Chitrakoot. Retrieved from https://hi-in.facebook.com/Vanangana.

Vindhya, U. 2013. 'Feminist Counselling For Domestic Violence: Some Issues Of Theory And Practice',in Bhate-Deosthali, Padma, Sangeeta Rege, and Padma Prakash (eds.) *Feminist Counselling And Domestic Violence in India*. New Delhi: Routledge, pp 93–125.

Walker, Lenore. 1979. *The Battered Woman*. New York: Harper And Row.

Worell, Judith and Pamela, Remer. 2003. *Feminist Perspectives In Therapy: Empowering Diverse Women*, (2nd ed.). New Jersey: John Wiley and Sons.

Notes on Contributors

Flavia Agnes is a feminist activist and women's rights lawyer who has worked on issues of gender and legal reforms. She is the co-founder of Majlis, a legal and cultural resource centre, providing quality legal services to women and children. She has played an important role in bringing women's rights to the forefront within the legal system and in contextualizing issues of gender and identity. A prolific writer, she has provided incisive analysis of many social trends and legal reforms including domestic violence, minority law reforms, secularism and human rights. After the communal carnage in Gujarat, she initiated a legal advocacy programme for sexually violated women in relief camps and subsequently has brought out a publication titled, *Of Lofty Claims and Muffled Voices* (2002). Some of her noted books include her autobiographical account, *My Story... Our Story of Rebuilding Broken Lives* (1990), *Law and Gender Inequality: The Politics of Personal Laws in India* (1999) and a co-edited volume *Women and Law in India* (2014).

Abha Bhaiya is one of the founding members of Jagori and has been active in the Indian women's movement for nearly 40 years. She has worked on a range of issues, notably: women's social, political and economic rights; the status of single women; women's right to health, bodily integrity and well being. One of the unique features of Abha's work has been the creation of linkages between community and international arenas. She has evolved a strategy for the convergence of many diverse women's groups, exposing the limitations of mainstream discourse by working on a synthesis between feminist theory and praxis. Her major contribution has been in the field of feminist training methodologies, with extensive experience in conducting feminist trainings for multiple constituencies across different countries. In 2002, she set up a feminist retreat TARA in one of the villages of lower Himalayas and also put in place a feminist community programme.

Anjali Dave has been a faculty member at the Tata Institute of Social Sciences (TISS), Mumbai for nearly 26 years and coordinates and teaches Women Centred Social Work. She initiated the Resource Centre for Interventions on Violence Against Women (RCI-VAW), TISS, Mumbai. It grew out of a field action project, entitled the 'Special Cells for Women and Children' located in police stations/offices. The project aims at developing an understanding and methodology to work within the framework of feminist social work on the issue of violence against women. Her work has been adapted into a scheme by state governments and contributed to the law for domestic violence. She has been member of National Resource Groups for Women especially for training, research and interventions on the issue of violence against women and education for girls and women.

Padma Bhate-Deosthali is an independent researcher and trainer working on gender, health and human rights. Padma was a member of the World Health Organization's Guideline Development Group for policy and clinical practice guidelines for responding to violence against women. She was also a part of the committee for drafting the 'Guidelines and Protocols for Medico-legal Care for Victims/Survivors of Sexual Violence', 2014 under the Ministry of Health and Family Welfare (MoHFW). She coordinated the setting up of Dilaasa, the first public hospital-based crisis centre in India. Her doctoral work looks at gendered patterns of burn injuries and the hospital responses to them. She has co-authored two essays, 'Responding to Sexual Violence', and 'Addressing Domestic Violence within Healthcare Settings', that have been published in the *Economic and Political Weekly*.

V. Geetha is a feminist activist who writes on issues related to caste, gender, education and civil rights. She is publisher and co-director of

Tara Books, Chennai. Geetha has carried out research on the nature and proliferation of NGOs operating in Tamil Nadu and has set up a federation of women's groups in the state. Some of her path-breaking works include *Patriarchy* (2007), *Gender* (2002), *Towards a Non-Brahmin Millenium* (1998), and *Undoing Impunity: Speech After Sexual Violence* (Zubaan, 2016).

Poonam Kathuria is the founder and director of SWATI (Society for Women's Action and Training Initiatives), based in Gujarat. She has over 20 years of experience working in the field of women's empowerment and leadership. Her work involves project design and management, situation analysis, action research and capacity development to promote the rights of women and other marginalized communities; and influence the drafting and implementation of gender just policies. She strives to bridge the divide between activists and academics and has written extensively for newspapers, magazines and published several books and research papers. Her latest work, *From Being Shelters to Becoming Homes - Situation Analysis and Recommendations,* is based on a study of shelter homes in Gujarat. Poonam was awarded the Dame Nita Barrow Distinguished Visitorship for 2014 at the Ontario Institute for Studies in Education, University of Toronto.

Corinne Kumar is the founder and coordinator of World Courts of Women. She served as the Secretary General of El Taller, an international NGO committed to women's rights, sustainable development, and both North-South and South-South exchange and dialogue across diverse cultures and civilizations. She was formerly Director of the Centre for Development Studies (CIEDS Collective) in India. She is a founding member of the Asian Women's Human Rights Council and of Vimochana, an NGO in Bangalore, India concerned with domestic violence, dowry-related deaths and sexual harassment at the workplace. A philosopher, poet, human rights theoretician and activist, she is editor of two human rights journals, *Sangarsh* and *The Quilt,* and *Asking We Walk: The South as a New Political Imaginary,* a four-volume set of essays. She has written and spoken extensively on refugees, violence against women, militarization, and the dominant human rights discourse, critiquing it from a gendered and Global South perspective.

Kanchan Mathur has 34 years of experience in applied research, evaluation and policy analysis in the field of social and rural development, with a focus on the issues of gender. Her areas of interest include understanding the politics of gender; women's rights and empowerment; gender based violence; gender, policy planning and education of marginalized girls and child labour. She is a professor at the Institute of Development Studies, Jaipur, and has published, among many works, a book titled, *Countering Gender Violence: Initiatives Towards Collective Action in Rajasthan* (2004).

Madhu Mehra is a feminist lawyer, founding member and Executive Director of Partners for Law in Development (PLD), a legal resource group working on women's rights and social justice. Her activism and writings, over 29 years, cover issues relating to gender, sexuality, identity politics, violence against women, access to justice and the law – including each of these in relation to UN Convention on the Elimination of All Forms of Discrimination Against Women (CEDAW). She has consistently pushed for decriminalisation of consensual sexuality – homosexuality, adultery, and adolescent sexuality. Her latest publication for PLD: *The Rape Law and Constructions of Sexuality* (2018) explores some of these areas at length. She works domestically and regionally in Asia Pacific as a trainer, technical advisor and researcher on the UN CEDAW and the UN human rights system. She undertook the review of 15 years of the mandate of the UN Special Rapporteur on Violence Against Women (1994-2009) for the Office of the United Nations High Commissioner for Human Rights.

Yashoda Pradhan is a senior programme officer at the Resource Centre for Interventions on Violence Against Women (RCI-VAW), TISS, Mumbai. She has completed her M.A. in Social Work at the Tata Institute of Social Sciences (TISS), Mumbai; and M.Sc in Gender from the London School of Economics and Political Science (LSE). She has written modules like 'Gender and Social Work' for the

School of Social Work, TISS. Yashoda has co-authored 'In Search of Justice and Care: How Women Survivors of Violence Navigate the Indian Criminal-Justice System' (*Journal of Gender-based Violence*, 2017). She has worked with various state and police departments, particularly in Delhi, Madhya Pradesh, Assam and Meghalaya to pilot demonstrate the Special Cell approach in collaboration with the National Commission for Women.

Sangeeta Rege is currently the coordinator of Centre for Enquiry into Health and Allied Themes (CEHAT). Focusing on training, research and advocacy on issues that lie at the intersection of violence against women and healthcare, her work involves leading initiatives that reform the response that the healthcare system has to survivors of violence; and the integration of gender in medical education. She was at the forefront of CEHAT's public interest lititgation on advocating for gender sensitive healthcare for survivors of sexual assault. Sangeeta has written papers and manuals pertaining to the violence against women and health care; and co-authored, 'Responding to Sexual Violence' with Padma Deosthali and Jagdeesh Reddy that was published in the *Economic and Political Weekly*.

Jaya Sharma is a feminist, queer, kinky, political activist and writer based in New Delhi. As part of a feminist NGO, she worked on issues of gender and education for over 20 years. She was also intensively involved in sexuality trainings for groups working with rural women. As a queer activist, she has co-founded and been involved with queer forums in Delhi. She is also one of the founder members of the Kinky Collective, a group that aims to raise awareness about Bondage, Domination, Sado-Masochism (BDSM). For more about Kinky Collective visit kinkycollective.com.

Taranga Sriraman has been a Strategic Coordinator at the Resource Centre for Interventions on Violence Against Women (RCI-VAW), TISS, Mumbai, since 2012. Her work is focused on gender, sexuality, violence against women, education, and feminist praxis with the State, in particular. She studied M.A. in Social Work at the Tata Institute of Social Sciences (TISS), Mumbai, and has worked in Bihar, Gujarat, Tamil Nadu and Delhi with various organizations and networks. She was National Consultant to the Ministry of Human Resource Development for Mahila Samakhya programme from 2008 to 2012.

Suneeta Thakur is a poet, author and feminist activist. She currently works as a counsellor and legal advisor at Jagori and has completed PhD from Delhi University. Her research work focuses on the writings of the Hindi author Vaidyanath Mishra (also known as Nagarjun), and on translation studies. Suneeta has been editor of the feminist journal *Sablaa* for eight years. She regularly contributes to Hindi magazines and web-publications. Among her publications are *Himanshu Joshi ka Kahaani Sahitya; Nagarjun ke Sahitya Me Antasambandha; Narivad Counselling: Siddhant aur Vyavahaar*. She has also authored multiple poetry collections, including *Kshitij ki Dhoop Me*, and *Do Pal Saath Saath*.

Saumya Uma has over 24 years of combined work experience as an academic, law researcher, trainer, campaigner and lawyer on issues pertaining to gender, law and human rights. She currently works as an assistant professor of Law and Legal Studies at the School of Law, Governance and Citizenship, Ambedkar University Delhi (AUD). She has previously taught at Maharashtra National Law University (MNLU) Mumbai, and at the National Law School of India University (NLSIU), Bengaluru, where she also completed her doctoral thesis. She has also worked as an international consultant for the UNDP for preparing a paper entitled 'Violence Against Women – Legal Responses in India'; with the UN Office of the High Commissioner on Human Rights (OHCHR) for preparing a tool on witness protection with an integration of gender concerns and with the International Commission for Jurists (ICJ). She has authored 12 books, including *Breaking the Shackled Silence: Unheard Voices of Women from Kandhamal* (2014).